William Clare Taylor

Jottings on Australia

With Remarks on the California Route to New York and Liverpool

William Clare Taylor

Jottings on Australia

With Remarks on the California Route to New York and Liverpool

ISBN/EAN: 9783337109875

Printed in Europe, USA, Canada, Australia, Japan

Cover: Foto ©Andreas Hilbeck / pixelio.de

More available books at **www.hansebooks.com**

JOTTINGS ON AUSTRALIA:

WITH

REMARKS ON THE CALIFORNIA ROUTE

TO NEW YORK AND LIVERPOOL.

BY

WILLIAM CLARE TAYLOR.

LONDON:
EDWARD STANFORD, 6 & 7, CHARING CROSS, S.W.
1872.

PREFACE.

TO MY SOUTH AUSTRALIAN FRIENDS.

As promised, I have kept and compiled, as well as circumstances permitted, a Journal of my journey from Adelaide, South Australia, *viâ* Melbourne, Victoria, and Sydney, New South Wales, thence by the California route to New York and Liverpool. Probably you may think that I have been too minute in some respects, and many little things may appear trivial at first sight; but as it is intended for inspection by friends in England and elsewhere, as well as yourselves, you will readily see my object. I wish to impress particularly on English friends the fact, that Australia is not such a wilderness as some suppose, and that one can travel from the Antipodes to the old country by steamboat and railway in comparative comfort and without fatigue: hence my frequent allusions to the style of colonial houses and buildings, fitting up of cabins and carriages, supply and quality of edibles and drinkables, prices, and so on. I myself gained 12 lbs. 4 oz. in weight between Sydney and Liverpool, notwithstanding the irritation, &c., caused by an accident at Honolulu to my left eye, which consequently led to some little trouble and anxiety at times, precluding me from making such ample notes as I desired to do.

WM. CLARE TAYLOR.

15, SALUTARY PLACE, ST. SIDWELL'S, EXETER.
19TH OCTOBER, 1871.

CONTENTS.

	PAGE
STATISTICS OF SOUTH AUSTRALIA	1
ADELAIDE	5
ADELAIDE TO MELBOURNE	18
VICTORIAN STATISTICS, 1870	23
MELBOURNE TO SANDHURST	32
MELBOURNE TO SYDNEY, NEW SOUTH WALES	47
SYDNEY TO AUCKLAND, NEW ZEALAND	105
AUCKLAND TO HONOLULU, HAWAIIAN ISLANDS	121
HONOLULU TO SAN FRANCISCO	173
SAN FRANCISCO TO NEW YORK	200
NEW YORK TO LIVERPOOL	258
HINTS TO TRAVELLERS BY SEA AND OVERLAND FOR THE CALIFORNIA ROUTE PARTICULARLY, AND STEAMERS IN GENERAL	266

JOTTINGS ON AUSTRALIA, Etc.

Statistics of South Australia.

South Australia, which was created a free British colony by Imperial Statute in 1835, and proclaimed under a large gum-tree (still preserved at Glenelg, Holdfast Bay, six miles from the city of Adelaide, the capital), 28th December, 1836, contains 245,000,000 acres, or 382,812½ square miles.

The colony was settled on what is termed "the Wakefield" system, land being alienated from the Crown at the upset cash price of 1*l.* an acre, but it can now be taken up on deferred payments at auction, or by private selection.

Population of the colony, 185,000 only, exclusive of aborigines. (N.B. Statistics are to end of 1870.)

Imports, 1,636,503*l.*; exports, 1,580,876*l.* 23 counties proclaimed, embracing with their boundaries 23,441,000 acres, of which not an acre is more than 100 miles away from the sea.

Land alienated from the Crown, 4,198,999 acres; quantity of land occupied by holders of the fee, 2,562,596 acres; entire number of holdings as farms, 13,098, giving an average of 283 acres to each; lands enclosed, about 8,000,000 acres; land brought under crop, 959,006 acres, out of which 604,761 acres were cropped with wheat, producing 6,961,164 bushels, 1870-71, being the

B

largest crop ever reaped in South Australia, the gross value, computed at 5s. per bushel, being 1,750,000l., and estimating 110,000 tons for export. The quality of the Adelaide wheat is very fine, and has led to the city being called by the Melbournites "the farinaceous village."

Average wheat crop, 11½ bushels to the acre; peas, 4385 acres, yielding 42,000 bushels; artificial grasses, 3712 acres; lucern, 3445; barley, &c., for green fodder, 2600 acres; flax, 186 acres; other crops, 829 acres; potatoes, total area planted, 3376 acres, producing 9563 tons.

Vineyards, total area, 6131 acres, with 6,168,758 vines; total quantity of wine made, 801,694 gallons. The area has gradually decreased since 1866, from not being established in the European markets; only 123,041 gallons have been exported during five years past. This is said to be owing to the duty on the light and cheap wines of the colony being the same as upon the costlier products of France, Spain, and Germany. But many attribute it to other causes, *viz.* its inferior quality; forcing it into the market before it is properly matured; lack of competent persons in the colony who understand the manufacture and manipulation of wine—the grower in most cases not only making his own wine, but preparing it in a fashion for use and sale; general ignorance of the process, several being retired tradesmen, who probably never saw anything of the kind out of the colony, converting themselves into amateur winemakers, having had no experience whatever, but relying principally on books for their guidance; and, in many instances, lack of sufficient capital. Quantity of grapes disposed of otherwise than in wine making, 35,847 cwt., a great quantity being shipped to Melbourne to be retailed at 1d., 2d., and 3d. per pound, the grapes being of admirable quality. Drying of raisins, hitherto on a small scale, increasing.

Return of horses to end of 1870, 83,744; cattle, 136,832; sheep, 4,400,655. Almost all these are bred and reared on "runs," many of them containing over 700 square miles.

Gold-fields exist at Echunga, Jupiter Creek, Barossa, Onkaparinga, Blumberg, and a few other places midst the settled districts, but have not been prosecuted with any great success, people generally not having had much faith in them, and no rushes having taken place like California, Victoria, and New South Wales. There are, however, several very rich copper mines, including the celebrated "Burra-Burra," at Kooringa, 98 miles from Adelaide by railroad, which has stopped working for some time, but about to be resumed by a new proprietary and fresh imported powerful machinery. 5000 men, women, and children are employed in connection with the Wallaroo mines alone. The latter are situate on Yorke's Peninsula, the townships being Moonta and Wallaroo.

Total length of railway and tramway lines under control of the Government, 190 miles; metalled roads, 614 miles; declared main lines, 1470 miles. Amount laid out under the "Central Road Board," the Commissioners of roads, in forming and maintaining main roads since 1850, 1,633,928*l*. of public money.

The Government are making a telegraph overland from Port Augusta, South Australia, to Port Darwin, Gulf of Carpentaria, called the "Northern territory," about 1794 miles, at a cost of about 100*l*. per mile, raised on 5 per cent. Government bonds, following the celebrated explorer J. M. Stuart's tracks as near as can be, on his successful expedition across the continent about nine years ago, to communicate with the British Australian Telegraph Company's intended submarine line from Java to Port Darwin, all to be completed 31st December, 1871, which will then connect the Antipodes with England.

The "Northern territory" is an immense tract of land, and was annexed to South Australia in 1862. It contains 800,000,000 acres, or 1,250,000 square miles. Its climate is tropical, and is said to be admirably adapted to the growth of cotton, sugar, and rice, and breeding cattle. Efforts have been made by the Government to colonize it, but with little success to the present time (although about 150,000*l*. has been spent over it), principally owing to disagreements between the Government officials who were sent up to survey the land and fix site for capital, &c., under the superintendence of B. T. Finniss, Esq., mismanagement and accidents, also law proceedings still pending between the Government and certain land speculators in London, who seek to get back their money. Capt. Douglas, R.N., is the present Government resident, at a salary of 700*l*. per annum. The capital town is named Palmerston.

ADELAIDE.

Adelaide, the capital of South Australia, is divided into two parts, known as North and South Adelaide, the shallow river Torrens running between, crossed by two handsome bridges. The population of the city and suburbs is about 27,000.

The streets of South Adelaide (the city proper) are very wide and well laid out. They are macadamized and kept in good order, and the footways in the principal streets mostly paved with large slabs of Willunga (colonial) slate, not very durable, but some pavements are of imported stone of a harder nature. It is lighted with gas by a public company, a rival company to which is being started, which it is said will bring the price down from a guinea to 14s. 6d. per 1000 cubic feet. There are a great many handsome shops and stores, plate glass being in great use. South Adelaide is about a mile square, or 640 acres, and is built on a flat, having on its outskirts four terraces, called North, East, South, and West Terraces, where there are mostly private residences, many of them detached and surrounded by open country called the Park lands or reserves, kept for the recreation of the public. The rifle butts for the volunteers are on the South Park lands. There is a beautiful range of hills at the back of the town, the highest of which is called Mount Lofty, visible from every point, from which trigonometrical surveys are taken. East Terrace is prettily situated, is of an irregular shape, and commands views of the racecourse and the hills. Plantations surround a great portion of the terraces and Park lands. The Government and other principal buildings are in South Adelaide. Unfortunately they are widely scattered, although not so much so as formerly, by which much valuable time is lost. The Treasury, Chief Secretary's, Crown Lands and Immigration Offices, Public Works, Land Office, Surveyor-General's Office, and Lands' Titles Registration Offices are, however, now together in King William Street and corner of Flinders Street. They are built of stone plastered and painted over, and are a fine lot of buildings, having bold elevations, the interior being well fitted up, principally with polished cedar, and the numerous suites of offices nicely finished and furnished. The cost of painting, in a hot climate, is a serious item in the expenditure, and, it is said, will lead to the Government using cut stone in future buildings, of which there is abundance in the colony.

Opposite, in course of erection, is the new Post and Telegraph Office, begun in 1867, having a frontage to King William Street of 150 feet, and to Victoria Square 160 feet, height from pavement to top of stone balustrading 57 feet 6 inches; the elevations are in the Anglo-Italian style, executed in cut free stone, the main portion of the walls is of Glen Osmond stone, an excellent building material, obtained three or four miles from town. At the south-east angle there is a splendid square tower rising 158 feet, or 179 feet 6 inches to the summit of the flagstaff. Estimated cost of the building 56,000*l*. The foundation stone was laid by His Royal

Highness the Duke of Edinburgh, on his official visit to South Australia.

The Parliament Houses (Upper and Lower) are built in a pit adjoining the Railway Station, North Terrace. The building is of stone, with brick quoins and pillars, very plain in appearance, and calls for no especial notice, except that the strangers' gallery is very small, and the space for reporters limited, and have been likened to the Blackhole at Calcutta.

The Supreme Courthouse, Victoria Square, is a substantial building over twenty years old, of cut stone, varying in colour from dirty yellow to light brown, approached by a few stone steps, with a heavy stone portico resting on high-dressed stone fluted pillars. The "Court" is lofty and has a gallery, but is not large enough for present requirements. A long, narrow room upstairs is used by the primary Judge in Equity for his sittings, which is too small for the purpose, and the Judge has recourse to the more commodious court below when not in use for general purposes. There is a robing room, law library, and numerous suites of apartments occupied by the master, prothonotary, and other officers. A second court is sadly wanted.

A very handsome building has lately been erected for the local, or Small Debts Court, at the corner of King William and Gouger Streets. It is of cut freestone with ornamental worked courses and facings, the interior well finished and furnished, having large rooms and ample accommodation. The offices of Registrar of Births, Deaths, and Marriages are in this building. The Police Court is a less pretentious, but good building of stone plastered and cemented over, adjoining on the south, but the elevation is very low compared with its frontage. The Superintendent's residence is portion of it.

The Government Printing Office is a new large stone building at the corner of North Terrace and the main road leading to North Adelaide. It is very roomy and contains many tons of type.

The Institute is a neat building on North Terrace, built of stone, stuccoed and painted over. Admission to the library, &c., free. The Museum is in this building, and is much too small for the exhibits, which are crowded together—in fact the whole building will have to be enlarged to satisfy the public requirements.

The Hospital and Lunatic Asylum on North Terrace, although very large buildings, have hitherto been insufficient for public wants. A new wing has lately been added to the former, and a very handsome imposing building is nearly completed in lieu of the latter. It is built of cut freestone, midst 134 acres of land near Parkside, in sight of the Glen Osmond road, and is a very conspicuous object at a long distance round. Most of the land has been trenched and planted by the "unemployed" midst a dull season, and there will be plenty of room for healthy occupation of the inmates.

The Horse Police and Infantry Barracks, Armoury, and Destitute Asylum, adjoin each other on the North Park lands fronting North Terrace; have been erected at different times with a seeming attempt at a Gothic style of architecture, but strangers usually take them for almshouses. There is a good gravelled level parade ground in front.

The Botanic Gardens are on the North Park lands, fronting North and corner of East Terraces. A Government institution, established in 1854, open to the public free. Very prettily laid out under directorship of the late Mr. Francis, and contained at that gentleman's death, a few years since, 2800 specimens of plants under cultivation, but increased, by the indefatigable exertions and tact of Dr. Schomburg, the present director, to 6000 species, besides the grounds and choice flower-beds being most tastefully and artistically beautified, rearranged, and increased. The ground is undulating and contains ponds of ornamental water, partly fed by a small creek which only runs a few months in the year, but principally by the waterworks, well supplied with tame and wild swans, geese and fowl, &c. There are also aviaries of birds, both native and foreign, enclosures and ornamental places with kangaroos (one a white one, a rare specimen), wallabys, emus, wombats, or native bears, and other native and foreign animals, including tigers, bears, racoons, male and female llama, American deer, a Brahma bull, &c.

The Industrial School at Magill, about six miles from Adelaide, is a Government institution, a very handsome large building of cut stone, lying on a plateau, healthily situated, and commanding an extensive view of the plains, the city, Gulf St. Vincent, &c. It stands in midst of about 130 acres of land; has its vineyard, fruit and vegetable gardens, and keeps sufficient cows for use of the house.

The Adelaide Town Hall, on which, with its furniture

and fittings, 24,000*l.* has been expended by the Corporation, with the assent of the citizens, is in King William Street, directly opposite the Post Office. It is built in the most substantial manner of solid dressed stone, and has a tower, rather dumpy in proportion to the main building, called the "Albert Tower," containing a nice peal of bells by Warner and Co., of London. The Hall, where public meetings, balls and concerts, &c., are held, is beautifully finished in ornamental plaster mouldings and tracery, with delicately enriched groups of pillars to gallery. Body of Hall is 110 feet long by 66 feet broad; gallery, 33 by 56 feet. The Hall will hold 1150 seated, and gallery 250 ditto—over 2000 can find standing room. It is unfortunately defective in its acoustic properties, speakers being imperfectly heard. There are large rooms for refreshments, and retiring rooms adjoining; also commodious rooms and suites of apartments below for sittings of the Council, Mayor's and Officers' rooms, &c. There is a balcony of stone in front over the wide pavement at the entrance, supported by massive dressed stone-built square pillars.

Adjoining, on the south side, is the Prince Alfred Hotel, built of cut stone; elevation very lofty, but frontage rather narrow; rooms lofty and well finished; excellent dining room with life-size photograph of the Duke of Edinburgh at head of room. The northern portion of this hotel is occupied by the Civil Service Club. The lessee is the well-known king of South Australian caterers, energetic but unfortunate George

Aldridge, formerly of Kissing Point, near Parramatta, Sydney.

There is also an elegant concert and ball room in King William Street, built and completed in 1855-6 by Mr. George White, one of the oldest colonists, an enterprising and successful Knight of the Thimble, on his own land in King William Street, with its "Shades" below, a cool retreat in hot weather; and a comfortable hotel called the 'Clarence,' at an expense of some 12,000*l*.; the principal room is 85 feet long, 45 feet wide, and 30 feet high, and there are cloak and retiring rooms; also a large room at the rear, called the "Masonic Hall."

Some of the Banks can boast fine buildings. The Bank of Australasia, King William Street and corner of Currie Street, is very lofty and imposing. It is built of stone stuccoed and painted over. The entrance is approached by stone steps leading to a portico supported by tall stuccoed pillars with ornamented caps. Additions are about to be made to the building on the northern side.

The Union Bank of Australia, in Pirie Street and corner of Freeman Street, is a fine edifice of stone, plastered and painted over; rooms very large and lofty, particularly the tellers' and ledger-keepers' departments.

The National Bank with the Imperial Fire Insurance Offices, &c., adjoining, in King William Street, are the gem of the whole, being built of cut freestone with ornamental mullions, &c., the elevation is very bold; the fittings of the interior of the Bank are very handsome and elaborate.

The Savings Bank adjoining on the north side is a neat, pretty building of stone stuccoed over; very ornamental in appearance, and having a frontage of about 40 feet by a depth of 90 feet. The Board and other rooms are commodious and substantially furnished.

The "Exchange" adjoining the Bank of Australasia is known as "Green's Exchange," having been erected in 1853 by Mr. George Green, a well-known land agent, at considerable cost. There is a balcony fronting King William Street, resting on square wooden pillars, affording shelter underneath from the sun and wet weather. The interior is very neatly finished and furnished, but is much inferior in style, size, and convenience to Melbourne and Sydney Exchanges. The Telegraph Office is here, but will be removed to the new building at General Post Office when completed.

There are excellent Produce Markets, one very extensive at the east end of the city, on private property, established at a considerable outlay by the indefatigable exertions of a Mr. Vaughan, in spite of opposition by the Corporation, who had neglected to provide proper accommodation for the public, but seeing Mr. Vaughan's market increase and prosper, have lately established a commodious Central City Market in Gouger Street, three quarters of a mile from the "opposition."

Hotels, public-houses, and churches and chapels are very numerous, more so than in many larger cities and towns. The latter, of every denomination, barring the Heathen Chinee, and Mahomedan. You can stand in Victoria Square and behold as many as nine places of worship in the immediate neighbourhood; the most imposing is the Catholic Cathedral, built of cut stone in the English style within and without, but not completely finished. It possesses one very large, loud, musical-toned bell, imported from Ireland, to many of the inhabitants a perfect nuisance. Trinity Church, at the corner of North Terrace and Morphett Street, with its dumpy tower and primitive appearance, is the oldest in the city. It looks like a country village schoolroom, but has one redeeming feature in the shape of an excellent clock in its miniature tower. The Stow Memorial Church in Flinders Street is the handsomest in the city; built of freestone well dressed, interspersed with imported Caen and Bath stone, elaborately embellished, carved, and so on. The Baptist Chapel in Flinders Street is a very pretty erection of stone, highly enriched in bands, mouldings, buttresses, &c. One chapel in Franklin Street has a very high ornamental spire—it is the primitive something—yet has a rather gaudy interior in the shape of an ornamented purple-coloured cornice. The floor has an incline of a few feet from the north door to the preacher's rostrum. Its minister is celebrated throughout the country for his Lectures on Chemistry, particularly a favourite one of his on the injurious effects to the constitution of "beef-steaks" and "apple-dumplings." He succeeded in getting some 20*l.* damages in an action against a chemist for furnishing some chemicals, said to be inferior in quality, which exploded in the midst of an experiment, doing some injury to himself and assistant.

St. Paul's Church, Pulteney and Flinders Streets, is a large but plain stone-built structure of Glen Osmond stone. The interior is commodious, and all the internal arrangements are exceedingly neat. There are choristers here in the Church of England style. The principal hotel is the 'York,' commodious and comfortable, but not elegant, having been much added to and improved at different times; in fact, there is no very large hotel in Adelaide, most of them being of a medium size. There is a large private club-house on North Terrace, substantially built of stone with brick facings, and a very heavy-looking portico of brick at the entrance. The elevation, however, is bold and lofty.

The Theatre Royal in Hindley Street, belonging to a small company, is centrally situated, but has nothing to take particular notice of outside. The street is not over wide, and does not give too much room to turn a carriage. The interior is very neat, and constructed in the improved modern style, so that the audience can see and hear from almost every part. There are large and extensive refreshment bars below for the general public, and a nice saloon upstairs on a level with the boxes, handsomely fitted up and furnished, and well supplied with edibles and drinks, with smart, lively waitresses in attendance. A large billiard-room at the side, generally kept going whether the theatre is open or not.

The Victoria Theatre, in the old style, in Gille's

Arcade, off Currie Street, has seen its best days, having done duty for many years. It was built by Mr. Emanuel Solomon, a very old colonist, at his own expense, who has been at a great loss from time to time in thus catering for the public; and who has also spent large sums of money in building, amongst other erections, Dorsetta Terrace in Flinders Street, an excellent row of large private houses; also a highly-finished terrace of houses in Franklin Street, near West Terrace, called Rosetta Terrace.

North Adelaide is on the north side of the "Torrens," and is situate on a hill overlooking the city, the buildings and shops being inferior to South Adelaide, but still there are several well laid-out streets and good buildings.

The Church of England Cathedral, according to the plans a very handsome one, is in course of erection at the foot of the hill, and will be gradually built in portions in the Early Decorated style. The total length internally will be 172 feet; width, 59; and height, 76 feet to the ridge.

Christ Church is a large imposing building on the top of the hill, doing duty for some years as a cathedral, adjoining which is the Bishop's Palace, a very comfortable Gothic residence.

The Congregational Church is a large building, said to be very elegant in its interior, but unfinished externally, and has been taken by visitors from other places to be a large colonial wine cellar.

Port Adelaide is the principal port of the colony,

and is connected by railway and main road with the city, about eight miles. It was laid out by the South Australian Company, who still hold many wharfs and much valuable property there. The streets are wide, and the footways are mostly formed with silt, raised in deepening the river and removing the bars of spongy limestone which impede the navigation and prevent vessels of large tonnage coming alongside the wharfs, until lightened, or at high tides. The Parade fronting the river has some good shops and stores, and the place generally is tolerably clean for a port. The river is not very wide or inviting, its banks being swampy in many places, midst mangroves and other stunted timber and growth. It empties itself into Gulf St. Vincent, about seven miles from the port. There are a great many villages and minor towns, named Thebaton, Bowden, Hindmarsh, Kensington, Norwood, Glen Osmond, Glenelg, Brighton, Gawlertown, Kapunda, Gumeracka, Strathalbyn, Willunga, Mount Gambier, and numerous others.

The foregoing are most of the public places and buildings deserving note, and with the statistics will show to a great extent the rapid progress the colony has made in a little more than thirty-four years from its foundation, when it was a wilderness in the hands of wild tribes of aborigines, many of whom are now extinct. The early settlers met with some privations, having at first to live almost in the open air on soup and bouilli, pork, cockatoos and parrots, and some fish, until a few lean sheep were brought over from Tasmania at 2s. a lb. Prime mutton is now selling for 2*d*. and 3*d*., and beef 4*d*. per lb. —a striking contrast.

Apparently 185,000 is a very small population indeed for such an immense territory. This is generally attributed to droughts and heat, there being sometimes three bad seasons in succession, which cause great drawbacks and stagnation in trade, rendering the progress of the colony slow, failing to attract people in sufficient numbers, many who have the means of doing so leaving for other places. Bad and restrictive legislation is also said to be a cause, the laws being subject to many changes, uncertain in their terms, and not liberal and elastic enough with regard to alienation of waste land from the Crown, and mining leases, as likewise the frequent ministerial changes.

The heat now and then is certainly considerable in the summer, about December, January, and February, but the atmosphere remarkably clear and much healthier than India. The thermometer has reached near roasting temperature, 161° in the sun, and as high as 112° in the shade; yet there are a great many beautiful days and the clearest of skies. A fair share of rain, and the "sunny land" would produce anything and everything, in fact, beat "all creation."

ADELAIDE TO MELBOURNE.

(*Sometimes called* PORT PHILIP). 520 Miles.

Wednesday, 1st February, 1871.—Weather fine. Left Port Adelaide at 4.30 P.M., per S.S. 'Penola,' 261 tons, Captain Snewin, for Melbourne. Passage in cabin, 6*l.* Several friends accompanied me down river, and to the Semaphore, about ten miles from the port, where there is a jetty, and there landed in pilot-boat. The Semaphore is on Lefevre's Peninsula, and only about two miles distant from the port by land. Ship and appointments, linen, &c., very clean; my berth (top one) scrupulously clean and comfortable; bottom one not occupied; small marble washing-stand and looking-glass, seat with cotton velvet plum-coloured cushion, hair and clothes brushes, comb and boot-jack firmly fixed in small recesses, brass nails to hang one's clothes on, &c., &c., all made "taut." I felt so jolly comfortable, the weather being moderate, the steamer now and then rolling gently from side to side, that I stuck to my berth for nearly eleven hours at night and morning; towards evening a nice breeze set in, with some sea on, and nearly all were sick in consequence. Steward very attentive. Hot grogs with lemon, 1*s.*; ale and porter, 2*s.* per bottle (quart); lemonade and soda, 6*d.*

Thursday, 2nd February.—Weather fine and cool; light sea breezes. Anchored at Guichen Bay, 185 miles from Adelaide; at 12.30 P.M., about half a mile from Robetown jetty. Sea very smooth and calm in this bay, which is well sheltered. Went on shore with most of the passengers in watermen's boats at expense of ship. The town is full of limestone, irregularly built on slightly-elevated ground, and has a splendid view of the bay, &c. On one side large rocks, and there are some good bathing-places and nice walks on narrow beach at foot of rocks, and some very good houses, banks, and large stores. Sir James Fergusson's, Bart., &c. (Governor of South Australia), summer residence is an excellent stone-built house, to which he has added some rooms of wood, the accommodation not being sufficient. The streets and approaches moderately wide and in good order, with the exception of a short piece of road leading from the jetty, in a very bad state of repair, the limestone projecting out of the ground in some instances a foot and 18 inches. The Government Central Road Board and District Council will not father it, owing to some dispute. Proposed that some of the inhabitants should turn out early some fine morning and do it themselves, but they cannot see the force of it. Met several whom I knew, among them, Mr. Young, late Governor of Her Majesty's gaol (a poor straggling building on top of small hill), some years ago in the horse police at Adelaide, also the solitary horse police-man stationed here, to whom the additional duty of gaoler has been transferred without increase of pay, who kindly showed me about the place. Three or four inns here—two of them very good for so small a town. Shipped several passengers, also some bales of wool, a four-wheel buggy, &c. Weighed anchor at 9 P.M.;

passed near large rocks visible from the shore, necessitating careful watches at night; nice evening, and comfortable sea, comparatively smooth.

Friday, 3rd February.—Fine morning; cool breeze. Anchored in MacDonnell Bay, 80 miles from Robetown, 7.45 A.M., about one mile and a half from jetty. Very inferior anchorage compared with Robetown. Entirely exposed to the ocean on all sides, except on the north a rocky promontory, not very bold or high. Township very irregularly built indeed. Buildings not so good as at Robetown; still there are some large stores. Has a pleasant appearance from the steamer, and commands a beautiful view from the promontory on shore. Good appetite at breakfast; never did rump-steak go down with greater relish; beef improves so much by hanging at sea. Lighters sailed to and from the ship, transshipping cases of brandy and gin, hogsheads of porter and ale; particularly a great number of chests and half-chests of tea, bags of sugar, and other wares for Robetown and Mount Gambier, and the settlers about; also a large piano. What numbers of hands these commodities have and will pass through before consumption! The lighters returned to the steamer with bales of wool and colonial produce for Melbourne, and all hands were very busy all day. Several porpoises knocking about, and a great quantity of sea-weed, the smell from which was very refreshing. A large hill, called Mount Schanck, visible from vessel, about 14 miles distant to the eastward, stands by itself in the midst of a run belonging to the Hon. W. J. T. Clarke, of Melbourne, no other hills being round or near it, with its top about the shape of the back of a razor, covered with timber and bush. In the morning it began to blow rather hard with a heavy swell on, and increased to a rough cross sea the remainder of the day and evening. The captain stopped receiving cargo at 5 P.M., as the lighters shipped so much water, and the gunwale of one of them went with great force against the steamer, the collision knocking a passenger by her down in the bottom, but no damage done. Some passengers during the day had gone to Mount Gambier, about 23 miles, and some persons came down for 'Penola.' A lighter (towards evening) got alongside with some difficulty, and the ladies had to be hoisted on board in a large wooden chair (the back shaped like a cask), by the donkey engine, swaying to and fro in the air like a swing in a fair.

Weighed anchor at 7.55 P.M; steamer pitching heavily in a rough cross sea, with strong head wind from south-east, which continued throughout the night. Mr. Johnston, a lively Scotchman, a "squatter" from beyond Mount Gambier, in the berth below me, tried to sleep, but was slightly sea-sick instead; says he never was so before.

Saturday, 4th February.—Fine cool day. Turned out at 7.30 A.M. Mr. Johnston did not; only nine put in an appearance at breakfast, about a dish to each one. At 8 A.M. wind moderating; sea still very cross; steamer pitching heavily, shipping water; wet decks. At 11 A.M. off Moonlight Heads, a rocky promontory Two bush fires in sight in scrub at the back, where the weather must be hot to occasion such fires, and yet we in the midst of summer can scarcely stay on deck, it is so cold. There is timber on the ranges at the back, at least, so I am told by the chief officer, for I cannot see it on account of the large sand hills. Most of the ladies have not shown up since we anchored in MacDonnell Bay, particularly five Sisters of Mercy (St. Joseph), from Adelaide, *en route* for Brisbane, Queensland, who have been and still are very ill. Two of the Sisters have with difficulty clambered up the companion to get some fresh air; not having been introduced, I could not do the amiable; indeed I had enough to do to keep on my pins, and if I had volunteered my services, I might have toppled over, and unpleasant consequences might have occurred. One fell forwards towards me, but, thank heaven, was saved by the stewardess, a slashing, tall, fine young woman from the Emerald Isle; a great relief to me, I assure you. At 1.30 P.M., abreast of Cape Otway, head wind stronger, with heavy sea—carrying mainsail and foresail now and then. Met steamer 'Omeo,' from Melbourne to Adelaide, with all sails set; a fair wind for her, going at a spanking rate. At 8.30 P.M. entered Melbourne Heads. Night dark, but lighthouses brilliantly lit up, and gas lights of Sandridge, &c., visible in the distance. Comparatively smooth inside, *i.e.* Hobson's Bay. Met steamer 'Alhambra,' for New Zealand. Anchored nearly half a mile off Oldtown Pier, Sandridge, at 11.30 P.M. Night being dark, and too late to land, all stayed on board.

The population of Melbourne and suburbs, 160,000; the population of Colony of Victoria, 700,000.

VICTORIAN STATISTICS, 1870.

Revenue, 3,244,601*l.* Protective Customs' duties prevail, interfering with intercolonial trade.

1,000 manufactories in operation of 70 different articles.

Total area of land occupied for pastoral purposes, 27,702,289 acres, equal to more than 43,284 square miles, divided into 999 runs, of which 552 had purchased land attached to them amounting to 2,375,922 acres. Area occupied for other than pastoral purposes, 9,530,638 acres. Enclosed land, 8,677,947 acres. Under tillage, 909,015 acres.

Produce of grain crops for the year, 5,456,577 bushels. 2,870,409 were wheat, and 2,237,010 oats.

Live stock upon farms: Horses, 144,000; milch cows, 182,000; cattle (exclusive of milch cows), 372,000; sheep, 3,838,000; pigs, 124,900. Live stock on stations or runs: Horses 23,132; cattle (exclusive of milch cows), 151,142; sheep, 6,923,518.

Value of machinery upon farms, 1,402,863*l.*

Approximate value of improvements effected, including buildings of all descriptions, fencing, wells, dams, &c., but not cost of clearing, 8,777,548*l.*

Value of gold taken from the Victoria Gold-fields, from 1851 to 1866, 155 millions.

Sunday, 5th February.—Very fine day. Landed in third boat (ship's), a small one, with the five nuns and a few others, and a pile of luggage. Nuns travel with very little luggage. I unfortunately sat on one slight box belonging to Sister ——, to which attention was called by the steward of the steamer, that I was crushing it in so, I had to remove to something more solid. No one at pier to receive the Sisters, probably on account of our arrival in the night, and Sunday being a heavy day for the Roman Catholics; but they had an address where to go, and being too early for the railway, Mr. Grice, jun. (a passenger), of firm of Grice, Sumner, and Company, kindly chartered a fore-and-aft car (*i.e.* one seat behind, and one before) for the Sisters, and they were dispatched in a jiffy in the care of a Paddy, a regular broth of a boy, who said, "Sure he knew all about it intirely, and faith he came a purpose for the leedies." Mr. Grice and I left in a similar vehicle for the city at half-past eight. Sandridge has grown to be a very large suburb, with well-built houses, hotels, and so on. Arriving at Tankard's Temperance Hotel, Lonsdale Street West, I was set down. Mr. Grice wanting to go a quarter of a mile farther on, cabby asked 7s. 6d. for our fares. Mr. Grice said, "All my eye—you won't get it;" and said to me, "Put 2s. on the seat, and I will polish cabby off." I did this, and bundled into the hotel with my leather trunk, at a pace that would have astonished my friends if they had seen me. My large box, &c., to come from the ship to-morrow, as I did not wish to desecrate the Sabbath more than I could help. I have a good bedroom here to myself, and tacked on the back of the door is a card signed by the Town Clerk of Melbourne (Mr. Fitzgibbon), pursuant to " Health Statute and City Regulations,", &c., that the " Room contains 891 cubic feet, one bed allowed." The bed is certainly large enough for two adults, and probably has and will be at some time made use of by man and wife, but not by me, I think. Very comfortable hotel, though built some years — very large, well-finished and furnished dining-room.

After a bath, passed the morning in the commercial room, reading with avidity the 'Argus' for the week, advertisements, telegrams, &c.; indulging in soda and raspberry, as no fermented or spirituous liquors are allowed on the premises, and a notice is on the walls, " Only brandy allowed to be taken medicinally." Anticipating this state of affairs, and that I must be a total abstainer at dinner, I swallowed two cups of " coffee royal" before I left the 'Penola,' and brought away with me a small bottle of stout, to imbibe just before dinner at half-past one; but, alas! for the weakness of human nature, at about a quarter past eleven I worked out the cork in my bedroom, thanks to the strength and capability of the knife which my friend Aldridge of Adelaide gave me, and I swallowed the contents in a twinkling, unaccompanied by the usual cheese and cucumber. The bottle I threw into a water-tank near, which probably some day may astonish the journeyman plumber, who will be called in to stop a leak or two, exclaiming, " What scoundrel could have dared to invade this sacred teetotal domain with a bottle of nasty, injurious stout—bah!" At dinner thirty-three sat down to an ample spread, and I imbibed a pint of ginger-beer and raspberry. All drank water, except one person, who indulged in ginger-beer, so that it was a bad look out for poor Tankard. What a misnomer his name is for an advocate of teetotalism! One man complained bitterly that he could get no brandy in the house, and he had landed late on Saturday night after a voyage very ill, not anticipating such a state of things, nor being aware such stringent laws existed in a British colony, *viz.* that no hotelkeeper or innkeeper in Victoria can sell from Saturday night at twelve till Monday morning. I told him what I had done, and that he ought to have provided himself with some brandy from his ship in a bottle or bladder. "Alas!" he said, "I was a stranger, and they took me in."

In the afternoon and evening still quiet in the commercial room, as I had not got over the roll of the steamer and the working of her screw, her machinery having been severely tried, and occupied in once more reading the 'History of the Beaus, Fielding, Brummel, and Nash,'—a most amusing book. The day and evening very warm and humid. This is a quiet street, with many good buildings in it; particularly nearly opposite a doctor has erected a large house of cut stone, with a tower or look-out at top, in part of which I am told he has a billiard-room; the side entrance is wide, and on each side of it are two pillars, with a brilliant gas-lamp to each; all this has been done to attract attention and get business. He drives a good pair of horses in a mail phaeton, a "tiger" being in the back seat. A great many very well-dressed persons passed to and fro, particularly during the afternoon, some for the railways, others for boats, steamers, vehicles, &c., &c., bent on their usual Sunday pleasure excursions; many for churches and chapels, all very orderly, and I only saw one policeman at a time near here. Some very good carriages and horses passed, many being elegant equipages.

At 9.30 P.M. I was taking a stroll down the street to see the effect of the numerous lamps lit up with gas, over a great portion of the city in view from here, when I "twigged" a man coming down an alley or narrow lane next to Tankard's, with a jug evidently containing fermented liquor; he went into a house the other side of Tankard's, marked "Lodgings," and no policeman, thanks be, was at hand, to interfere with his movements. I am told that the law is evaded, and drink sold on what is termed "the sly," particularly at the watering and other favourite resorts on Sundays, where police are few and far between.

Monday, 6th February.—Fine day. Went to an elegantly-fitted up hairdresser's shop in Swanston Street, to have "a crop" and brush up. Operator a tall, stout, good-looking fellow, with light curly hair, about 30, fit for the Life Guards. After careful inspection and observation, "Air sadly neglected, sir," "Yes, waited for a sea voyage; not been to Eymer's lately" (the head friseur in Adelaide). "Eymer, sir, I knew him well—

his day's gone by, sir; requires an artist now-a-day, with undimmed eye, quick perception, a delicate touch, and who understands nature and the feel, sir; by-the-by, I would suggest, sir, a patch bout the size of a crown piece, and a bottle of our Balm of Elixer, for the top of your ed, sir; a sovereign remedy for baldness." Declined with thanks. Paid a shilling to the barber's clerk at the counter and exit, looking ten years younger. Saw Mr. Klingender, solicitor, formerly and for many years at Adelaide, who gave me a note to the Town Clerk to obtain admission to the Town Hall. Then went through the Royal Arcade, a very commodious building about 200 feet in depth and 40 feet wide, full of shops on each side, and wares of every description for sale. Went through Swanston and streets adjacent, and took a cursory view of the magnificent shops containing goods, &c., of every description under the sun; then to the Public Library for two hours, which stands on rising ground, with beautiful entrance, an immense building of cut stone, magnificent pillars, &c. The extensive library itself, with its handsome highly-finished gallery, contains a multitude of books of every description, and moreover a law library, all to itself, containing the reports, &c., &c. In the afternoon I visited the large buildings adjoining and connected with the library (but, like most public buildings in Melbourne, in an unfinished state, or something more to be added at a future period), one the Industrial and Necrological Museum, an immense arcade, with very lofty imposing roof painted purple and yellow, and handsome stained-glass windows at sides, &c. A magnificent collection of statuary in two very large lofty long halls; nice and cool promenading, &c. Extensive and splendid collection of oil-paintings, prints, sketches, &c., in a very long room. In fact I spent all the afternoon there, and in the evening again in the gallery of the library, where there are books to suit every taste ; and I doubt whether any single British colony can produce the like.

Tuesday, 7th February.—Wet day. Began to rain very hard at five in the morning, and continued with little variation all day and throughout the evening; lower parts of streets temporarily flooded. Most of the cabbies on the stands placed their horses in the running streams through the wide gutters, which the animals seemed to enjoy very much. Very little summer weather this season throughout the colonies. Went round the large brick building in course of erection for "Mint." Quoins and buttresses of Melbourne cut stone, very durable, will form a square when finished, *i. e.* it will be like a barrack square (barring the "canteen"); only the back part and two sides nearly completed; is being roofed in and pushed on to begin to coin as soon as possible. Front with a tower intended to be gone on with at once. Three chimneys about 100 feet high already completed, of white firebrick, ornamented now and then with red brick, interspersed with crosses of stone of a black colour. A man on the works told me it was too late; the Mint ought to have been up sixteen or seventeen years ago, as gold is getting year after year much scarcer. More closely inspected that magnificent group of (Melbourne cut stone) buildings, the General Post office, with pillars elaborately worked, &c.; its numerous boxes in arcades for posting, registering, and receiving letters, &c., to and from all parts of the world, are wide and very extensive, in fact there is room enough for all; still one end (where there is a temporary money office of galvanized iron) has yet to be built. Went round a handsome church with very tall spire of brick, ornamented at the angles, which cost 16,000*l*., called the Scotch Presbyterian Church; minister, the Rev. Robert Henderson; it is in Bourke Street, pleasantly situated on the top of a hill (near Bourke and Wills', the explorers, monument). It is erected of brick with white worked stone quoins. Introduced to Town Clerk in afternoon, who sent Town Hall porter round with me to see the interior of the building. The large hall in hands of painters and decorators, as walls have not been fit to allow this to be done until now. Large organ partly built. When complete the Hall and buildings will cost from 100,000*l*. to 105,000*l*.

Length of Hall, 166 ft.
Breadth „ 71 ft. 6 in.
Height, about 60 ft.
Will seat about 4000.
Hold, standing, about 6000.

Beautifully ornamented and embellished, particularly caps of pillars; extensive gallery.

Splendid supper-room, retiring rooms for ladies, carpeted and handsomely furnished, large cloak-room for ditto, large concert-room, and more retiring rooms; rooms for gentlemen to change, &c., ditto to wash in, &c., fitted up with mahogany and white marble stands, &c.; also a smoking-room. Town Clerk's and assistants' apartments above and below. Town Hall porters' room, carpeted, with sofa, chairs, &c., and other rooms, &c., too numerous to mention. In evening went to "Theatre Royal"—as large as the Haymarket, with about half-a-dozen bars and eighteen barmaids, some very smart, business not active—to see Mrs. Gladstone, an actress of much merit, but not so good to my mind as Mrs. Kean, Madame Celeste, &c.; attendance medium.

Wednesday, 8th February.—Morning opened with slight showers. Went and more closely inspected General Post Office. Then on the Exchange and to Exchange room, reading rooms, &c., upstairs; a large but not a very good building, new one much wanted. Great commotion and stir among the brokers and money lenders on the "Pavement," some very "seedy"-looking individuals amongst them, but commissions appeared to be at a discount. Went on board S.S. 'Penola,' lying at the Queen's Wharf, about ten minutes' walk from the Exchange, to look for my missing memoranda book. "Where is it?" Steward and stewardess searched everywhere, berth included, but without success. Went to see Botanic Garden in afternoon. Cab to Prince's Bridge, South Yarra, for sixpence; then walked about a mile in a pathway running by the banks of the Yarra, a narrow stream throughout, but deep enough for boating, several skiffs being on it; the pathway beautifully shaded by trees and shrubs; a splendid cool walk. Grounds very undulating, plenty of ornamental water-courses, ponds, &c.; very picturesque. It is bounded on one side by the Yarra. It is full of all kinds of beautiful trees, flowering and other shrubs, but with regard to the hothouses and flowers, arrangement of the parterres and so on, is infinitely inferior in its ornamental character to the Adelaide Gardens in care of Dr. Schomberg, which are not near so old, and not half so much money expended upon them. The "Victoria Regia" not equal to the Adelaide one. It is a large spot, about six times more so than Adelaide, but, properly speaking, is a "Park," not a "Garden." Grass and walks well kept. It is said that over 90,000*l.* has been spent since the appointment of Baron von Mueller as Director, but no adequate return for the money. Occupied all afternoon. Evening again at Theatre Royal. Saw Mrs. Gladstone in 'Frou Frou;' rather a tedious tame affair; good actress, but few to support her. Could barely be called a "good" house. Business at the extensive bars still appeared to be slack. Was told scarcity of money was the only reason.

MELBOURNE TO SANDHURST.
100¾ Miles.

Thursday, 9th February.—Fine weather. Chief town of the Bendigo Gold-fields. By railway, a double line. Railway station in Spencer Street. The ground occupied by this station at first was 50 acres, now increased to an area of 100 acres. Land fenced in by a substantial galvanized iron fence about 7 feet high, occupying about a quarter of a mile in length to Spencer Street.

The present station, although a well-finished structure

of wood, is only a temporary one, it being intended to build a substantial stone one soon. There are commodious refreshment and other rooms for the accommodation of passengers, nicely papered and painted. Station roof is of galvanized iron. Length of platforms, 730 feet. There are at present four large galvanized-iron sheds. A large shed in course of erection of brick, nearly ready for roofing, to be of galvanized iron. There will be two platforms to this shed, about 870 feet in length. Left station 6.45 A.M. Got to Sandhurst in 3 hours and 55 minutes.

1st Station, *North Melbourne.*—Three quarters of a mile; an insignificant one (train did not stop). For about 2 miles passed through flat, swampy land, not at all inviting, and uncultivated. Houses of an inferior description here and there.

2nd Station, *Footscray.*—Three miles; same sort of station as North Melbourne; crossed, on a bridge, over Salt Water River. Same description of swampy country, succeeded by a plain.

3rd Station, *Keilor Road.*—A small plain station of wood. Stopped here a short time. Scattered township about a mile away; nothing worthy of notice; flat open country follows.

4th Station, *Diggers' Rest.*—Twenty and a quarter miles from Melbourne; a small station, so called from the diggers camping near there in the early period of the diggings, before any coaches were started. The land about there belongs to the Hon. W. J. T. Clarke, one, if not the largest landed proprietors in the colonies

D

(120,000 acres in Victoria, 50,000 in Tasmania, 75,000 in South Australia, and 45,000 in New Zealand; besides valuable town properties and shares in companies and banks), supposed to be worth at least two millions sterling; was formerly a butcher in Somersetshire. The railway runs through his land, and there were two large flocks of sheep, each running in a very extensive fenced-in paddock. About this spot "the Plains" end. They commence near Footscray, mostly poor land, scarcely any timber, not cultivated, and sparsely inhabited, there being very few cattle and horses about. There was a station about twelve miles from Melbourne called Albion and Darlington, abandoned some time ago, there being so little traffic to it. Between Footscray and Diggers' Rest, and at a few other insignificant places, women and children turn themselves into "signal-men" to save expense. A woman or child rushes out of a cottage door on the approach of a train, and holds up a stick with a small square piece of white linen attached, indicating "all right." From Diggers' Rest the country becomes more hilly and of better description, with farms and some large vineyards. The Industrial Schools are visible on the top of a large hill, from which a fine view must be obtained. The buildings are large and detached; I counted twelve and a house about the centre, the superintendent's residence, all visible from near Diggers' Rest station. There are over 500 children there, I am told.

Stopped at all following stations.

5th Station, *Sunbury.*—A small neat station, with

township close by; nothing to speak of. Shortly after leaving, crossed Jackson's Creek (water plentiful); better country, well timbered, some nice houses now and then, plenty of good gum and shea-oak trees, &c. (Down train passed.) Some very good country between this and the next station, for the greater part level, nearly all grass land; in fact, there is nothing in view cultivated.

6th Station, *Lancefield Road.*—Township not visible, a few sheep here and there, plenty of goats near straggling cottages; good level, well-timbered country.

7th Station, *Riddell's Creek.*—Very small station, of wood. Township close by; small, and houses poor; low hills near; a little church visible nearly on top of one hill. Went through three cuttings of rock not very deep. Some beautiful wooded hills visible in the distance through some slight cuttings. Country rather hilly; a monster hill, and very long called "Mount Macedon," seen in the distance, seemingly covered with timber and growth, very bold appearance, and runs away to a short point at its north end; but I am told there are roads and pathways all over it, that there are a few farms there and steam saw-mills, that nearly all the largest trees have been cut down for years, that comparatively few "big" ones now remain, but still a brisk trade is carried on. Mount Macedon is connected with a long chain of hills many miles in length, on the south side, but mere babies compared to her.

8th Station, *Gisborne* (new).—A small wooden station, and township near; few wooden houses, but neat, at this place. Scrub land called the Black Forest commences, a great deal of which has been cleared within the last twenty years, especially so near Gisborne; the old township not visible. In the old times diggers used to camp about this forest, on their way to Forest Creek Diggings, &c. Several parties would camp out near each other to prevent being robbed, and I was pointed out a favourite camping place where, my informant assured me, he had seen on more than one occasion from 100 to 150 drays camped out, and sometimes many of them detained for days on account of heavy rains and the boggy nature of the ground, &c.

9th Station, *Macedon*.—So called after the Mount, and about five miles from it. This station is a very small one, of wood, about 25 feet in length, and the station-master's house is built of wood, the opposite side, very neat in appearance. Small township, the cottages mostly wooden ones. Splendid view of the Mount from this station, with the "ranges" attached to it. Plenty of split timber, &c., &c., in yards, ready to be sent off by rail, principally to Melbourne. Country hilly; many cuttings, some deep, the soil mostly soft stuff. Country pretty well timbered; no cultivated land in sight.

10th Station, *Woodend*.—Small, partly galvanized-iron and wood. Formerly called the Five-mile Creek, and stopping place for drays, &c., in early digging times. Township scattered, poor buildings, mostly wood. There is a good hotel close by, called 'Victoria Hotel,' by H. Thornburn. Woodend, so named from its being the depôt for cut wood, posts and rails for fencing, palings from iron, bark, and gum trees, &c., felled at Mount Macedon and the forest, and shingles and slabs for roofs and buildings, poles and props and bark for cool roofs. There was an immense quantity ready all round the station to be taken away, some three or four acres covered with material; the shingles, sawn timber rails and palings, were nice and white, and turned out well and comparatively smooth. Country level, train going about thirty-five miles per hour; only went through one cutting, and that not very deep. A few poor crops of wheat now and then to be seen, some cut and in sheaves, apparently spoilt from the wet, of which this district, it is said, has had more than its share; also a few standing crops, but I could not see more than five or six bushels to the acre. I am told that very little wheat was sown last season on account of the unfavourable weather, the land being inundated at times. Saw a few potato crops looking remarkably well.

11th Station, *Carlsrue.*—Fifty-three miles from Melbourne. First stone-built station; small but neat. Country nearly level, and very good land. Lots of potato crops in blossom, and looking well. Some cattle and horses now and then to be seen.

12th Station, *Kyneton.*—A well-built, handsome station, of dark Melbourne stone (large square pieces), hammer dressed, &c., up and down station. Platform on each side, about 100 feet long. Sheds, &c., of similar stone. Handsome verandah to both platforms. Commodious refreshment room; one pretty girl, one plain ditto. Good English ale, 6d. per glass. Cauldfield's Farmers' Hotel close by, well built of stone. A wooden house near; an inn called 'Samson's,' not at all looking like " Samson " contrasted with " Victoria." The township is a large one, about a mile from station; some very fine stone buildings there. A public garden, not long laid out, and bounded on its west side by Corlevan Creek (plenty of water in it) towards the railway. The ground just sufficiently hilly, and the walks appear to be winding and well laid out. Very good country, and almost level, exhibiting signs of the late heavy rains and floods. Substantial farm-houses and some steam flour-mills visible now and then. Said to be a good wheat-growing country, but very little sown last season on account of the wet. One paddock of wheat reaped; appeared to be spoilt. Country looks as if it has had a soaking for some time. One paddock wheat standing, very light, not six bushels to the acre. The Malmsbury water reservoir close by, running over with water fed by the Corlevan River, now a fine swollen stream. The reservoir is so close to the river that it almost looks to be part of it. Crossed a fine viaduct over the Corlevan before entering next station.

13th Station, *Malmsbury.*—A good stone-built station, about 80 feet frontage. Township good; many well-built houses of stone; a few of wood. About 40 miles of good bold forest seen to the west, about 15 miles off. Good country, but very little under cultivation. Fine potato patches on sides of embankments not far from station, belonging to railway employés. A few horses, cattle, and some pigs and goats about. Passed over a bridge near the station on a large creek flooded with very dirty water.

14th Station, *Tarradale.*—Nice, well-built station, of dark Melbourne stone in large squares, hammer dressed, with good shed of stone, and other buildings; about 70 feet frontage. Scattered township, very pleasantly situated in a valley on west, with some very good houses in it, and the customary wooden ones. Passed over viaduct on nearing the station. A decent church in the distance. Passed through scrubby land growth, &c., for several miles. Many flocks of goats about.

15th Station, *Elphingstone.*—A small neat brick-built station; brick goods shed, &c. Township very scattered, close by; poor buildings, principally of wood. Near this station is a spot called Saw Pit Gully, near which was formerly a camping place for diggers. Still scrubby land, but a great many nice young saplings springing up. Went into a very deep cutting of rock, and then through a tunnel about a quarter of a mile long (the first I have been through since 1852). Country well wooded. Hills within two miles. Old Forest Creek Diggings in sight, and shortly afterwards the train ran close by. Appeared to me to be abandoned, only one man fossicking about. Appeared to be full of water-holes and water from recent rains, but I am told they are still worked by machinery. It is a long scattered township, of mostly small houses of every description, a sort of tumble-down affair. Mount Alexander visible in the distance; a very bold appearance.

16th Station, *Castlemaine*.—Great digging place formerly; little doing at present. A splendid large brick-built station, stone quoins; up and down platform; handsome verandah on each side; about 120 feet frontage. Large town partly on a hill, but mostly in a valley, through which runs a very good main road. There are numerous large well-built houses, buildings, with churches, chapels, hotels, &c. A splendid brewery visible from the railway. Her Majesty's gaol on the top of a hill, looking down on Her Majesty's subjects below. A few gardens in and about the town, but the soil in view appeared to be very heavy clay, sort of diggers' washing stuff. This place is now said to be very dull, very little going on in prosecuting search for gold. Went through several deep cuttings. Country rough and hilly. Now and then the remains of diggers' work seen. Several water-courses, and surface water lying about, the low-lying lands having been inundated by unprecedented floods for the season of the year. The Ballarat coach had been detained at Glengower for half an hour before it could cross a creek. Fruit gardens near creeks also suffered, and the fruit lying on the ground, which the wind had shaken from the branches, was washed away. A few miserable hovels seen. Again through deep cuttings of stone and some rather soft stuff. Up to this station I was indebted to Dr. ——, a passenger, for some information as to locality, &c. The Doctor, a middle-aged man, carried with him a soda-water bottle filled with brandy-and-water (rather highly coloured), at which he swigged with great gusto, and honestly confessed that he seldom had an appetite for breakfast, but was ready for anything at 11 A.M.

17th Station, *Harcourt.*—Very neat station, of brick and stone. Only a few good houses to be seen. A chapel in the distance. Still hilly and rocky; rocks cropping out of the land, appearance of granite. Through deep cuttings of splendid granite.

18th Station, *Ravenswood.*—Very small wooden station. Only a few small houses near. Country more open, and pretty well timbered; no cultivation, only a small bit of garden to a cottage here and there. Large blocks of granite cropping out of the land. Heavy granite cuttings. Now rather hilly; land poor; a range of hills not far away. Very deep cutting through a sort of slate or rotten-stone, and then went through a tunnel of about 250 yards, and into deep cuttings of slate or rotten-stone again. Now signs of the diggings on every side, with tall, smoking chimneys, machinery, &c., in the distance, but no one was working near here, and the country appeared to have been lately flooded. Water very yellow and dirty.

19th Station, *Kangaroo Flat.*—Formerly a great digging spot, now little or nothing doing there. Pretty brick-built but small station, with a few wooden houses of the better class about. Land scrubby, no large timber, only saplings, &c. Again signs of diggings; chimneys and shafts, &c., on hills (not very high), part of Sandhurst, a very large scattered town. Some very good buildings visible, also a large school-house of brick on the top of a hill, with bell, &c. The line from Melbourne to Sandhurst is fenced off on both sides (plenty of land left on either side to add to or make a line) with a post and three-railed fence of wood, in some instances with two wires added; most of the posts capped with a piece of iron, the posts and rails, &c., being neatly cut and finished. On sides of the embankments lucern has been sown to protect them, which is growing vigorously and beautifully green, like in spring time, owing doubtless to the very wet autumn and summer. The line is well ballasted with the dark Melbourne stone, broken to a small gauge, and must be everlasting. The bridges &c., are built in the most substantial manner of the same kind of stone, and some unnecessary, lavish expenditure has taken place in dressing, quoins, &c., as if they were bridges in a city or town. Officials much better dressed than Adelaide, in fine dark-blue clothes with gilt buttons; crown in cap, worked in gilt, &c., and looked a superior class of men.

20th Station, *Sandhurst.*—The capital town of the Bendigo Gold-fields. This station is beautifully built of red and white brick, and with its sheds, &c., occupies a frontage of about 250 feet, *i.e.* the buildings. There is more land attached to it, fenced in with galvanized iron, &c. The town is a very large and extensive one, the houses and buildings being very commodious and exceedingly well built. Places of worship of almost every denomination; a savings bank and all the other banks; splendid well-made wide roads and footways flagged with stone; in fact, everything you might see in a large city or town in England. There is also a fruit market and a cattle and pig market separate. I must say they are in the old-fashioned style, very dirty, not well built; in fact, the worst I have seen. From the top of a hill I saw houses, diggings, machinery, &c., as far as my eye could reach, and I am told that the Bendigo district is more than 20 miles in extent, and that similar appearances run all over the district. After taking a cursory view, I went in a car for 6d., about 1½ mile, to the Eagle Hawk Gully, so celebrated in years gone by for its enormous yield of gold. We drove along a beautiful wide road, passing by the old Ironbark Gully Diggings, Long Gully (once known as Commissioners' Point), and Windmill Hill, and so on to Eagle Hawk. No surface digging going on, but quartz reefing is progressing, and parties are now doing well, although it is a great risk, having to go down 200, 300, 400, or 500 feet, and sometimes more. I could see gold in many of the stones brought up in the large tub the shape of a cask, by a whim drawn by one horse. In the afternoon I went with a friend to the quartz workings on California Gully close by, and saw some splendid specimens taken out of the "Britannia," and I had four presented to me. My friend, Mr. Gard, said I may as well go down the shaft by the ladders; it was only about 300 feet deep. I declined this, observing that though Britannia rules the waves, she shouldn't rule me on the diggings. There are a great many claims now working. I also inspected the stamps and machinery at two places, very extensive and very expensive ones. I was driven nearly half the afternoon over the diggings, and then into Sandhurst. The day fine, and but little remains of the late flood, the largest and heaviest ever experienced there. A great many persons were walking about, females particularly noticeable in large force, mostly by themselves; a great many of them dressed in the most expensive fashionable style. The brokers on Change under the "Verandah," as it is termed here, seemed in excellent spirits at the prospect of better times, creating a great din in transacting their business of buying and selling shares, &c., and many of them appeared to fancy that ere long they will be in a position to cast aside their seedy-looking garments and obtain new. My friend and I went first to the pig market, a very primitive, dirty spot. It was nearly over. The pigs were mostly dark-blue or black, and appeared to be very well bred.

After a long talk with an old Paddy, offered him 2*l.* 17*s.* 6*d.* for a black sow, but he wanted 1*l.* more. Then went to the fruit market, where an auctioneer was busy in "knocking things down." Fruit said to be plentiful, and selling very cheap—greengages, peaches, &c., 2*d.* a dozen, and so on. Then adjourned to an oyster shop, where we had a dozen each, fresh and good, at 1*s.* 6*d.* per dozen—all brought up from Melbourne by railway. A few years since these luxuries were not to be got here for love or money. The chief supply is obtained from Sydney. Shops containing general merchandise very good, and well supplied with everything one could wish for—plate-glass window fronts to several shops, and business steadily going on, as if no gold-fields were close at hand. In the evening the town and shops were well lighted with gas. Slept at a splendid hotel called 'The Shamrock.' It has a balcony 100 feet to Pall Mall—a wide open place—and 40 feet to Williamson Street, with balustrades to it of fancy iron-work, &c. House built of stone, plastered over, and nicely painted; beautiful large dining and breakfast saloon, well finished and excellently furnished; waiters in the "London" style. A clerk kept, who has an office immediately inside the entrance to diningroom. He had a book with the numbers of the bedrooms in it. After a Welsh rarebit and a bottle of stout, when I wished to "turn in" at 10.30, the clerk asked the waiter what bedroom I was to occupy; he replied, "No. 18," then wrote my name opposite 18 in the book. "What train do you leave by?"—"The first to Melbourne at 6.30." He then wrote, "To be called at 5.45 A.M." Slept in a comfortable bed, so enveloped in mosquito curtains that I had some difficulty in getting inside without making holes in the muslin.

Friday, 10th February.—A beautiful morning and day. Woke at 5.30, much refreshed, but rather "dry." Boots were outside, ready cleaned, at 5.45. Boots knocks at the door. "All right!" was the reply. Breakfast things were laid, but no guest down but myself. Had some excellent ham, rusk, bread and butter, and coffee. Paid charge for supper, bed, and breakfast, 7s. 6d., and went immediately away to the railway station, about 10 minutes' walk. Arrived at Melbourne station at

10.20 A.M. The day being very clear, distinctly saw several roads laid out over Mount Macedon, but no houses visible, being hidden by timber and growth. Went over the station, and saw new large goods shed in course of erection. Called at engineer-in-chief of railway's office, and obtained particulars of area, &c., of the land occupied by the station, &c.

Evening, went to Theatre Royal, and saw Mrs. Gladstone as 'Leah.' She was very correct and good, but was said not to be equal to Miss Cleveland in that character. Have only been able to see the outside of the magnificent pile of buildings, the Parliament Houses, Parliament not being in session, as no one can gain admittance without an order from an M.P., most of whom resided out of town, or were engaged in new elections. The hospital is an immense structure of brick, &c., having a frontage of over 210 feet, and occupying an acre of ground.

Must pass over the markets, which are not much to boast of, although extensive, and on Saturday nights as noisy as Billingsgate, going by the name of "Paddy's Market." Very bustling was told. But taking the city and suburbs together, they infinitely surpass any of the capitals of the other Australian colonies—the superior character of the buildings, the streets being so well kept in repair, the footways paved with flat stones, and the kerbing and guttering of stone, all dressed. Menzies and the Port Philip Club are two magnificent, commodious hotels, and there are also many other handsome ones.

MELBOURNE TO SYDNEY, NEW SOUTH WALES.
580 Miles.

Saturday, 11th February.—Beautiful day. Left Hobson's Bay Railway Station for Sandridge Pier, 3 miles, at 3.15 P.M. First-class fare, covered by steamer ticket. Station up and down, very large, there being branches to several suburban places. Passengers for suburbs cross from booking-office to their side over a small iron bridge, approached and descended by iron steps railed off. Went on board Australian Steam Navigation Company's steamship 'City of Adelaide,' register tonnage, 615; burthen, 1000; horse-power, 220; iron-built on the Clyde by J. and G. Thomson, of Glasgow; captain, J. B. Walker, a regular stout-built, kind-hearted British tar. Saloon fare, 5*l*.; cabin berths much larger than the 'Penola's,' with wide horsehair sofa or seat, long enough to lay on at full length. Two berths in each cabin, with a separate washing place; toilet set, &c, fixed in mahogany case, over washstand; 2*s*. 6*d*. charged for a bottle of ale or porter; 9*d*. for hot grogs with lemon; 6*d*. per glass for anything else, *i. e.* wine, lemonade, seltzer, tonic, soda-water, &c. Left wharf punctually at 4 P.M., there being opposition on the line. This steamer had only arrived in Melbourne the *night* previous. Extra hands were put on; cargo discharged; another shipped, and she was ready for sea again in a few hours. Just after leaving the wharf, an excited elderly gentleman hove in sight, and by voice and gesture, waving an umbrella, and so on, tried to stop the steamer, but without success. A travelling agent for an opera company on board soon explained the reason why. The gentleman's (a Melbourne merchant) daughter was on board, having clandestinely left her home to go to San Francisco, being "stage struck." She had attempted to do so before, and was taken off one steamer. But this time she had eluded his vigilance, and succeeded in getting away with a considerable quantity of wearing apparel. Before evening she was dubbed the "mysterious young lady." She was plain in person, about four or five and twenty years old, but very affable, chatty, and vivacious; particularly interesting in her conversation, and fond of argument at table, having evidently read a great deal; in fact, the very life of the ship. At times abstracted, as if something hung on her mind. Very childish on one point—dress—often changing her costume during the day; in fact, to use a colonial expression, the lady had evidently "a shingle loose." Overhauled steamship 'Blackbird,' 531 tons, for Sydney (she had a quarter of an hour's start of us), before we got half down the bay. Her passengers looked a rather low, scabby lot. At sunset, off Queenscliffe, a favourite resort of the Melbournites, and particularly newly-married couples. Very good hotel there, with a tower and look-out to it; well-built houses, a lighthouse, and jetty. Passed close to it. It had a very pretty appearance at sundown, when we cleared the heads, about 30 miles from Melbourne. Abreast of Cape Schank at 9 P.M.; a lighthouse on it. Rounded the cape at 9.45; in open ocean at 10 P.M.; sea comparatively smooth; threw up rocket and burnt blue-light; answered by steamship 'Derwent,' for Launceston, Tasmania, by burning a blue-light; the night being dark, it had a pretty effect. Slept heavily; knew nothing about the night's doings. Sea was middling smooth according to log.

Sunday, 12th February.—Morning and throughout day very fine. At 4 A.M. passed the cleft rock, cropping out of the sea, not very large, but dangerous. About 5 A.M. passed large conical-shaped rock called 'Redundo' —top about shape of a round corn-stack. 7.15 off the sea rocks, four in number, with range of bold rough rocky hills at back, called the Gipps Land ranges, about 115 miles from Melbourne Heads. The shore appeared to be very rough and rocky. Some passengers sick, and did not put in an appearance at breakfast. Several during the morning, both ill and well, were lolling about the poop, wrapped up in opossum and other rugs. One, a Jewess, with a female companion, was stretched out comfortably on the skylight, busy reading novels; others with newspapers, and so on. A passenger jocosely observed to Rachel, who was a native of Goulbourn, New South Wales, "Ain't you going below to nurse your husband?" who was in his berth awfully sea-sick. "Oh dear, no," she replied; "fiddlesticks and nonsense, we've been married over six years." A Wesleyan minister, also from Goulbourn, afforded a fund of amusement. We saw by the newspapers that he had only been married a few days before at Melbourne. He was tenderly nursing his young wife, carefully wrapped up in shawls and rugs; in fact, he stuck to her so close that they appeared to be part of each other; he fondled, and read at intervals selections from some laughable work of a lively author—one of Dickens', we guessed—trying to allay the awful feeling caused by her sickness. Slept over this reverend gentleman, *i.e.* I had top berth, and he had the bottom one. His wife was in the ladies' cabin. In colonial steamers a large roomy cabin is set apart solely for females, thus separating the males from the females, and keeping the saloon more select, as colonists had been in the habit of taking any persons' wives but their own from one place to another. A few absentees from dinner, which was a splendid spread, the "mysterious young lady" being very well and particularly lively in her conversation. After dessert visited the unfortunate "Jumping Moses" in his berth. He had managed to put on a clean shirt, but felt too ill to turn out. He looked as white as a sheet, in fact a perfect Lazarus. Persuaded him, after some bother, to swallow a glass of raw brandy, and then left him to his fate. Nothing sighted after Gipps Land till 4.45 P.M., then land visible many miles off called the Snowy Ranges, New South Wales, very lofty and bold, and distant from Melbourne about 250 miles. Shall see nothing more of Victoria; only New South Wales from thence. Weather hazy towards and in evening. Wesleyan minister held service in saloon in evening; about sixty attended; rather lengthened service, singing and sermon. Head steward very wroth, as he couldn't brew a drop of grog till 'twas over, and he was afraid his pocket would suffer. Was for sewing the poor parson up in a bag with a piece of lead and pitching him overboard. Cleared 90 mile beach, which had been in sight for some time, and Ram Head, a bold rocky promontory, at 8.45 P.M. No light shown there. Now plenty of sea room. Cleared Cape Howe at 11 P.M.; a lighthouse there, and telegraph lately opened from thence to Sydney. Night dark and hazy; captain afraid of a north-easter; a lively sea on, but nothing to prevent sleeping.

Monday, 13th February.—Turned out at 7. Morning cloudy, but at 7.30 sun came out, weather got clear, and sea middling calm. Main land, part New South Wales, visible; had been so from 12.30 at night, and will be so nearly all the way to Sydney. Passed large full-rigged ship, all sails set; also a large barque in full sail, looking well in the distance. Land consisting of very high hills still visible. Coast bold and rugged; an immense lofty mass called "Mount Dromedary," a beautiful sight. Abreast of Dromedary at 10.30 A.M.; appeared to be covered partly with small timber and scrub. Passed Montagu Island, 160 miles from Sydney, very low, small, rocky, and barren, at 11 A.M., but long and narrow, uninhabited, only some rabbits and goats being there, with good fishing round and outside. A succession of very high peaks and spurs at the back, of every shape and form, extending for miles, called the Goulbourn Ranges, a noble, picturesque sight. At 12.30, abreast of entrance to the Clyde River, near two or three diminutive islands, seemingly all rock; being closer in shore could trace the entrance of the river through rocky headlands. Weather still hazy, with a tolerable sea on. Rained from 3.30 to about 4.30 P.M., with head wind and rather heavy sea on. At 5, abreast of "Cook's Pigeon House," a remarkable cone of rock at the top of a lofty mountain, called after Captain Cook; a very large hollow at the foot of this mountain, looking like a huge bowl; some term it "The Devil's Punch Bowl," and the cone "The Lemon." Cape St. George and Jervis Bay became visible with its lighthouse at sundown. At 7.45 saw its revolving light of red, white, and green; very pretty appearance. Out of Jervis Bay, and cleared Cape George at 9 P.M. A rubber or two of whist at night; my partner a crusty, rheumatic old New South Wales settler, known on board as Captain Cuttle, who had been to Melbourne to get some minerals found on his property tested. We lost four glasses of grog, and he continued growling until he had made two palpable mistakes himself, when he "shut up," and would play no more, being afraid of losing again. Weather looked "dirty," and was comparatively so during the night. Land still in sight, and so on to Sydney.

Tuesday, 14th February.—Morning beautifully fine and clear; day turned out oppressively hot and humid. Turned out at 5.30. Entered Sydney Heads at 5.45 A.M. The harbour, with its picturesque inlets, a bay here and a bay there, a variety of nooks and crooks, of creeks and corners, with numerous queer-shaped rocky promontories, on which native shrubs and wild flowers cluster among the rocks and little islands, looked more beautiful than ever, with lovely sea and town scenery mingled together. Besides, since here in 1853-54 numerous villa and other residences have been erected on the rocky eminences, hills, and slopes on each side of the harbour, adding much to the beauty of the scene. Little fleets of small steamers and boats running from shore to shore and all parts of the harbour; also several batteries, some in midst of the harbour, one called "Fort Denison," another, "Fort Macquarie Battery," is on a point in sight of Government House, manned with eleven guns, and "Pinch Gut," a small island or chaos of solid stone, rising up in the centre of the harbour, now and for years bare of trees and soil, with ten guns.

The outlay has been over 80,000l., and some (supposed to be) scientific men, shake their heads and exclaim, "Money thrown away!" "No practical defence at all!" &c., &c., the Government and its officials being, of course, a set of noodles. Some neat wooden bridges or viaducts have also in late years been erected from shore to shore. Got alongside A.S.N. Company's wharf, Sussex Street, at 7 A.M., and no sooner had the landing-stage been "placed," than the "mysterious young lady" was escorted by a gentleman passenger, and popped, with her luggage, into a hansom cab, which drove rapidly away, the driver being well paid to act "mum." A minute had scarcely elapsed, when a tall elderly gentleman in gold spectacles, and stick with silver head and tassel, hurriedly came on board and spoke to the captain. The telegraph had evidently been at work between Melbourne and Sydney. The captain called down below, "Steward, is Miss H. in her cabin?" well knowing all the time that she had left the ship. "No, sir, she went ashore five minutes ago." Exit elderly gentleman, rather chagrinned, midst the suppressed laughter of all. Went to Oriental Hotel, Circular Quay, with my luggage in a van, about a mile for 2s.

My attention was called immediately to a ship over 2130 tons burthen, called the 'Sobraon,' quietly anchored alongside the wharf, within fifty yards of the hotel, a magnificent vessel, with some other "wollopers" near her, and my thoughts went back to Adelaide, and her insignificant river and port (so-called). The City of Sydney, with islands in Port Jackson, contained in 1870 65,463 inhabitants; suburbs, 59,675. Estimated population of the colony of New South Wales, exclusive of crews of colonial vessels at sea, and roving aborigines, 500,000. (In lunatic asylum, Tarbarn Creek, at Ryde, 204 males, 133 females.) Walked up and down George and Pitt Streets, the two principal ones, on each side, nearly two miles; they looked old, and so narrow after Melbourne and Adelaide, that I could scarcely believe I was in the principal streets of the city; also visited several adjacent and cross streets.

Many of the stone footways full of holes, and in the most dilapidated condition; the streets very dirty, and certainly not in good repair; the metal not broken to a proper gauge; particularly noticed the footway full of dangerous holes outside Mr. Dawson's and other lawyers' offices in Pitt Street; a sign of lucrative practice.

Was informed that the Corporation are "hard up;" but why they don't compel the owners of properties to mend their ways in front of their houses, as in most other colonies, couldn't ascertain.

The omnibuses generally a shabby lot to look at, many of them small, narrow, and dirty, with no stuffing to the seats; drivers often breaking in horses, and racing and loitering about. Many of the drivers, and most of the 203 boy conductors, very shabbily dressed, having no clothes but borrowed coats. Many of them clothed in an absolutely indecent manner, and apparently didn't often wash themselves. Informed that these matters were about to be brought before Parliament by a Mr. Lunt. Pair-horse hack carriages cleaner and in better condition, although several getting old.

The Church of England Cathedral is a noble building of cut stone, highly ornamented, fronting George Street South, at its widest part. Should say it is the finest in the Australian colonies. The Catholic Cathedral is being rebuilt on the old site, looking on Wooloomooloo; the old tower being still standing, not having been damaged by the fire which destroyed the old cathedral a few years ago. The banks, particularly the Commercial, in George Street, are finer in appearance, and much better built—of Sydney stone, beautifully finished and cut pillars, with ornamented caps—than the Melbourne or Adelaide banks, except the present City Bank, the Union Bank, and one or two others, which are of brick, or stone and plaster painted over.

The English, Scottish, and Australian Chartered Bank is a fine lofty building in George Street, having an ornamental cornice of wood and plaster, then brick upwards from the cornice, the bottom being of stone, plastered over and painted. The building is nicely finished and ornamented, especially the cornices, window sills, &c. The new City Bank, in Pitt Street, nearly completed, will be a magnificent pile of cut stone, the colour of dark amber, from Pyrmont, suburban to Sydney (workable as easily as Bath stone), with beautiful cut ornamented stone pillars, &c., yet I have not seen to my mind a single bank building to surpass the "National" at Adelaide, taking in "Imperial Fire Office," &c. The present 'Royal Hotel' (Charles C. Skurratt, proprietor) is built on the old site in George Street, and is very imposing. Front elevation about 70 feet, frontage 60 feet; but this includes a building occupying 15 feet frontage, and running the whole depth of the hotel, 200 feet, used as a warehouse by C. Newton and Co. It has three balconies, supported by wooden pillars, painted to imitate the grey spotted Moruya granite, near river Clyde, Goulbourn district, with similar pillars at the entrance. Splendid entrance hall and large bar, with two lively barmaids.

About 100 bedrooms at the 'Royal.'

Wednesday, 15th February, very close and sultry; and *Thursday, 16th*, cloudy morning; drizzling rain all day, until 6 P.M.

Occupied the principal part of these days in perambulating the city. Went to Hunter Street and paid first-class passage, 40l., to San Francisco, by the Californian, New Zealand, and Australian mail line of steam-packets.

The new Town Hall adjoins the Church of England Cathedral. Frontage of main building to George Street, about 50 feet; depth to Druit Street, over 200 feet. It is being built principally with the beautiful amber-coloured stone from Pyrmont, with richly ornamented stone pillars and caps; massive cut stone pillars to two entrances from George Street, which is distant from main building about 30 feet; handsome iron railing fixed in dressed stone, already erected all round. The new Post Office in course of erection on the old site in George Street (Mr. Barnett, colonial architect) has a frontage (the principal one) to that street of about 78 feet, with an elevation of· 70 feet and a depth of 170 feet. It will face on one side a street, to be made by pulling down shops, &c., intended to be a chain wide, and to be called St. Martin's Lane. The Post Office will be called St. Martin's-le-Grand, the back yard opening into Pitt Street. The roof will be of slate.

Here again the Pyrmont stone is principally being used. Very tall highly-polished, dark-grey, spotted granite pillars (Moruya stone) in front and at sides, particularly to St. Martin's Lane, where they looked very massive and imposing. Base of pillars of same stone, dressed but not polished, and being of a lighter colour (grey) than the pillars themselves, had a very pretty effect. Caps to pillars richly cut and embellished. Interior walls and roof of solid stone (amber) beautifully carved, &c. There are vaults all through the building below. In richness of style it is infinitely beyond the Melbourne Post Office, but not so large or extensive; the back part, however, towards Pitt Street, looks ridiculously narrow, but perhaps it is intended to add to it; at present it cuts a very poor figure when contrasted with the beautiful New South Wales Bank in course of erection opposite. There is a temporary wooden post office near Wynard Square, having a frontage of about 200 feet, and containing every accommodation. The clerks already complain of the new building, and say it will not be large enough.

Went over the markets on Thursday afternoon; they are the same old buildings in appearance as in 1853–54 (when last in Sydney), but some additions have been made in the centre, and handsome new iron gates to the entrances fixed in stonework arched over and elaborately cut, carved, &c., not harmonizing with the dirty old buildings. The stonework or dwarf walls, above which are the shops, particularly towards George Street, is decaying, and much out of repair. The markets cover a very large space of ground, and were full of fruit of almost every description. Cartloads of pine apples, bananas, oranges, &c., very cheap; pine apples, 2d., 3d., and 4d. each; bananas, 9d., 1s., and 1s. 6d. per dozen. Poultry alive and dead, rabbits (some lop-eared), hundreds of cockatoos, parrots, and other native birds; dogs old and young, monkeys, opossum and other rugs; native fur muffs, earthenware, and other commodities too numerous to mention, and this every day. Barring wheat, the Adelaide annual "show fair" in February is not to be compared to it in extent of space and wares. Called on Secretary of Sydney Exchange, Mr. Ebsworth, on introduction from his brother at Adelaide. Kindly presented me with free admission ticket. Building very substantial, of cut Sydney stone; good elevation, imposing from street; commodious exchange and reading rooms, &c. Numerous brokers and others have offices, and can communicate by telegraph from there.

Friday, 17th February—Day fine; cool. In morning went from north end of George Street in a 3*d.* 'bus to the Glebe at end of Parramatta Road, in fact a continuation of Sydney, over 2 miles, containing 6007 inhabitants, and inspected the Sydney University, standing in its own grounds, apparently about 50 acres, on an elevated spot commanding an extensive view of the city and suburbs. Grounds well fenced in with wooden railings neatly cut. Lawns very green and well kept, enclosed shrubberies of valuable trees, plants, &c.; ornamental sheets of water at bottom of slope. The University is a splendid building of cut stone—frontage over 300 feet—highly ornamented quoins, &c. Tower in centre of building, with pillars elaborately embellished; one wing of building not yet completed. One room about 40 feet square contains only fifteen oil-paintings, but appear to be very valuable. The large hall is a magnificent spectacle, about 135 feet long, with a gallery; all solid stone walls, with a very lofty, handsome cathedral style of roof about

60 feet high, elaborately carved, &c.; eight full-length oil-paintings of Sir W. Manning, Deas Thomson, Sir Chas. Nicholson, and others; beautiful stained-glass windows, altogether superior to Melbourne University, *i. e.* the buildings, but not the exhibits. Only one statue; it is of white Italian marble, of W. Chas. Wentworth. Library upstairs, about 30 feet square only, contains very rich old bookcases of oak, carved, &c.; books handsomely bound; one presented by Her Majesty, "the principal Addresses and Speeches of the Prince Consort," with H.M.'s autograph; also 'Life in the Highlands,' and 'Early Life of Prince Consort.' Some few oil-paintings and statuary about upstairs in landings, passages, &c. In two rooms, not very large, an Egyptian mummy, splendid ancient specimens of small mummies, statuary, coins, &c., 220 ancient coins (presented by Sir John Young), one suit ancient armour, copies of all the seals of the Kings and Queens of England to present time. The exhibits, a myth compared with Melbourne, but the hall, library, &c., more elegantly finished—very costly, particularly the stained-glass windows. Lawns kept close cut by a mowing machine. At 11 A.M. went to Parramatta, 17 miles by water, per paddle-steamer 'Adelaide,' 107 tons, from wharf bottom of King Street. Near here a wooden viaduct crosses over the harbour to Pyrmont, and another one just below to Balmain; when here in 1853 used to cross over in boats for 3*d*. Cockatoo Island looked as usual, only no prisoners are kept there now. Now used as a dry dock, excavated

out of the solid rock; very extensive—docked the 'Himalaya,' the 'Galatea,' and other large ships. There is a steam factory about 300 feet long, for repairs, &c.; appeared to be all rock, with here and there very coarse grass. Small house, and garden containing peach and other fruit trees, enclosed by a dry stone wall close to the river. A landing stage here; stopped and landed some passengers. Stopped at Gladesville, where there is a small landing stage; beds of rock all round, slightly timbered here and there. Stopped at "Kissing Point" landing place; station of wood, 20 feet by 12 feet; twelve panes of glass in the two windows broken out of eighteen. The landing stage and station present rather a dilapidated appearance. Six bags of wheat and twelve of flour landed for the ninety-seven starving inhabitants.

Many nice residences, orangeries, &c., on the sloping hills near here. A nice stone-built church visible on top of hill; it is in the township of Ryde. Beautiful little bays opposite, and on a grassy slope near one of them stands a lovely house, the property of Mr. Thos. Walker, merchant, Sydney, with look-out tower, &c. The shrubs and trees beautiful in appearance, and the captain says all indigenous. Lawn very green and well kept. Orangery and garden, &c.; altogether a perfect *bijou*. Orange groves and vineyards now visible in the distance, with nice villas, &c., on slopes and hills in every direction.

I can say no more in the fruit line, as my attention is now diverted to a large cockle and mussel bank, the tide being very low, and more service to the inhabitants,

I imagine, than "Cockle's Antibilious." Landed a mile from Parramatta, on an estate called Redfern (no houses) into the bush, containing a great quantity of beautiful, tall, straight timber, &c., the land being the property of Mr. McCarthy, of Sydney. Went through the bush in a three-horse 'bus to Williams' Family Hotel, George Street, Parramatta; road not made, very dirty and slimy; river occasionally seen, but very narrow from Redfern to Parramatta. About 1¼ mile. Mr. McCarthy allows this bush road to be used, as no harm can be done; it is about three-quarters of a mile through Mr. McCarthy's property. One nice piece of land, leased by the latter for twenty-one years (he won't sell an inch, or allow a stick of timber to be felled), contains thousands of young orange-trees for planting. Some good grass land about on entering Parramatta; quite green and fine. All the way from Sydney to Parramatta, on both sides, the land is generally low, sloping, and very rocky, with occasional bushes and trees, and some trouble and expense must have been gone to in clearing, planting, &c. The scenery is delightful, with its little islands and numerous bays, residences with their well-kept lawns, orange groves, vineyards, &c. The tide very low to-day, bringing to view numbers of mussel backs or beds, covered with mussels lying about. It was 1.30 P.M. when I arrived at this comfortable hotel, and dinner was nearly over, so I dined by myself in a well-furnished, large parlour, carpeted, sofa and chairs to match, of walnut, and green damask covers with variegated stripes of red, &c.; also a very large square-shaped piano; good prints on walls, and so on. The landlord, a young man; his wife about twenty, nicely dressed, dark hair, cocked up behind. I was well attended to by this lady and two young ones also, about fourteen and sixteen, with beautiful light-yellow hair hanging down their backs (no sham stuff). Colonial girls, especially New South Wales, have *real* heads of hair in profusion as a rule. A roast fowl and haricot, cabbage, and potatoes, winding up with cheese, lettuce, celery, and a pint of stout in a pewter—all for 3s. 6d.; the cheese wrapped round with a napkin in the orthodox style. I had also a napkin, for the first time since I have left Adelaide. I then sallied out to see the town, containing 5577 inhabitants; the district, 9980. Two of the streets, George and Church Streets, a chain and a half wide, generally in good order; kerb stones to nearly all the streets, the footways flagged in many instances, otherwise well gravelled. A very large brick-built tweed factory, an immense pile, but only works three days in the week, as the proprietors cannot compete with English importers. Driver of 'bus is of opinion that a small duty ought to be put on imported cloth, &c., to regulate manufactures. There are two churches belonging to Church of England; one of them, called St. John's, stone built and commodious, with two spires cased with galvanized iron; other Church of England large and more modern, stone, with galvanized-iron spire 160 feet high. The Scotch Church, of stone, large main building with a very low tower, making it a ludicrous sight contrasted with the main body; besides well-built chapels, of medium size, belonging to various denominations, all of stone like the Sydney stone. A great many well-built houses, but very few shops; a very large brick hotel, called Payten's, two stories, elevation not much, but which has a frontage of about 150 feet, and stands in a small well-kept grassed lawn containing shrubs, &c., fronting George Street. Attention called to a small wooden building off George Street, kept as an inn by an elderly widow, and called 'Babes in the Wood;' had a peep at it, and for the first time since I left England, had a glass of mild ale for $1\frac{1}{2}d.$; suggested to the old lady and a young one, a relative, that they and myself should remove with the old wooden house into some romantic spot in the bush, in sight of the river, and become real babes of the wood; declined with thanks. Immediately after caught sight of a gentleman with a real barrister's gown and wig, standing talking to three gentlemen in middle of street; inquired and found it was Mr. Wilkinson, the Crown prosecutor; that Mr. Judge Simpson was trying prisoners at District Court House, called Parramatta Quarter Sessions; went after Mr. Wilkinson. Court House of cut stone from neighbourhood, similar to Sydney stone, tall fluted pillars at entrance; Court House about half the size of Adelaide Supreme Court. Heard latter part of charge of receiving two stolen gold rings. Husband, called Yuman Nursery, a black, said to be a native; wife, nice-looking white young woman, only seventeen, also native born. She was discharged by the judge, and up to the time of the jury giving their verdict, kept up a continual low moaning, shedding abundance of tears. After she had exhausted her pocket-handkerchief, she had recourse to the bottom part of her spotted muslin dress, and used up both sides of that before the judge had finished summing up, which he did decidedly against prisoner. The jury retired for twenty minutes, and returned "*not* guilty." I observed some Paddies on the jury, which may account for the unexpected verdict; so blackey and wife hurried away to paddle their boat to their home, some place on the river. I then went to see the Parramatta Park, a domain in which stands a large old-fashioned house, called Old Government House. It had got much out of repair, and a miserable ministry of the day said that if the then Governor, Sir John Young, wished to make use of it, he must put it in repair at his own expense; this he declined, and it is now let to a retired squatter, Mr. Blake, of considerable means, from the Maitland district, an invalid suffering from paralysis. A friend, Captain Gwynne, a retired army officer, lives with Mr. Blake as companion, and there they are in this barrack of a building, with three servant girls, leading a very secluded life. I saw the captain, who regrets selling out, as he lost all his money in "squatting." He tells me the park is about 350 acres. Formerly the Government reserve was 20,000 acres, but when Sir John Young would not live there, the Government disposed of all but the present park; it is walled in, the greater part with large square blocks of stone; a small lodge at the entrance, then through an avenue of

English oak, about three-parts grown, for 100 yards, and covered with acorns.

The house and most of the park is on an eminence, commanding a beautiful view of the town and river. Trees, mostly of oak, large and small, and valuable shrubs and trees, natives and others, are scattered over the park wide apart, so as not to obstruct the view. There are trees of the pine tribe in one direct line and regular distances for a quarter of a mile. Rose-trees, shrubs, &c., but very few flowers, are enclosed by neat white painted palings, in fancifully-shaped parterres. There are also some small lagoons, surrounded by weeping willows, rushes, &c. All the park splendidly grassed. Two men constantly kept on, but there is very little garden work to attend to, as there is not much round the house, and very few flowers. Two or three little "Joeys," a solitary emu, and a few brown ducks and some fowls is all the live stock I could see in the park. Some magnificent oak-trees scattered over the town, and particularly adjoining George Street, in front of houses, about half-size of English-grown oaks, leaves green and covered with acorns.

Town very quiet place; little business doing; very few shops; some machinists, wheelwrights, &c., depend on country people, and Saturday is their day. No cabs or carriages (except two 'busses, but not on any stand), plying for hire; but vehicles can be obtained from a livery stable. Observed three pair-horse, low, old-fashioned carriages, at railway station, in which I should not care to be seen in the city.

Good pasture land in and round Parramatta, quite green, with cows, horses, and sheep, &c., grazing, putting me in mind of England, with some plots of maize about. There are numerous orange groves, gardens, &c., in and round Parramatta.

The station, within five minutes' walk of George Street, is of brick, with convenient waiting-rooms, &c. Frontage, 120 feet, and answers for up and down traffic; and goods shed, of brick, about 100 feet long.

Left at 5.30; Parramatta station to Parramatta junction, 1 mile; to Sydney, 14. A well-dressed lady in black, over fifty, evidently an educated woman, brought with her a fine bouquet of flowers, particularly some splendid dahlias; and a young lady in white (rather confiding), who I soon discovered came from about 42 miles north of Goulbourn, also came into the carriage with an enormous bouquet of flowers, particularly dahlias, verbena, roses, &c. The lady in black and the lady in white entered into conversation as to the relative beauty and quality of their several bouquets, and it was, after an animated conversation on all sides, decided that the dahlias of the lady in black were better than those of the lady in white, but the palm for roses was carried off by the lady in white; and considering the disparity in the ages of the ladies, the rose-tint on the cheeks of the lady in black apparently fading, while those of the lady in white (about eighteen and very interesting) appeared to be daily improving, the lady in white certainly had the best of it. Observing that the lady in white was evidently tired in handling

F 2

about and holding her large bunch, I relieved her by quietly suggesting that it might be placed on the seat (there being plenty of room), which she politely allowed me to do.

Good pasture land all round; some slight cuttings through soft strata ; then through some bushes, young stuff growing up, looking like plantation.

Parramatta Junction to Haslem's Creek, 4 miles ; very small brick station there; through two miles of scrub, the rest good land, particularly in grass; a few wooden houses ; one with bark roof, very poor.

Haslem's Creek to Home Bush, 1 mile; small brick station and little verandah over; scrub and lightly timbered ; some tall gums, then grass land. Two marble masons' shops near station ; a very large and pretty cemetery close by ; walks laid out and flower beds, &c. A church seen at the top of the cemetery on an eminence ; also a chapel.

Home Bush to Borwood, 1 mile; small brick station ; one rather deep cutting through soft soil ; nearly all open grass country; some nice cottages with gardens, &c., planted with orange and other fruit-trees ; a brick-built church.

Borwood to Ashfield, 2 miles ; small brick station with verandah ; long but not very deep cuttings, through slaty strata and soft stuff.

Ashfield to Petersham, 2 miles ; station same as Ashfield. Some good houses and gardens here; neat Catholic church of stone, and cemetery adjoining ; a large chapel on top of the hill in sight.

Petersham to Newtown, 1 mile; small station, wood, with galvanized roof and verandah; large town; every description of house, good, medium, and bad.

Newtown to Sydney, 2 miles. This (Sydney) station is built of wood, and is the meanest I ever saw in a city or large town, and was described to me by a porter as "a shed;" heard, however, that 30,000*l*. had been on the estimates some time to build a new one, but the money was not forthcoming. It is a long station of about 225 feet, and its platforms, inside station and without, 450 feet; station only on one side for up and down trains; goods sheds very mean. There is a very handsome mortuary of cut stone, with dressed stone pillars beautifully embellished, the caps of pillars being carved. Slate roof and ornamental "fringe" at its top, about 50 feet frontage. It belongs to Government as well as the railway, and corpses are deposited here, and the funerals take place at Haslem's Creek Cemetery, also belonging to Government, as Camperdown Cemetery is closed except to those who have vaults or walled graves there. Entered short tunnel shortly before coming to station; splendid view of the city from station, &c.; arrived 6.15 P.M. What became of the lady in black I don't know or care, but I took possession of the bouquet of the young lady in white; this she wouldn't hear of, and would only allow me to carry her brown silk umbrella, so we walked on together, talking on various topics, particularly as to her place of birth, the neighbourhood thereof, &c., until we got outside a nice house, about three-quarters of a mile from the station;

there we shook hands as if we had known each other for years, and parted, and I suppose we shall never see each other again. I walked towards George Street as I thought, and after a mile and a half inquired, and found I was going towards the Surrey hills, the wrong way altogether, so I had to retrace my steps. I am afraid that I was thinking of the young lady in white. Went to Prince of Wales's Theatre, King Street East, a very commodious, handsome one, with well fitted-up bars, but small. J. B. Howe very good as 'Rip Van Winkle,' but not "up" to Jefferson the Yankee.

Saturday, 18th February.—Morning warm. Afternoon hot. In morning at Exchange, reading up Adelaide news. Afternoon at Upper Paddington, suburb; houses all the way now. Portions of first and second companies of volunteers, about 100 men (Scotch), many of them very athletic men, in full Highland costume, bonnets with large handsome black ostrich feathers, assembled at Victoria Barracks (very good for colonial barracks), and attended funeral of one of their comrades, called James Bannerman. A number of Masonic brethren also assembled, but no regalia, and they were in carriages and Hansom cabs, about thirty in number, *i.e.* carriages and cabs. The driver of the last trap, a Hansom, carried an umbrella over his head, and caused some amusement to the juveniles, and adults also. Went over Wooloomooloo, a suburb, now connected with the city by houses all the way. It has grown to be a large place, with over 20,000 inhabitants. Houses of every description, many of the first class, built on hills, rising ground, and in a flat. Evening at market. Immense quantity of fruit, &c.; quite a glut. A large attendance; yet not much was got rid of, and pine-apples were as low as 2*d.* each. Went to Victoria Theatre, in Pitt Street. Very large. Much out of repair. No dramatic company, but Frank Hussey's Excelsior Minstrels. Only the latter (Bones), tambourine, and Hussey's wife (pretty Miss Blanche Clifton), of any account—Rainford and the bass being much missed.

Sunday, 19th February. — Bright day. Afternoon very humid and warm. In morning went to Church of England Cathedral, St. Andrew's; all open seats, free. Seats in nave of polished New Zealand pine, with a kind of cross at top, cut out of the wood, at entrance to each end. Chancel, of imitation oak, ornamented. Pulpit low, base of worked stone, top part carved oak; handsome crimson velvet cushion; reading desk very low; very handsome crimson velvet covering to altar-table, worked in centre; beautiful stained-glass window, high, but narrow in comparison with height. Powerful organ, highly gilded, embellished and painted with different colours, good tone. The walls and most of the vaulted roof is of solid cut Sydney stone, some portion seemingly of wood, painted purple and yellow. Pillars of cut stone, very high and imposing, said by some persons to be too large and too near some of the seats, but I do not think so. Small twisted brass pillars, about 8 feet high, with brass ornamented branches at top, light up the place with gas; very neat, and exceedingly light in appearance. Fourteen choristers (boys), in the usual Westminster gowns; no adults, full chorus being in afternoon. Two clergymen did whole service; one handsome young man, about thirty, with splendid voice. He preached a good sermon, and was very loud and distinct. Had on white surplice, black sash in front, black and blue on his back. A fair-haired young lady lent me her Prayer-book, and shared with her sister another one. Soon took an opportunity of knowing who she was. Turned to fly-leaf, and found her to be one Miss J. E. S., a gift from her Pa. Had difficulty in finding the places, not having been in a Church of England Cathedral since 1852. Miss S. did everything for me; and when it came to the chants, hymns, &c., this energetic, kind gal, popped me between her sister and self, and the trio held one hymn-book. Collection after service. A voluntary played all the while. Wood plates, with crimson cloth at bottom; about six vergers engaged in the collection, who handed the plates to the elder parson, who took charge of the loaves and fishes. Full congregation, and many pounds must have been given. In afternoon went over 'Sobraon,' 330 feet from stem to stern. Saloon about 60 feet long, splendid accommodation for passengers. Also 'Carlisle Castle,' about 1458 tons, a beautiful liner. 'Patriarch,' 1500 tons, fine vessel, and 'Glendower,' of London, all large ships, but 'Sobraon' bears away the palm. Went in a third paddle steamboat from Circular Quay (close under Government House, and near 'The Earl Belmore Hotel') to Milson's Point, North Shore, about one mile. Many respectable persons on board. Amongst the motley group a middle-aged lady, of good address, but from her face and little turn-up nose, showed evidence of Irish extraction, though apparently not born in the " ould counthry," and two young ladies, who called her Aunt. Being warm, Aunty took off her lemon-coloured kid gloves. I found that she was a very old maid indeed; no engaged or wedding ring visible. The youngest wore her light hair in its natural state, *i.e.* loose, hanging down her back; the other sister, a style I never saw before. About nine inches of curls at back of head, three inches plain, and the rest long curls, plenty of it, and the colour of the cocoon of the silkworm. A warm conversation ensued on the Continental War; old Aunt backed up the French, the girls the Germans. Before we got to the wharf the Aunt gave in, rather reluctantly, and acknowledged that the Germans had shown great forbearance towards the French, and that the latter had certainly brought it on themselves; "but, my dears," she added, "you should not be so harsh against France. I lived there once. I liked them very much." I may be uncharitable, but a thought came across my mind that Aunty had been disappointed in love there, or jilted. North Shore is a mass of rock and a succession of moderate hills and gentle slopes, with here and there stunted trees and scrub, and occasional patches of sandy soil: pretty little bays and coves on every side. Portions cleared and covered with gentlemen's, merchants', and retired tradesmen's residences, &c., everywhere commanding extensive views of the harbour, city, &c. The grass of lawns, with a few exceptions, rather inferior, being mixed up with wire grass, &c. Some good gardens, with a few orange and lemon trees, and a few large apple, pear, and peach trees, &c. What is called the town is about a mile from the landing place. Some inferior two-horse open carriages and 'busses run for 6d. Main road or street in good order, about a chain wide. Footways kerbed with stone for some distance up the road, and also portions in the town. A steep pinch from landing, and up hill and down dale to the town. Some stone-built houses and shops—many of the latter with their doors open—a few houses of wood; neat Church of England, of stone, with spire covered with small pieces of shingle, and roof of ditto, very pretty, perched on top of the hill. Roman Catholic church of wood, very small and plain. Seeing a flag flying from an elevated staff, and being thirsty, and no water at hand, mistook a retired sea-captain's residence for a public-house. Subsequently discovered that some of the inns were partly concealed by trees and shrubs, and that there is no less than nine in the town, all third-rate houses, one of them a mean, dirty place, of brick, bearing the appropriate sign of 'The Rag and Famish.' Two of them built of weather-board, as also Her Majesty's Post Office. Stone very good, same strata as Sydney, and easily worked, as I tested some blocks with my pen-knife. In evening went to Roman

Catholic church of St. Mary's, close to Hyde Park, and in sight of Wooloomooloo. The tower of old cathedral (burnt down some three or four years ago) is intact, with its eight bells. This tower will form portion of the new church in course of erection, and will be more lofty and handsome than Church of England Cathedral. Some of the walls and pillars are up, all of cut and dressed stone, &c. The temporary church is built of brick, close by the new building, about 160 feet long, nave about 60 feet wide, chancel 75 feet, there being a recess on each side of the latter resting on iron pillars. The roof is lofty, and is a diagonal one, of polished Kauri pine, from New Zealand, varnished over. This wood is a good imitation of bird's-eye maple, and is used in Melbourne and Adelaide for second-class railway carriages. The roof is supported by small iron rods. For a temporary building it is one of the neatest I ever saw, very much like some of the country railway stations in England. All open seats. The place was full. I was introduced to a seat, with cushions, by a tall young woman, native born, but of Irish parentage, whom I met near, of whom I made inquiries, as I could not find the place. She dipped her hand in the holy water at the entrance. I followed suit, but with my glove on, which she did not observe. At the corner of the pew she bowed, as all others did, in a slanting direction to the Virgin at the altar. I did the same. She went down on her marrow-bones. I did the like. She lent me her book of prayers, half in Latin and half in English; so I got on very well, and followed the chants, &c. The music good. A powerful harmonium. Priest, stout and fat, preached an extempore eloquent sermon. Loud voice, and he gave his congregation a pretty good dressing down, especially with regard to future rewards and punishments. He also forcibly reminded them of Ash Wednesday, Good Friday, and Easter week services, strictly enjoining them to come to High Mass, Sacrament, &c.; to give freely, &c., as he would take no excuse. If the altar had been closed up, and the parish priest had had on Church of England attire, I must have taken his sermon to have been a High Church one. He has very little Irish brogue. All the morning and partly in the afternoon pleasure-parties seemed to be the order of the day. Numerous boats and small steamers were plying in the harbour. There are 750 watermen on the water-police books; some of them as long as thirty years. Many of the boats dirty and rotten, and some of the men too old and infirm to do the work, who make extortionate charges and shirk night-work. The regulations over forty years old are not strictly enforced, and a Mr. Tunk has lately brought in a Bill for regulating public vehicles and boats. Carriages, 'busses, &c., in and around the city were running everywhere. The doors of chemists' shops open all day; as also, with few exceptions, the side-doors of public-houses, and oyster and fruit shops—the very reverse of Melbourne—and there is no difficulty in obtaining anything you want in the shape of drinks, oysters, fruit, and other edibles.

Monday, 20th February.—Day hot and close; sun very warm in afternoon. Went over Hyde Park, near St. James's Church and Regent Street East, about 1730 yards long (nearly a mile), about 700 yards broad, well grassed and kept; beautiful avenues of pine-trees, &c., &c.; pathways wide and properly gravelled; many oak and valuable trees and shrubs scattered over it, not too close together; elevated position, and splendid views of the city and Wooloomooloo and portion of harbour. At entrance near Regent Street is a magnificent large statue of bronze of the Prince Consort, on large pedestal of hammer-dressed granite, erected 1866; also near the Museum is erected in the Park a fine obelisk to Captain Cook (the discoverer of New South Wales); base very large round, of dressed Moyura granite, with splendid polished pedestal of ditto, and a flagstaff at top. To be replaced by a statue of the Captain to come from England, and shortly expected.

In afternoon went to Clontarf in a paddle-steamer full of passengers, situated in a delightful land-locked bay, close to the Heads, the place where Prince Alfred was shot at. This is a gala day of the Catholic schools. The children, with their friends, left Circular Quay in two steamers this morning, near where I am staying, with two good bands (reed and brass). Clontarf is a beautiful spot—a favourite resort for pic-nic parties, &c.—a large grassy flat, evidently well patronized, as the grass was very short and close. Scenery beautiful —a perfect paradise—being surrounded by moderate hills and ranges of solid rock, small timber, and scrub, and little bays about; roundabouts, &c., in full swing, and other amusements for the children, superintended by the priests and teachers, who paid every attention to the youngsters that possibly could be. A neat wooden building, called a pavilion, where dancing was going on with great vigour, was full of people, old, middle-aged, and young, principally Irish Catholics, generally well behaved; none intoxicated in the room. This erection is about 200 feet long, 50 feet wide, and 30 feet high, the shingle roof being visible on the inside. Printed rules and regulations as to conduct of dancing parties, &c., posted up, such as "No man allowed to dance with another," "No obscene language," "No drunken person allowed in the room." Only one policeman from Sydney in attendance, and services not required. At one end, with a short space between, is the bar—a long one—of the public-house, of wood, kept by two brothers, called Moore. Very good liquors and fruit is obtainable here; and little apertures being left at end of pavilion in sight of the bar, the proprietors and their servants can see everything that goes on in the room. Really an enjoyable afternoon. Returned by paddle-steamer at 8 P.M., as full as she could hold of men, women, and school children. A few rather tight and sleepy on board. Fraternized with one of the female teachers—a young woman evidently of a strong mind, by the way in which she disciplined the children. Nothing very remarkable about her except a small wart on one side of her nose; dark hair and complexion; splendid cage of manipulators; very chatty.

Went to Madame Sohier's waxwork exhibition in a large room, 267, Pitt Street; about 200 figures. Amongst other celebrities were Lord John Russell, Mr. George Peabody, Garibaldi, &c., &c.; bushrangers and a murderous set of villains upstairs, including Morgan, of course, and a fellow who killed a whole family in England at a blacksmith's shop. A brass band, making as much noise as seven performers could possibly do, were in attendance.

Tuesday, February 21st.—Steady rain from 5 A.M., and at intervals throughout the day and night. In morning went to public free library, built of large blocks of Sydney stone, two different shades; lofty cut stone pillars, with ornamented caps; elevation, about 60 feet; frontage to Macquarie Street and looking into domain, about 80 feet, partly of an oval shape, to Bent Street, the rest in a line with that street, about 80 feet frontage; pillars lofty and handsome, about 5 feet from bottom all round; exterior of building is relieved by ornamental work in stone; wide entrance up twenty stone steps; then into entrance hall, about 30 feet by 15 feet, with two recesses, 8 feet 3 inches and 7 feet 8 inches, covered with cocoa-nut matting. The library is 80 feet by 40 feet, with a gallery round, supported by ornamental painted pillars of wood, with ornamental ironwork to railings; at one end a large gay specimen of the lion and unicorn, &c., about 6 feet at bottom, running narrower above, painted in gorgeous colours —purple, yellow, and gilt; height of library to ceiling, about 50 feet; height to gallery, 18 feet 9 inches;

gallery, 13 feet 7 inches wide. About 20,000 volumes in library.

In afternoon visited the Museum near Hyde Park; a very lofty Sydney stone cut building (large blocks, dressed, &c.); frontage on public road, next Hyde Park, 170 feet; large hall, square pillars, ornamented caps; frontage to shrubbery, being main entrance, about 170 feet, and depth about same—nearly a square building; handsome fluted stone-dressed pillars to entrance up a few steps. Building stands on an eminence, with good views. Signed name in visitors' book. First gallery, near entrance, over the hall and gallery next mentioned, runs all round, and is about 14 feet in depth, containing numerous specimens of native and other war implements, &c., curiosities, and stuffed birds. Floor of hall is of wood, and is 100 feet long; width, 30 feet; glass cases all round, of polished cedar, about 10 feet high; also cases throughout the hall, and large glass cases of cedar, &c., in gallery above, all round it; handsome iron railing to gallery, with polished cedar top, and every 6 feet carved polished cedar posts let in; very numerous stuffed specimens of birds and beasts—English, foreign, and colonial; Master Reynard, Miss Puss, and a host of others; skeletons of animals, &c.; stuffed wild boar from Harz Mountains, North Germany (brown), also a white bear (the latter the largest I ever saw); five skeletons of human race—1 Corsican, 1 Mongolian, 1 American, 1 Malayan, 1 Ethiopian or Negro —one a Clarence River (New South Wales) aboriginal; 79 skulls of various human races. Following cases, which are 2 feet deep on each side:—Insects, 57 feet long; ditto in bottles, 12 feet long; shells, 72 feet long; mineral specimens, fossils, &c.; models of nuggets, &c., 123 feet long; French ditto, 18 feet long; French shells, 18 feet long; butterflies and moths, 36 feet; beetle tribe, 36 feet. Gallery, an immense collection both sides; and at end of specimens of stuffed birds— English, colonial, and foreign—large New Zealand mat and war implements in centre. Up nine steps to another large room, called the Upper Hall, 90 feet long, 40 feet high, 50 feet wide, with recesses (two); thirty-five without pillars, plastered over and coloured; caps ornamented; walls plastered and coloured stone colour; ceiling partly wood painted and the rest coloured white. Beautiful coloured diamond-shaped tiles form floor of this room. Full-length oil-painting of Duke of Edinburgh; statuary, twenty-five in number; two cases South Sea Island and New Zealand war weapons, &c.; case skeletons of Australian pouched animals; one case West Australian native war weapons and personal ornaments; ditto of old English household utensils and weapons; one case fragments of bones, &c., of kangaroo and other native animals; two cases fossil remains of extinct mammals, formerly inhabiting Europe and America (somewhat similar to lobsters and crabs); one case war implements, pottery, &c. (Fijis); one ditto Australian fossil remains; several cases of minerals and shells of animals and fish; one case beautiful white and red coral; one case fossils (native cat tribe); two cases fossil remains, and jaws, &c., of native bears

G

(wombat tribe), opossums, &c.; one case stuffed fish from Pacific Ocean, &c.; splendid oil-painting in a sitting posture—Alexander Macleay, F.R.S.; two very large cases snakes, preserved in bottles; large high cases, about 110 feet long, of Australian stuffed animals; one case of frog tribe, preserved in bottles; skeleton of Australian sperm whale from Pacific Ocean, 35 feet in length and of immense girth; one stuffed walrus, 12 feet 6 inches long, with two sharp tusks over a foot in length; one sea leopard, about 10 feet long (this animal is spotted all over with small yellow spots); one shark, about same length, caught in Port Jackson (Sydney); one Macleay's sperm whale, 15 feet long; skeleton of a famous sire (Sir Hercules), presented by C. King Cox, Esq.; preserved skin of a very large snake, about 35 feet long; and of an immense boa. Then up wide staircase of seventeen steps to a landing paved with ornamental tiles, same as in last room. Two approaches from here to a room over the hall, about same size. Staircases are winding ones, consisting of twenty-seven steps each—are of iron, with ornamental iron railings and polished cedar banisters; capital floor of wood; gallery same size as under, with pretty iron railings; numerous cases of minerals, fossils, wood, eggs; two cases fish preserved in bottles, both foreign and colonial; one specimen skeleton of a "moa"—a gigantic extinct bird from New Zealand—from claws to head over 15 feet; two cases skeletons of birds; two plaster full-length statues—"Aristides" and "Canephora." Average annual attendance at this museum, 90,000.

In evening went to "Masonic Hall," York Street, at a concert and musical soirée, for benefit of Catholic schools—admission, 1s. This is a very large handsome stone building, containing numerous rooms. It is opposite the market, and presents a very imposing appearance from the street. The room in which concert was held is 80 feet × 40, and about 40 feet high. Walls painted light stone colour, relieved by miniature niches only about a foot deep; neat wooden cornices painted stone colour, ceilings papered. Strong beams to ditto of wood painted white, five large Gothic-shaped windows, gallery at end of room whole width of building, and about 20 feet in depth, supported by wooden painted pillars, with Sydney cedar caps at top, and ornamental iron railing, painted dark green, with cedar top; five small glass chandeliers on each side of room and two at end, and two in the gallery, each containing three gas-burners; 50 gas-jets in a sort of round cage let in the centre of ceiling inside the cage formed of glass; portions cut in small round pieces had a pleasing effect; five Gothic-shaped windows at back of gallery; very low platform for performers. Brass band with one big and two kettle drums; twenty performers played at intervals first-class music, but too loud for size of room. A Mrs. Cordner (professional), of French extraction, and a charming widow of little over thirty, presided at the piano (an excellent square one of walnut) as accompanist, with much grace and artistic ability. She also sang some very sweet songs, in a loud, melodious voice; a Miss Kearney, and also a Miss West (amateurs) sang well, and contributed largely to the harmony of the evening, and were loudly applauded; some good recitations were given by amateurs, and promised an entire success, until an amateur, a basso, whose name I could not find out, attempted to sing 'The Mill Wheel,' whose discordant voice almost spoiled the whole affair, there being no merit in his singing at all. Slight hisses, with murmurs of disapprobation, were heard, such as "Why didn't you stay at home?" "Go to bed," "You can be heard at Parramatta," &c.

Wednesday, February 22*nd.*—Rained all the morning, so went to Exchange and read the papers. Afternoon fine, but warm and close; rained again in evening and night. Went in very small paddle steamer to Athol Gardens, about 2 miles from Circular Quay; called at Wooloomooloo Bay, $1\frac{1}{2}$ mile = $3\frac{1}{2}$ miles, and back to Circular Quay for 6*d.* only. Wooloomooloo Bay is in the shape of a horse-shoe, is about half a mile broad and 1 mile in length. It is part of Sydney harbour, and is perfectly land locked. Excellent villas on each side, on gentle hills and rocky slopes, &c., with nice shrubberies, &c. Wharfs on strong wooden piles, sheathed with copper, running the whole of the frontage the shape of a bow. One middling large vessel discharging colonial coal, several small craft, pleasure-boats, &c. Water very smooth. A great portion of the town of Wooloomooloo in view, looking like a vast amphitheatre. Passed the training ship for destitute boys, called the 'Vernon,' from 800 to 1000 tons. Boys taught almost every trade, including navigation, sailmaking, and row-ing. Eight small urchins, with coxswain and teacher, were out in a boat practising. It must be washing week, as the rigging, spars, &c., were covered with articles of clothing. Primitive slippery landing place at Athol, of timber of all shapes; very rocky, middling lofty hills; went up a steep winding path, sometimes over bed rock, to an inn kept by a Mr. Clark, formerly a dancing master at Sydney; he also rents the small steamer, I am told for about 3l. a day, and he trusts to the custom of his house (he is lessee of the hotel and grounds) to make up for the lowness of the fares. The hotel is pretty good, but wants repairing and painting inside; about 45 feet frontage, with a verandah nearly the whole length resting on plain white painted pillars; a well-furnished large parlour, also a dining and sitting-room, with a piano much out of tune. He trusts to visitors to make a living, as there are no houses about. Liquors very good, but double Sydney prices. Good view of harbour, &c., from house. The so-called gardens (?) are not extensive, containing very few flowers, are full of fruit-trees, a few oranges and lemons, plenty of quinces, and some apples, peaches, &c.; looks more like an orchard than a garden, grass and weeds being abundant. Two very large pear-trees in lawn in front; says he never sees any of the fruit on his table, as visitors begin to pluck them from about the size of a nutmeg. Five pines and some large specimens of indigenous trees and shrubs, and large red-flowered oleanders. Two (so-called) saloons for dancing, of wood, sloping roofs of shingle, one 100 feet × 25, the other 52 feet × 22;

apertures left on each side about 5 feet square in place of windows; good floors of wood. Several wooden arbours about. There is also a small house at back of hotel of square blocks of stone roughly dressed. Hotel itself plastered over and coloured white. An animated conversation took place on the subject of dancing between the landlord and a friend from Balmain, whom he had not seen for eight or nine years, and both came to the conclusion that colonial dancing was much faster than British; in fact, the steps were a sort of fast shuffling walk, the British being slower, more steady, and pretty in effect.

Inspected three batteries in course of erection at three different places, commanding the harbour, at and what is called "The Point," to be mounted with 68-pounders. The foundations are cut out of the solid rock, the whole of the neighbourhood being all rock, hilly, scrub and small timber. A new road being made to connect the three batteries. I walked through the bush over a steep, rough, rocky, and dirty path (from late rains), about one-third of a mile from hotel. Not one battery will be able to be seen by an enemy, being concealed by bush; the scenery and views are beautiful from here. Some of the stonecutters live in calico tents, but most of them go home by cheap steamer on unfavourable evenings. A small blacksmith's shop was working.

Went to School of Arts, Pitt Street, in evening, when rain came on again. It was established in 1833, by Robert Baird, Esq. This is a very noble, lofty building, of cut stone, with pillars, ornamental caps, stone cornices worked and embellished, frontage about 90 feet; and about the same depth. The library contains 13,000 volumes; a spacious hall or lecture-room, also used for concerts, exhibitions, &c., holds 800. There are reading rooms and school-rooms; dead and other languages taught, &c. A diorama of the American war was being exhibited in the large room. Saw similar panorama at Adelaide a few years ago, but now much improved upon; entrance 1s. and 2s. Went in, found room well-lighted with gas, lower parts of walls wainscoted and varnished in imitation of oak for about 4 feet from floor, then wood (plain) for over 4 feet, then plaster, coloured light pink; four round windows on one side near ceiling, other side dummies, three windows at back; four plaster busts against wall on each side, resting on brackets, of notables I could not identify, no names being appended, and I was not near many of them. Square plaster work about 6 inches deep with ornamental caps, about 10 feet apart, to relieve, &c. Sixteen ground-glass lamps, with brass branches resting on brackets; ceiling in large squares coloured white, relieved by square girders of timber painted white; long cedar seats with backs to them; brass chandelier, a single one, shape of hoop, suspended from centre, with sixty gas jets. A gallery supported by fluted Sydney cedar pillars, and under it a platform of raised seats of wood. I was well satisfied with my shilling's worth.

Thursday, 23rd February.—Raining heavily from early morn to night. Went to Union Bank twice; got drafts on London for San Francisco and New York.

Large room at Union Bank well furnished and ornamented, but low ceiling. At Custom House with Mr. Ebsworth to pass entry of large box with papers, &c., for England. Sorting papers and things, packing, &c. Got painter to put on name and address, &c., of a relative at Wellington, Somersetshire, which he did very cheap, for 2s. 6d., and spent a great portion of it at the bar very soon after. In evening went to Prince of Wales's Theatre,—'Behind the Curtain,' and the 'Irish Emigrant.' Howe very good; but miserably supported; noticed several actors and actresses I had seen at Adelaide and Melbourne.

Friday, 24th February.—Day very warm and humid. Left, by 8 A.M. train, Sydney station for Bowen Fells, 97 miles, per Western line; arrived at 2 P.M. Left on return journey at 4, and arrived at Sydney 9.50 P.M. Very good line, well ballasted. Stone, available for permanent way, enough for centuries, in fact inexhaustible, in a great many places adjoining the line.

Parramatta Junction, 13 miles; *Parramatta Station*, 14 miles. After leaving this station several deep and some long cuttings through rotten-stone and soft stuff. Large orangeries, and apples, pears, peaches, &c., on fruit-trees in orchards. Some maize about, quite green. Mostly grass country, not much scrub. Some tall timber-trees, but not large. Great quantity of melons in blossom. Passed on large culverts over several small creeks and one large ditto of running water.

Seven Hills Station, 20 miles. Small, built of wood. Houses about small and inferior. One middling deep cutting through soft strata. Mostly grass country, very little bush or timber.

Blacktown Junction, 22 miles. Built of brick, slate roof; a neat station, but small. Platform about 105 feet. Middling hotel of brick, and a few small brick and wood houses, with a few gardens and fruit-trees, &c. A small cutting, two long but not deep ones through rock. Passed over large culverts, middling-sized creeks running. Country not much cleared. Some good pasture, and cattle and horses on it.

Rooty Hill, 25 miles. Small brick-built station, slate roof, galvanized-iron verandah. A large lot of split timber and firewood at this station; a few wooden houses visible, with bark roofs; very poor. Passed several large vineyards and orchards; some light cuttings, except one very long one, through deep but soft strata. Country about same as Blacktown, but much dead timber about.

South Creek, 29 miles. Built of brick and stone, with slate roof; platform about 80 feet long; two other very small buildings of brick; one good wooden house, with shingle roof; several visible in distance, with large gardens. Over very large culvert or bridge, passing a large creek. Maize about; some long light cuttings, some deep ones, but all soft strata. More bush and saplings and light-timbered country than cleared land; few cattle and horses about.

Penrith, 34 miles. Built of brick, about 100 feet long, with refreshment and waiting rooms; platform whole length; large goods shed of galvanized iron;

large straggling town; good and inferior houses of miscellaneous materials; good gardens, churches and chapels, &c. Some orangeries, both old and young; one apple orchard; immense high ranges in view, very thickly wooded; good flat land, nearly all pasture, all about station; and shortly afterwards, visible as far as the eye could reach, similar pasture, quite flat, and called Emu Plains. Houses about mostly of wood, and poor; lots of maize; some large water holes; then on a very high embankment, and over a very long splendid iron bridge, under which runs a large river called the Nepean, and shortly after a branch of the same river came in sight.

Emu Plains, 36 miles. Small wood-built station; galvanized-iron roof; some beautiful land, full of grass; plenty of cattle and horses about, and a few sheep; some good stone and brick buildings; some small, of wood; large orangery; plenty of maize. Over high long embankments; deep cutting through soft rock, &c.; very steep gradients now and then, also some cuttings through hard rock, portion of same range as Lapstone Hill. Some cuttings through hard rock; two very deep and long cuttings through solid rock. Passed over splendid stone bridge, a very deep ravine under; splendid views of Emu Plains and Nepean River, with bridge across it, in distance; commencement here of what is termed the "zig-zag," to enable the train to get up this mountain. The ascent begins about two miles from "Wascoes," then went backward through rocky cuttings on branch line, then forward again on embankments through deep cuttings, rock, sand, pebbles, &c.; splendid views of the plains; roughly timbered wild place, midst immense hills; small cuttings follow; little slab huts with bark roofs visible at a spot we stopped to water the iron horse; rather more flat country here, but very little indeed cleared; after heavy gradients, long embankments, though not deep, country moderately hilly, and deep cuttings through soft rock, at last we reached the plateau or top of this range.

Wascoes, 42 miles. Only a very small platform with railing; didn't stop.

Springwood, 47 miles. Only a very small platform with railing; didn't stop.

Woodford, 56 miles. Only a very small platform with railing; didn't stop. Old mail road visible. Wascoes old brick and wooden inn at right of it looking very shabby; passed and repassed this place on main road in 1853. Some inferior houses of brick, wood, bark, &c., about, still on top of range nothing cleared; short but heavy cuttings through solid rock; small embankments, but long, not deep; again cuttings through solid rock. Passed two good Gothic stone cottages, one shut up (meant for a public house, but railway has "shut up" most of the inns on old mail road, which passes very close to it nearly all the way), and a wooden one. Good views of extensive deep valleys (one called James' in the Valley); more embankments and long but not deep cuttings; some land cleared, and good stone and wood houses about; one public house of wood and shingle roof, much out of repair, on old main road, with little garden of flowers, &c.; gradients now not so steep;

more rocky cuttings, but not deep; beautiful views now and then, and steep gradients; very deep cuttings through solid rock; very lofty ranges and mountains visible on right side of railway, and fearful deep gullies; very high embankments now and then; short heavy cuttings; some very short tunnels; good Gothic stone house; a few small patches cleared; now and then fine views, particularly on passing through 18 miles hollow; very deep stone cuttings and high embankments; then through 17 miles hollow; some very good houses seen near here; walls generally plastered over and whitewashed, with galvanized-iron roofs; some patches of land cleared and looking green; very deep long cuttings through the solid rock; extensive views of a very rough country; some flocks of goats about, and slab and bark huts; now up an incline into a cutting through rock, but not very deep, and into Blue Mountain station.

Blue Mountains, 58 miles. Station built of wood, itself very small; platform about 150 feet long, but a refreshment room, also of wood, about 25 feet long, with little verandah of galvanized iron outside, takes up the greater portion; room plainly but neatly furnished; coffee, tea, ale, of hops only, teetotal drinks, sandwiches, biscuits, cakes, &c., and fruit to be had here, presided over by a black-eyed, dark-haired, good-looking young Jewess. I stuck to the ale mixed with ginger-pop. As we stopped 20 minutes nearly all the passengers partook of refreshments, as they would not have the chance to do so again for a long while, and mountain air makes one feel hungry. Quite a treat to be on the top of a mountain enjoying a nice breeze, it being very warm and close coming through the deep cuttings. Some plots cleared; two or three nice wooden houses, and a good garden near the station. On leaving went through very heavy deep cuttings through solid rock and over long embankments, now and then with steep gradients; distant mountains and ranges again visible; no land cleared up to the Weatherboard, all scrub, and for the greater part of the way we were hemmed in on each side by the bush, and could see very little beyond a quarter of a mile.

Weatherboard, 62 miles. Only a small platform and one bark hut. Went over a high bank and large culvert, running stream underneath; scarcely any open country round, only scrub and timber; one long cutting, not very deep, through stone strata; others of comparatively soft stuff; some very high embankments; extensive views of rough scrub land and huge ranges and mountains and immense rocky headland to left of line; very extensive look-out, a splendid sight. Passed two bark huts and a small garden; used to be stone crushing machines there to provide metal for the roads, now abandoned; steep gradients followed; timber inferior and scrubby on hills and mountains' sides, being so exposed to the wind; larger and better timber in valleys, but generally very scrubby, poor country; nothing cleared. Came on more extensive and beautiful views to right of railway; very wild and bold scenery; actually one bay horse in a small plot, and very green too, so there may be a hut or house concealed somewhere in the scrub, or the animal may have strayed from a distance. Easy gradients, and we are "going it." Here and there, patches of grass; several large flocks of sheep being driven on old mail road; splendid view on left of line, very extensive. Little Blackheath commences about a mile from Blackheath.

Blackheath.—A platform only, about 60 feet long. Old wooden public house I slept at in 1853, in going to Sofala on the Western Diggings, very near railway line; it is dilapidated, and most of it has fallen to the ground. A new house of cut stone with galvanized-iron roof, of good appearance, has been discontinued as an inn, in consequence of the railway taking the traffic off the old mail road. It is occupied by a man or two who fell timber, &c. There is a paddock of about ten acres partly fenced, plenty of feed, and some good indigenous trees in it; a large flock of sheep there, who, if they remain a few days, will nibble it down close, but there is plenty of bush and scrub at back for them. Slight embankment shortly after passing this place, and rather heavy stone cuttings follow. Extraordinary views of bold rocky headlands, very high perpendicular rocks, scrub, &c.; extensive deep valleys, an immense extent being visible as far as the eye can reach, also scrub and lofty ranges to right of railway.

Mount Victoria, 79 miles. Substantial station of rough dressed stone, about 60 feet frontage, platform a few feet longer; neat lamps; refreshment and waiting rooms; large galvanized-iron shed.

Hartley Vale, 80 miles. Did not stop; only a small

platform. Huge rocks to right of line, and ranges and ridges full of stone, scrub, and small timber. High embankment. Some cuttings through soft stone and not deep. A few bark huts. Country not cleared, timber scrubby. "Going it" now down an incline. Some bold rocky heights and ranges to right of line. Immense hollows and very deep, very long embankments now and then. A great hollow visible, like the Devil's Punch Bowl under Captain Cook's Pigeon House, but twenty times as large, with steep craggy rocks all round, and near it noble wild scenery on both sides. Now through a very deep cutting of solid rock at entrance of a tunnel about half a mile long, and also at end of it, and then down a steep incline. Very deep embankments and valleys; immense ranges, hills, and rocks. The railway winding about the side of the mountain up and down in all directions to reach the plateau; over very high viaducts of hammer-dressed white stone, very handsome, and immensely high embankments; a most wonderful work. (Mr. Mooray, of Sydney, the engineer, has only received 700*l.* for this, he asks for 1500*l.* more, which the Government demur to pay.) Now we commence the second zig-zag, run backwards slowly and shift on to short line; a pathway seen threading throughout the long deep valley below; a creek and some little waterfalls from the rocky cuttings above. Now we run through a short tunnel, then shift to the main line and forward again, still up a very steep incline on the edge of steep precipices; large masses of very high rock all round and on ridges, &c.; some large masses have and are in course of falling down—tons of it. A few cockatoos about. Very few birds seen to-day, probably too hot to show up. This zig-zag is supremely grand, but produces a sickening sensation at first sight on looking out of the carriage. On top at last, and then gentle inclines ensue. Country more level, with some few slight cuttings. Four green flats; cattle and horses about, and some three or four good houses and gardens, and several bark huts; then into Bowen Fells station; a dead level.

Arrived at *Bowen Fells*, 97 miles, at 2 P.M. Substantial stone-built station of rubble-dressed square blocks of light stone; good deep coping of worked stone; roof of slate. About 100 feet frontage, with waiting rooms, &c., but no refreshment room. Verandah front and back on painted wood pillars and galvanized-iron roofs. Station flagged with light-brown flat, smooth stone, in squares properly dressed. Platform about 160 feet. Galvanized-iron goods shed, 80 by 40 feet. Station master has one of the neatest residences I ever saw at any country station, built of same stone as station; erected in the Elizabethan style, with a nice garden, &c., round it, a mixture of shrubs, flowers, and vegetables; amongst the latter noticed some red cabbages and early York cabbages. Bold and lofty hills and ranges, with rocky ridges and sides, &c., in sight of station. Land cleared some distance all round here, and fat cattle and horses, &c., depasturing. A few stores and houses about, some partly stone and wood, some with galvanized-iron roofs, bark huts, and so on. One nice large residence, with extensive outbuildings, grounds, garden, &c., belonging to a Mr. Brown, a squatter, in a beautiful valley with running stream, in sight of the station, with high hills and ranges at back; a very pretty landscape. There are also some other good residences with gardens in same valley. Township two miles and a half from station, and no vehicle plying. Not sufficient time to walk it. Offered some tea, but did not care about it in the middle of the day, and had to content myself with biscuit and water, until return to Blue Mountain station. Plenty of coal, very slaty looking and close in the grain, said to be good, found near here, but principally at Hartley. Left at 4 P.M.; getting cooler. Did the second zig-zag slowly and carefully. Lamps lit at Mount Victoria, although sun far from being down. At Blue Mountain stayed ten minutes. The keeper of refreshment room "fossicked" out and favoured me with a small bottle of Bass's pale ale "on the sly," as he cannot afford to pay 30*l.* a year for a licence. Relished this very much with a sandwich, for 1*s.* 6*d.*; and took away a dozen peaches at 6*d.*, which I considered would last me to Sydney. Dark when we arrived at first zig-zag, although there was the moon rather young, but then she was often of no service to us, being hidden from view by the dense scrub and deep cuttings. The lights at Penrith looked very pretty as the moon went down. Arrived at Sydney station at 9.50 P.M. Went to Prince of Wales's Theatre late, and saw Howe in part

H

of 'Shamrock of Ireland' and farce of 'Spectre Bridegroom;' not of much account; poor attendance.

Saturday, 25th February.— Morning warm and throughout day. At Wooloomooloo to get opossum rug lined, &c. Afternoon through lower part of domain or Botanic Garden. Dwarf wall of dressed stone for a quarter of a mile to Macquarie Street, with tall iron railing, then common paling fence. There is a row of gigantic Moreton Bay fig-trees next this street for about 150 yards; then follows on rising ground a pathway all bed rock, facing the harbour, and Government House of cut stone, with its castellated stone towers, &c. Also on brink of this portion of the harbour, and in front of Government House, is Fort Macquarie with its three castellated cut-stone towers mounting fifteen large guns, built on bed rock and constructed of very solid masonry. Then by the water for a quarter of a mile on a pathway rocky and sandy; then inside, passing through a small entrance-gate and a lodge of brick in the Elizabethan style, you find very wide, well-kept pathways, almost carriage ways, with borders of verdant grass 18 inches wide, and in some instances gutters of brick. The trees, particularly the pine tribe, are gigantic; pretty ornamental wooden arbours formed of crooked trees, branches, &c., in their natural state, thatched and so on, with nice seats within; mostly a paling fence all the way. Grass a lively green, and near the water well cut and close. Every variety of shrub, some flowering, with flowers intermixed, but I did not notice any beds of flowers, though

I am told there are in the upper part of the domain, which I must see another time, having exhausted four hours in this varied and extensive portion, wandered round to the extreme point, and found myself looking on Wooloomooloo Bay and its environs, with St. James's Church, &c., on an eminence in the distance, a very pretty prospect view. In the evening at Prince of Wales's Theatre, Howe's farewell; selections from 'Richard III.,' Act 2nd; 'Hamlet,' 3rd Act; and 'Rip Van Winkle,' 3rd Act (Rip waking after twenty years' sleep). Mr. Howe splendid in Rip. After repeated calls the actor came before the curtain and made a neat but sarcastic speech, during which he pointed to the almost empty boxes and thanked sincerely those who had patronized him, *viz.* stalls, pit, and gallery.

Sunday, 26th February.—Morning, afternoon, and evening, occasional heavy showers. In morning viewed upper part of domain, with its broad and well-kept walks and magnificent trees and shrubs, foreign and colonial, with parterres of flowering shrubs and flowers covering an immense extent of ground, something like three miles round, yet I feel bound to observe (which view is corroborated by several visitors to the colonies whom I have met with) that Adelaide bears off the palm for the beautiful artistic arrangement of its fairy beds, &c., of flowers. Then went round to St. James's Church, King Street East, a large old brick-built edifice, erected in time of Governor Macquarie, in 1820, with spire metalled round; several handsome entrances by cut-stone steps, with dressed lofty pillars, particularly to

King Street East. The brickwork of main building rests on about six feet of cut Sydney stone, with high iron railings all round, fixed in dressed stone. Interior of the fabric is square in form, about 150 feet deep, 50 feet broad; ceiling about 30 feet high, of plaster and whitewash, slightly ornamented, and cornices ditto. Enclosed old-fashioned pews of Sydney cedar, about 3 feet 6 inches high, wainscoted against walls about 4 feet 9 inches high. Ledges to rest books on. Some pews square, but the greater portion about 10 feet long and 3 feet wide. Cushions and carpets in some few seats. A gallery nearly all round, in the shape of a horse-shoe, of Sydney cedar, and over the east end, supported by large wooden pillars painted to imitate white marble. Plain glass windows. A very good powerful organ, and good chanting and singing. About thirty very handsome tablets, mostly of white marble, some resting on black ditto. About fifty ground-glass gas lamps resting in bronze brackets. Chancel and its furniture plain; it is round in form and is in body of church, about 20 feet from east end, but has a handsome white marble font. Pews at east end, where communion table, &c., is usually put in most churches. Reading desk of cedar, and lofty pulpit of ditto. Was shown into American Consul's seat, that functionary being absent from the city. Observing that I had no books, a handsomely-dressed, fair-complexioned little girl, about ten years old, whom I afterwards discovered was called Ada, whispered to a young lady older than herself, called ———, and then the little lady passed a Prayer and Hymn Book to me. The lessons and part of the communion service were read by a middle-aged short clergyman, a very correct but tame reader. The other clergyman, who assisted him at communion and afterwards preached, was the Rev. Mr. Allwood, an elderly gentleman, who has been connected with this church from the beginning; an excellent reader, and very distinct good voice. He preached, in a white surplice with plain black band, an impressive sermon, with no High Church about it. In afternoon strolled about Miller's Point, where I used to live, and on the eminence called the Flagstaff. Handsome new stone bridge over Fort Street, and new approaches to Flagstaff, rather steep, but cut stone boundary walls. In evening went with an old Sydney friend, Miss Anna J——, to Trinity Church, Miller's Point, built of cut stone, about 150 feet long and 50 broad, with very lofty roof of dark timber, about 70 feet high; immense archway of worked stone forms entrance to chancel. Chancel window very large, of stained glass, as well as all the other windows. Good organ, presided over by an amateur, gratis. Five female amateur singers (Miss J——, leader), also without pay. I was in organ-loft, and the singing was very good. An elderly clergyman, Rev. Mr. Rogers (a great favourite), a distinct reader, preached an excellent sermon. Occasional heavy showers during evening and at night.

Monday, 27th February.—Morning hazy and dull, very slight showers, and turned out warm in the afternoon. Great procession and demonstration by working men of all trades, in favour of eight hours' system of labour, came down Pitt Street at 10, *en route* for steamers from Circular Quay, with large banners; naval brass band in front, and one ditto in rear. The fête took place at Ivanhoe, Manley Beach, an inlet, bow or nearly horse-shoe shaped, in sight of Sydney Heads. Went down at 11 A.M., when everything was getting clear, in a chartered steamer; return ticket, 1s. 6d. Good landing stage and approach to an excellent hotel up a gentle slope, quite green, covered with indigenous trees and flowering and other shrubs. Hotel built of cut stone from neighbourhood, similar to Sydney stone. Galvanized-iron roof; extensive verandah with galvanized top. The best and most commodious pavilion for dining, dancing, &c., I have seen in any watering place in New South Wales. It is very large, of stone, wood, and galvanized iron. Picnics being held on the moderate hills and gentle slopes adjacent; cricket, football, and other adult and juvenile sports were indulged in. Scenery delightful. Several good houses and gardens about in the scrub. A fine white sandy beach, bow-shaped, about two chains wide, nearly all round bay. Returned at 6 P.M. Walked round, but was too late to go inside, the infirmary and dispensary, Macquarie Street, a large brick building, but ascertained that there was over 1200 in-door cases, and 3000 out-door during the year, about 200 actually in hospital at one time, The Mint is part of this building, or rather was taken from it, having formed part of the female hospital, and was detached for sake of economy. The exterior of the Mint calls for no special notice.

Tuesday, 28th February.—Fine day. Engaged in writing to friends from 6 A.M. to 11 A.M. Called on

Registrar-General of Deeds, &c. (an old Adelaide friend), who showed me over the commodious suite of offices and large "strong or fire-proof" room for protecting the legal documents against fire; also saw the oldest law documents of the colony, the first Crown grant of land issued, and entry of birth of first child born there. Inspected exterior of ragged and industrial schools, three in number, but not of much appearance; supported by voluntary subscriptions: about 420 children on books; average daily attendance about 200. Saw Exhibition building in Prince Alfred's Park, which is nicely laid out, but contains only ten acres. It was built for colonial exhibitions of 1870, and is situated near the Haymarket, George Street South; erected of stone, brick, wood, and glass, and is the largest building in Sydney; the exterior not prepossessing, but the interior well finished and has very large rooms for meetings, balls, &c. Went round Darlinghurst Gaol, standing on high ground overlooking the city from the east; walls 20 feet high from base course; area about $5\frac{1}{2}$ acres; lodge for warders east side of entrance gates; will hold over 600 prisoners. Commands good views of the city and harbour, as indeed do most places, almost wherever you choose to walk. In evening went to Corporation baths, Dawe's Point, close on the harbour; cost the corporation several thousand pounds; exterior a nice elevation of cut stone; interior not excavated to proper depth; bottom uneven and rocky, and bathers in plunging had received severe injuries. Sarcastically reported in a newspaper that the lessee, with a philanthropic regard for the comfort of visitors, had provided a supply of sticking-plaster and other remedies for cut and bruised limbs, and suggested a "resident medical officer" as the next desideratum. Since being here I have swallowed a considerable quantity of "Sydney rock oysters," 6d. to 1s. per dozen; small, but very sweet, about the size of "natives," mostly patronizing G. Clarke's saloon, Market Street East, a very clean, old-established place; the proprietor, an elderly man, with snow-white apron, about half a century at the business. The walls in many places adorned with attempted rhymes, in frames; one was as follows:—

> "Ladies all, we come at your call;
> And when on the table you knock,
> We please, if we can, and serve you well;
> Bid you 'Good night!' at twelve o'clock.
>
> "Gentlemen all, we come at your call;
> And when on the table you knock,
> We please, if we can, and serve every man;
> Bid you 'Good night!' at twelve o'clock.
>
> "Gentlemen, one word, 'tis not too late;
> To find fault we are loath;
> If you cut your bread upon your plate,
> You will not cut the cloth."

Wednesday, 1st March.—Fine sunny morning. Left Sydney with regret; the inhabitants certainly much "slower" than their Victorian or Adelaide neighbours, but exceed them in attention to business and extreme politeness; in fact, their habits are more like England than the other colonies; still their "ways," in many instances, want mending sadly. Also particularly noticed a perfect nuisance, which the police in Melbourne or Adelaide would not tolerate, nor the public either, such as blind men with their dogs, and a string of beggars, annoying one from morning till night; with now and then a female "fortune-teller." Also observed more open distress than seen in the other colonies. Men, some of them appearing to have been well off at one time, some in the last stage of seediness, others in rags and tatters, no boots, &c., sleeping they know not where, and not caring much. When I went to Parramatta saw one specimen, at 9 A.M., evidently belonging to some profession formerly, asleep on the slimy wharf stairs, and only was aroused by the noise on the arrival of the up steamer.

SYDNEY TO AUCKLAND, NEW ZEALAND.
1300 Miles.

Left Circular Quay at 7.30 A.M. in wherry belonging to and paddled by one James Potter, a native of Exmouth, Devon, and boarded S.S. 'City of Melbourne,' sister ship to S.S. 'City of Adelaide,' built in 1862, John Grainger, commander (a good-looking, stout, strict man, about fifty; couldn't touch malt liquors for the life of him, only wine and spirits). Only 200 tons cargo on board, but 800 tons coal, she consuming from twenty-eight to thirty tons a day. Licensed to carry 900 within Sydney Heads; 198, including crew, at sea; ship's company, men and boys, all told, 55; 80 adult passengers and 10 children on board, the latter, as luck would have it, all "forward." Lying in Johnston's Bay, a quiet nook about one mile and a half from Circular Quay. Breakfasted on board at 8. Great excitement and confusion on small steamer and boats continually arriving with passengers and their friends, some as close as two minutes to starting; particularly through an excited elderly female, who only got alongside about half a minute before departure, her boxes being pitched on board anyhow, to her great annoyance. Seven "locked-up" German ships were close by, afraid to go to sea, on account of French man-of-war from New Caledonia cruising about on the lookout. Weighed and left at 9 A.M. precisely. An exciting chase took place by four or five watermen after a tame goose, which by some means had got into the sea. After half an hour's bother it turned out to be a wild-goose chase, as the bird at length got close to and flew on shore, near habitations, a present for the first landsman who might come across it. Water as smooth as glass in harbour, &c., as far and until through the Heads; then a nice sea on and comfortable weather. S.S. 'City of Hobart,' for Hobart Town, Tasmania, a larger and more powerful boat than ours, overhauled us half-way to the Heads. Shoals of immense jelly-fish about; very pretty in the clear water. Passed three steamers, packed like sardines with Catholic school children, to a picnic in Manley Beach pleasure grounds. Through Heads at 10 A.M. Viewed from North head a continuation of light sandy beach, under low rocky hills. Scrub land, with small timber scattered about, many miles in extent, and was visible to us up to 1 P.M. At noon fresh breeze, but little ahead; now carried spanker, main trysail, and foresails. Freshened in afternoon, with rather heavy sea on; shipped a sprinkling now and then. No land visible since 1 P.M., and will not be till about Sunday next, perhaps Monday. Nearly all more or less sick. No lady, and only thirteen or fourteen male cabin passengers came to lunch at noon; same at dinner at 4, and nearly ditto at tea at 7 P.M. Course E. and N.E. Cabins rather closely packed; three berths in some cabins, four in others. I had top one, No. 1. One of my companions, Mr. Geo. A. Thompson, of Nelson, New Zealand, was on poop ill, afraid to come below; other one, Mr. Trennery, a Cornish gentleman, late of Ballarat, Victoria, for England, in his berth all day very ill. Heavy cross sea and head wind on all night. Steamer shaking, rolling, and pitching heavily; did not sleep much. Afraid of being pitched out or toppling over. To prevent this had to lie most of night on broad of back.

Thursday, 2nd March.—Fine sunny morning. Turned out at 7. Both my companions still ill. Not much sea on; continuous head wind. Lieut. Verney, of Her Majesty's service (infantry), an entertaining, spirited fellow, *en route* to Queenstown, and thence to his native place in Ireland on a visit, mounted a net hammock of Indian grass, attached by cords to boom of spanker on deck, flung himself into it *au fait,* and passed the morning comfortably smoking cigars and reading the 'Home News,' a monthly publication expressly for the colonies, sent out from England every month. Noticed large glass case, protected by wood and wire, lashed to deck, of plants, &c., from South Australia, through Anthony and Bartleet, of Port Adelaide, for "His Majesty the King of Hawaiian Islands, Honolulu, care of Josh.

Planta, Esq. More sea on in afternoon, with head wind, &c., making her roll very much; a greater proportion sick than I ever saw in any ship I have been in before. One lady, Mrs. Pinnell, wife of ex-United States' Consul for Melbourne, expected to succumb; hoped her husband would not have her body thrown overboard, as she thought she could not survive it long. He promised to take her home to his "thoroughfare" in the States dead or alive. Says he is a doctor; was born in the Southern States; had a plantation; got disgusted with slavery; left, and went to Northern States. Said he was engaged as an army surgeon in the late American war. His brogue was Yankee, such as "Yes," pronounced by him "Ya," "Y-a-a-s," &c. I asked him what "remove" Sam Wright, the second steward, was from a negro—a very good and attentive man, with light-brown curly hair and brown complexion, a native of Kingston, Jamaica, but similar features and "wool" to the negro race. The Doctor answered, "Every man who has the slightest stain of negro blood in him is called in the States 'a nigger.'" Weather and sea day and night about same as Wednesday, with a few light showers. Bright moonlight, beautiful night. After tea fell asleep on poop in a reclining wooden chair, not lashed fast, but luckily fixed aft corner of skylight by accident.

Friday, 3rd March.—Woke in my chair all safe at 1 A.M., much refreshed; went below and turned in, almost in the dark. Three or four children crying and screeching awfully from sickness, and some adults moaning, &c., ditto. Head wind still, and very cross sea. Steamer rolling heavily, no sails set; raining in afternoon; rough rest of day, evening, and all night; perpendicular pitches, rather. Yankee doctor calls her very unruly; his wife still fancies she is dying. Sam Wright, who had overheard the conversation about "nigger blood" yesterday, observed to me, "If she does kick, she will be sewn up and pitched overboard in the usual manner, as we have no rum to spare to preserve a Yankee dried-up piece of old junk like her."

Saturday, 4th March.—Early morn fine till 8 A.M., when a squall came on; heavy rain till 10; jib and main trysail set, making her run easier; shortly after wind almost fair, all canvas spread, then fair wind all day; pitching heavily at times, but two ladies actually appeared at dinner; shipped a few seas; doing 10 to 12 knots. In evening and all night wind still fair.

Sunday, 5th March.—Wind fair but rather light; not much sea on; captain read prayers for an hour in saloon; full attendance (except sick). Rev. Fletcher, a Congregationalist minister, from Richmond, near Melbourne, was to have "spouted," but sea-sickness took the wind out of his sails, and he was a spectator only. Three immense rocks, called the Three Kings, with numerous other rocks adjacent and between them, &c., cropping out of the sea, one of the Kings running for some distance to a point or small promontory, sighted at about 6 P.M. Passed at 9 P.M., and from thence it is about 280 miles to Auckland, and 1020 from Sydney. Land (part New Zealand coast) sighted at 10.30, a long way off. North Cape, an immense mass of rock, &c.,

passed in dead of night; bright moonlight; weather cool; wind veering N.W. to S.W.

Monday, 6th March.—Squally morning and cold; rough sea on; fresh gale and squally; wind within a point of fair, and carrying nearly all her sails; made her steadier; some with great coats on, &c. Sailed about 14 or 15 miles from coast on starboard side, a bold and rocky one with lofty peaks and ranges, but no beach visible. At 8 P.M. abreast and within 2 miles of a very high rocky promontory, called Cape Brett, with two large rocks outside it, cropping out of the sea; wider open space between one of these and the cape, the latter a mass of solid rocks, with thick scrub, &c., on sides and top of ranges. The warlike hostile Hau Hau tribe (against the Britishers) occupy this cape and country round. Still similar rocky ranges, peaks, &c., in continuation on starboard side for miles. At 9.30 a barque in full sail (except top-gallant and mainsail), 400 or 500 tons, said to be for Sydney, passed us on starboard side, the first craft we have seen since leaving Sydney Heads. At 10 A.M. passed three rocky, barren islands on port side; heavy squalls now and then, driving all below; during these squalls land hardly distinguishable, being as if enveloped in a mist. During the morning passed the Bay of Islands, four in number, with very large rugged rocks cropping out of the sea, on port side; at 11.45 abreast of the Three Knights, one large rocky island and two small; some very rugged; one rock particularly high and craggy, near a large bay; a white sandy beach on starboard side, near to which were some elevated rocks and peaks called "The Hen and Chickens." (Rather a large hen that.)

Opposite side of the bay, and outside "Hen and Chickens," are several islands almost all solid rock, no vegetation visible, with narrow entrances between and round them from open sea. Up to 2 P.M. numerous rocky islands, large and small, outside the main land; also a few on the port side. 2.15, abreast of a sandy beach, with scrubby land in view, said to be good agricultural country, at back of the ranges. Then passed "Rodney's Point," not very imposing, succeeded by rocky ranges, becoming gradually less bold and much lower. For miles on starboard side, a large rocky range or island, called "The Little Barrier," cropping out of the ocean, top of range being apparently very scrubby and like a (huge) turtle in shape, ending abruptly at one end like its head, and the other similar to its tail (a rather long one though). Great Barrier not to be seen, being much more to starboard, and the weather getting hazy. Little Barrier was visible up to 4 P.M. At 3 passed a large bay called "Cowie Bay," and some very pretty small ones. Ranges getting much lower, some with coarse grass on them, approaching to green. Plenty of friendly Maories about here and in country at back, who grow potatoes and go out fishing. Two boats were out, of English build, bought up by Maories; breeze freshening; heavy sea on and squally. Purser observed that no one but Maories would have come outside in such weather.

The wind is fair, and we are comparatively steady

under steam and canvas. 3.15, "Large Barrier" now plainly seen about three times the size, length, &c., of its little sister, but considerably more to starboard. At 3.30 a lofty spar or pole visible about 15 miles ahead, called the beacon of warning. Passed it at 4, and at 5 we were abreast of "Tiri Tiri" Lighthouse, on a cape of rocky strata, scrub, &c. Ranges of rock, scrub, peaks, and spurs ahead, peculiarly shaped; some of the country said to be good, and one portion forms an immense bend almost in the shape of a horse-shoe, now looking as if we were near the entrance of an immense bay, out of which there is no apparent outlet on N.E. and W. sides, yet one can go all round it. It is called "Rangitoto." Every now and then passed barren islands of all sizes and shapes. At 6 P.M. off Flag Staff on north shore, on starboard side, fixed on top of a curious large mound of volcanic formation; other similar mounds near, covered with growth, said to be tea-tree scrub, with picturesque hills adjacent, and mountains in distance at rear. Now about three miles from a rocky point, on rounding shall be about ten miles from wharf. Some excellent houses and gardens on north shore; a few on land to port. Amongst others, a curious long island, the shape of a racing boat. Pilot boarded at 6.15, and we got alongside pier at 7 P.M., near dusk.

Very "dirty" afternoon and evening, squally and rainy, yet there were many persons along pier, anxious to have a peep at us. Only a few went on shore, the weather being damp and disagreeable; night rather dark. The Yankee doctor, however, nothing daunted, rushed away to the nearest barber to get shaved. On returning he said that the room appeared to him to be turning upside down, as he still felt the roll of the vessel. Atmosphere so damp that decks were quite wet at 10 P.M., more than three hours after any rain had fallen. In Australia they would have dried up in twenty minutes after rain. Amongst the numerous visitors to the saloon during the evening, one of the "oldest" (white) inhabitants told us that he never knew such a wet summer, and that this had been the most moist day he had ever seen here, coming down in spouts, &c.; that as a general rule the climate of Auckland was like spring weather the greater part of the year; seldom any winter. Slept on board very snug and sound. Short summary of voyage to this place as supplied by the ship's purser to the Auckland papers as follows:—"Experienced from Sydney first part, light variable weather, with heavy N.E. swell; latter part strong S.W. and W. winds; from Three Kings fresh gale, attended with heavy squalls; wind veering from N.W. to S.W."

Tuesday, 7th March.—Beautiful mild morning and day, only a few drops of rain.

Auckland and suburbs. Estimated population at present time (census to be taken again shortly), whites, 30,000; Maories, 8000. Turned out at 6.30 A.M. Fine sun-shiny morning. Very fine commodious harbour, land-locked north and south sides, with a bay on the east and mountains and ranges in the distance; a few houses only seen from deck on north side; at back, on

I

south, a high hill called "Mount Eden," commanding a beautiful view of the city, suburbs, and harbour. This hill is volcanic, and has a crater at top, and one can walk in its hollows and fissures, without any danger, as within the memory of whites and blacks it has not emitted any fiery volcanic matter. The pier, so called, is substantially built of timber, resting on wooden piles (*à la* Goolwa, South Australia). It is 40 feet and upwards wide throughout; turns, after running some distance west, at a right angle, thence continuing south to Queen Street, altogether about half a mile of it, the platform being well finished, of wood, except a small portion next Queen Street, which is macadamized. This pier cuts the harbour in twain, for there is a continuation of it on west side, at end of which is a very wide entrance to the Waitemata River, in midst of which entrance is a small island called Watchman's Island, so named from formerly being used by hostile river tribes when at war with hostile tribes in east, where a Maori sentinel was placed to watch for the approach of the enemy's canoes up harbour from east. Mostly small craft around us, the largest a composite ship called "The City of Auckland,' nearly 800 tons, lately on fire in consequence of ignition of portion of cargo—native flax; and another, 'The Queen Bee,' of London, 726 tons. Viewed from the poop, on the hill sides and gentle slopes, as also facing the harbour (all on south side), are numerous very well built houses, a few of stone, principally of brick, and many of wood— "Kauri pine"—commanding from the hills a view of the harbour and north shore, and distant mountains and ranges. There are also several churches and chapels about the hills and in the city, some with brick spires. There is a breakwater to the south-east in course of erection (nearly finished) from the harbour to a nice elevated point, on which stand several large wooden buildings and a stone one or two, some time since used by Government as a fort, now abandoned. After breakfast, at 9 A.M., I sallied forth with Mr. Garside (a cabin passenger, formerly of Manchester, late a storekeeper at Ballarat) to see what we could in the limited time (five hours). After traversing the wharf, and observing two masculine Maori women, with their broad bare shoulders and picaninnies at back, pumping out a decked fishing-boat, their lords and masters, most of them of gigantic proportions, lying about their boats doing nothing, and some of the women half naked, ditto—this being their morning costume till about the middle of the day, when they don an English style of attire, barring stockings, and boots and shoes—we came to the end of the wharf at the entrance of the principal street, Queen Street, about 1¼ mile long, hilly at the end of it; chain and a half wide; road macadamized, and in fair repair; very wide footpaths, formed of a dark-coloured coarse gravel and sand, well calculated to wear holes in one's boots on a short acquaintance, kerbed with dark spongy-looking stone. Some very excellent buildings in this street, being a great many warehouses, banks, good shops containing merchandise of every description, and hotels—in fact the business street of the town, as I could see no private dwellings—principally built of brick, stone, plastered stucco, or painted over, and several wood ones. I only noticed one cut-stone building in the street, near the Thames Hotel. One very fine building is nearly completed for the New Zealand Insurance Company; lofty elevation, with ornamented tower at top containing a large clock with three faces—east, north, and south. The main building of brick plastered over, and well finished with handsome ornamental pillars, ditto. Narrower streets, some of them particularly so, and very sharp ascents and descents branch off Queen Street on east and west sides. Several banks in this street, large and lofty, but plain; the Bank of New Zealand is one of them. The Union, higher up the street, nearly at the top; good elevation, the base course of very dark stone (similar appearance to Melbourne stone) partly hammer-dressed and partly rubble masonry; the main building stuccoed over, painted, &c., with very high, large plain pillars at entrance; lofty, large bank room, &c. The Post Office is in Shortland Crescent, off Queen Street on east; it is an imposing, good building of brick and cut stone, about 80 feet frontage, with worked stone quoins, &c.; handsome worked light stone arches next street, to an arcade, 70 feet long, fronting the various letter and newspaper boxes, &c.; the ceiling of the arcade, about 30 feet high, being of polished Kauri pine, very neat and pretty; worked stone arched windows, &c. Went to a good stationer's and bookseller's shop kept by a Scotchman, near Post Office, and purchased some newspapers and stamps; came to 2s. 7d. Waited half an hour for change for a sovereign; then short 1s. 11d. Said silver was horribly scarce; that everybody was very "hard up"—"if you dare ask for money, chances be you get knocked down"—notwithstanding the new Thames Diggings shares, which, he expressed his opinion, would sell like wildfire, only people hadn't the money to speculate. Could I look in again in an hour or two? I could get my change. There being very little silver on board the steamer, I thought I had better lay in a supply, so I invested 1s. at Phillips' ironmonger's shop, in a chamois leather bag; went to the Union Bank, where the teller kindly supplied me with 5l. worth, and ten half-sovereigns in exchange for sovereigns. I subsequently knocked 2s. out of the stationer, giving him back a stray penny which I had brought from Adelaide. Then went into some of the branch streets and skirted the hills, finding numerous excellent houses (many with slate roofs), good shops, several neat hotels of Kauri pine, some of them extensive ones, scattered over a very large area; some streets had a few vacant spots for building, more or less, and a few back ones were not metalled. Mount Eden, towering far above its lesser neighbours, looks over everything round about. The old barracks and Volunteer Office, &c., at top of hill to south-east have been handed over by the Imperial Government to the New Zealand Government, who are having most of the old wooden buildings pulled down, and intend selling the land, which will be built on. The old citadel, a very poor attempt at defence, the wall, about 12 feet high, of rough dark stone, might be easily scaled by Maories, and one 18-pounder would knock the whole affair down in twenty minutes. Near this place, lower down the hill to the east, is the entrance to Government House, along a wide well-kept carriage drive, standing in a small domain of 10 or 12 acres; nice walks, trees, and shrubberies. The house is very large, with a good elevation, and is built of Kauri pine, well painted, carved facings, ornamented, and so on, and at first sight one would take it to be built of stone or brick plastered over and painted, it is so well finished; it has a nice view of the harbour, &c. The Supreme Court House is a handsome building of brick and cut stone, with a tower of same materials, situate in Waterloo Quadrant, opposite Government House and grounds, the public roadway dividing them. The club house is a very good but plain building in Princess Street, at top of a hill and nearly opposite to the entrance to Government House; it has a large entrance hall. The steward a very gentlemanly, well-dressed, civil young man. The church on the hill that I noticed from the poop before breakfast, we now ran against, is the chief one here belonging to the Church of England. The main building is large and lofty, but old, sadly wanting repairing and whitewashing; the brick spire is much too short and infinitely out of proportion to the main building. No cathedral in existence here. Farther south, and in view from the old barracks, is the public park and garden, on a slope; about 100 acres of it looking, in the distance, full of trees and shrubs. We had not time to go there, and were informed that they have been rather neglected of late years. The grass in the suburbs on the hills and places not built on was very thick and green, and most luxuriant, like in England. The principal hotel is the 'Waitemata,' corner of Queen and Custom-house Streets, nearly opposite to the entrance to the pier; has two frontages, well-finished, lofty building, and interior containing good accommodation. Paid a visit to an old digging friend of Mr. Garside's, called Vance, formerly of Ballarat, now a wine and spirit merchant here. After tasting some of his liquors and talking over old times, the conversation concluded by Mr. Vance remarking that this is the most poverty-stricken place he ever saw, and that the "old hands" are extremely jealous of new arrivals "settling," and try all they know to work against and keep them out. Very little business appeared to be doing, and persons did not generally appear to be in a hurry.* Observed a few good pair-horse carriages, also some Hansom cabs, and an omnibus or two, but nothing bustling. Charge for pair-horse carriage, 5s. per hour. Taking into consideration one thing and another, many of the buildings here are imposing; indeed it is a very pretty, healthy-looking place.

More Maories knocking about in the middle of the day. They don't appear to "turn out" very early, especially the men, as the women do nearly all the work. Met with several not pure, some very light-brown complexions to very dark-brown, &c.; both sexes mostly dressed like Europeans, generally without

* Sir G. A. Arney, Kt., Chief Justice, in his charge to the grand jury on 6th March, congratulated them on non-increase of crime of a serious nature, considering "the unparalleled depression, and the great amount of distress prevailing during the (then) last quarter."

showing bare feet and legs; many had boots on. Very tall, masculine, powerful men and women as a rule, but some of them appeared to be decaying and wasting away; faces greatly disfigured by tattooing, on cheeks, noses, and even round their monstrous thick ugly lips, chins, &c. Immense masses of jet-black hair on the women, some straight, others with curls hanging about their shoulders. I went into the bar-parlour of the 'Waitemata' to take the last pewter of half-and-half on shore here, where I saw a strapping robust Maori girl, about twenty. She made a motion to leave. I beckoned to her to stay, and asked her if she would have a drink. She didn't seem to comprehend, but turned and looked modestly out of the window. I then called in the barman and explained matters. He spoke to her in her language, and she replied "shandy-gaff," with much clearness twice. So shandygaff she had, and we exchanged bows at the first draught, and presently I got from her that she was born a long way beyond Mount Eden, and had come to town by coach to see the sights. She had on a little dark-straw hat with black feather—looking like a mouse on a mountain on her monstrous "nut"—red-and-black-striped frock and shawl, feet and legs bare, limbs immense. Having only twenty minutes to spare to get on board, I parted from the copper-coloured young lady, she giving me such an awful squeeze with her shoulder-of-mutton hand, that I winced for half an hour afterwards. Got on board four minutes before the time of departure; rather too close, if anything. Pier crowded to see her leave.

AUCKLAND TO HONOLULU, HAWAIIAN ISLANDS.

About 3858 Geographical Miles.

Cast off at 2.10 P.M. Took about a quarter of an hour to wear round. Saw north shore more closely; noticed some nice green slopes, on which stood the houses and a few well-kept grounds and gardens; also a splendid avenue of trees running north to south towards the sea. Beach partly of dark rough sand and stones, remainder of white sand. A jetty there about 350 feet long, on piles. Two small steamers lying off, which ply about and near harbour; keeping same course as on entry, fair wind, all canvas spread. Passed warning beacon at 5.30 P.M.; the Great Barrier, the last land seen, at night. About 11 P.M. wind chopped round, all sail taken in; steamer pitching now and then in a short cross sea. Being tired after a heavy day's work, having had a great deal to see and do in a short time, turned in at 9 P.M., and slept heavily till morning. Had a few additional passengers from various parts of New Zealand; one a very mild young Catholic priest, Father Byrne, who had been also in Australia, but was on his way back to Ireland, as colonial life did not suit his taste, his hearers being generally too fond of whisky. Also a Mr. Schaw, a stipendiary magistrate, from Hokitika, west coast, on a visit to England, and Colonel Whitmore, late of New Zealand Volunteers, who holds a sheep station, a wiry, determined man, of about forty, with a fine sharp grey eye, plenty of dark hair, and rather dark complexion.

Wednesday, 8th March.—Morning fine. Still light head wind and cross sea. At 11 wind slightly veered round, and hoisted foresail.

At Noon, Observations taken.—Run 199 miles from Auckland. Distance from Curtis Island, 285 miles. Latitude, 34° 12′ S.; longitude, 177° 9′ E. Lovely weather all day, quite mild; latter part slight head wind. At 5 P.M. a barque sighted about fifteen miles off, bearing southward, supposed for Auckland.

Evening and night calm, still a light head wind. During day much annoyance on account of smut from dense smoke of funnel falling on deck and on one's clothes, face, &c., even penetrating into the saloon.

Another Wednesday, and 8th March, to equalize time on approaching tropics (Thursday in Auckland). Weather fine and balmy all day. Scent something " changeable " gradually approaching. Continuation of light head winds. No canvas spread until evening, then two forward only.

Observations, Noon.—Distance run, 224 miles (*i. e.* since noon of yesterday). Latitude, 31° 22′ S.; longitude, 179° 57′ W.

Curtis Island distant 61 miles, but not seen. At 9.30 abreast of an island with conical-shaped top, about ten miles off, starboard side, called Macaulay Island, but not clearly distinguishable. Bright moon, and starlight, cool night. In afternoon a large shoal of porpoises on each side of us, and then right across bow, racing, sporting, and jumping like mad out of the water for some distance. When porpoises kick up this fracas, the general supposition is that a whale is in chase.

Thursday, 9th March.—Cool day. Heavy showers of rain from 6.30 A.M. to 7.30. Wind approaching fair, but almost a head wind; carrying foresails. A nice sea on. At 10.45 breeze freshening; all sails set.

Observations, Noon.—Distance run, 245 miles. Latitude, 28° 1' S.; longitude, 177° 16' W.

Savage Island 675 miles distant (but will not be sighted at all. It is inhabited, and has a mission station there. Passing ships sometimes call for provisions). Evening and night cloudy; occasional showers, good breeze, fair wind, all sails set, nice sea on; ship pitching gently now and then; a few sick again. Rats knocking about the saloon at night. Ate holes and took away some fur from a Mr. Kitchener's rug (from west coast of New Zealand); the captain says to make their nests with. Was glad to lend my opossum rug to a Mr. Mitchell, a chemist and druggist, a native of Cornwall, who was about to settle at Honolulu, and was very sick; he used it on deck almost all day and night, which preserved it from the attacks of the rats.

Friday, 10th March.—Heavy rain from 6 A.M. to 1 P.M.; fresh breeze, fair wind, and all sails set till 2 P.M., when light head wind and cross sea, which lasted all afternoon, evening, and night. Ship pitching heavily. A few flying-fish seen this morning. Captain couldn't take observations, weather so cloudy and close. Very few showed on deck to-day. Quite warm below, like being "stewed up"; vivid lightning in long sheets on starboard during evening. Night very close.

Saturday, 11th March.—Sudden squall and shower of rain at 7 A.M., lasted only half an hour. Wind still ahead.

Observations, Noon.—Distance run two days, 450 miles. Latitude, 22° S.; longitude, 172° 11' W.

From Savage Island 223 miles. Day cool, with occasional slight squalls. Wind-sails let down from poop, which moderated the close atmosphere in saloon. Sea comparatively smooth; warm night below.

Sunday, 12th March.—Morning warm. Engines stopped working at 8 A.M.; slight disarrangement of machinery. Engineer's assistants "tapping" at it till 1 P.M., when steam up again, progressing at first moderately. In mean time all sails set, with very little wind to keep her moving barely three knots an hour. Rev. Fletcher read Church of England Service in cuddy, and then "discoursed" a short amusing episode on the relative qualities of a live dog and a dead lion. Shortly after which a shark about six feet long was descried close astern, with its two faithful pilot fish ahead, beautifully striped all round their bodies like the zebra. A hook baited with pork was thrown overboard; he swallowed the pork, but not the hook; baited again, which he took voraciously, hook and all. A general hurrah and haul at the rope; the captain leader. The brute was within two feet of the gunwale, when it "shook" itself and dropped safe into the briny, apparently not the worse, but it did not trouble us again.

Observations, Noon.—Distance run, 175 miles; latitude, 19° 47' S.; longitude, 170° 8' W. Savage Island distant 46 miles, but not visible to us at all. Afternoon, evening, and night cool. Ship progressing favourably under steam and sail, wind being nearly fair.

Monday, 13th March.—Morning fine but warm. Wind nearly fair; fore and aft sails set; sea smooth.

Observations, Noon.—Distance run, 225 miles; latitude, 16° 43' S.; longitude, 167° 51' W. Nassau Island distant 340 miles. Current, east 15'. Afternoon and evening dull and cool; night warm below. Fresh breeze; all canvas spread. Some slight seas shipped at night. Port-holes had to be closed.

Tuesday, 14th March.—Morning fine, but a north warm wind blowing. Breeze freshening; all sails set. Nice sea on. Squall for a short time at 10 A.M. Shipped a few seas; fine wind afterwards. Weather cool latter part, and at night.

Observations, Noon.—Distance run, 234 miles; latitude, 13° 18' S.; longitude, 165° 54' W. Nassau Island distant 110 miles. Afternoon and evening showery and squally, with rather a heavy sea on, but not an angry one. Shipping water continually. Steamer rolling evenly, yet driving females below, as also some sea-sick males, individuals who ought not to venture on the briny unless compelled to do so; probably, however, their misfortune, and not their fault. To sailors and convalescents this is a delightful time.

Wednesday, 15th March.—Morning dull and cool. Head wind and nasty cross sea all day, and throughout night; no canvas spread. Ship pitching heavily; cook's assistants well "washed" in bringing breakfast to saloon. Many persons were surprised in afternoon to find that a young hog, about 80 lbs., had been slaughtered; no one in after part of ship having heard a squeal. But ships' butchers, as a rule, knock their pigs on the head in an orthodox manner with a marlingspike, and cut their throats instantly, not giving them the ghost of a chance to cry out—to several on board a most un-English mode of hog-killing, their wails being generally heard a mile or so distant in the old country. This exemplary method might be followed with advantage to the general public on shore. Too cloudy to take observations at noon.

Thursday, 16th March.—Early morning fine. Wind veered round to within a point of fair; fore-and-aft sails set. Nice sea on, which, with the wind, increased in afternoon and evening.

Observations, Noon.—Distance run, 400 miles; latitude, 7° 13' S.; longitude, 163° 9' W. Fanning Island distant 700 miles.

Friday, 17th March.—Morning bright; slight shower at 6 A.M. Wind not so fresh as yesterday, but in same quarter; all canvas spread. A pleasant, cool day.

Observations, Noon.—Distance run, 205 miles; latitude, 3° 56' S.; longitude, 162° 15' W. Fanning Island distant 500 miles. Cool night.

Saturday, 18th March.—Morning sunny but cool. Wind slackening; nearly all canvas spread; nice sea on.

Observations, Noon.—Distance run, 208 miles; latitude, 0° 36' S.; longitude, 161° 15' W. Thirty-six miles from the equator. Fanning Island distant 281 miles. Rest of day, evening, and night cool.

Sunday, 19th March.—Morning cloudy. Slight squall and shower at 8 A.M.; afterwards a clear, sunny day; beautiful refreshing sea on. Wind about same as yesterday. Ship pitching occasionally, inclining mostly on port side. She is getting much lighter in the water, as a large quantity of coal has been consumed. Rev. Fletcher officiated as on last Sunday, and extemporized on Christian charity, suggesting good feeling (barring sea-sickness) one toward another on board, attention to the sick, and so on.

Observations, Noon.—Distance run, 222 miles; latitude, 2° 59' N.; longitude, 160° 19' W. Fanning Island distant 78 miles. Evening and night occasional showers and squalls, high wind, rough weather. Steamer "shaking" and careening to port very much.

Monday, 20th March.—Cloudy, squally morning, with showers; nasty cross sea. Steamer pitching heavily, but behaving well, not shipping any water. Almost a head wind; all canvas spread, more to steady her than to increase her speed. Evening and night moderate weather. Observations could not be taken.

Tuesday, 21st March.—Morning and day fine and sunny. Almost a head wind; all sails set; nice sea on.

Observations, Noon.—Sun crossed line about this time; distance run, 440 miles; latitude, 10° 6' N.; longitude, 158° 38' W. Honolulu distant 679 miles. Mail bags (of canvas) taken out of hold for inspection and sorting. Rats had eaten holes in four of them, all newspaper bags, and had attacked some of the papers, luckily not doing much damage. This in some degree may account for missing papers now and then. The rats usually attack those with paper covers pasted together; the safest way is to use string only. A rat in the night consumed a part of an address-card pasted on my trunk. Breeze freshened evening and night, blowing hard, and a heavy sea on. North-east trades, or equinoctial gales, now on.

Wednesday, 22nd March.—Squally morning, occasional showers. Wind more moderate than yesterday, but still a heavy sea on. Shipping water now and then, but seldom on poop.

Observations, Noon.—Distance run, 214 miles; latitude, 13° 40' N.; longitude, 158° 31' W. Honolulu distant 460 miles. Evening, afternoon, and night rather rough, with head wind.

Thursday, 23rd March.—Fine clear morning, still nearly a head wind. Sea calmer; light breeze; nearly all sails set.

Observations, Noon.—Distance run, 222 miles; latitude, 17° 22' N.; longitude, 158° 23' W. Honolulu distant 239 miles. Day beautiful. New moon visible at 6 P.M.; went down at 9; fine clear evening. Wind chopped round dead ahead at night; sails had to be taken in.

Friday, 24th March.—Weather about same as yesterday. Wind veered round a little. Nearly all canvas spread. Land sighted at 6.30 A.M., not clearly distinguishable. After breakfast we were gradually

approaching the group commonly called the "Sandwich
Islands," very mountainous in appearance, one very lofty
and bold, towering over 13,000 feet above the level
of the sea, called Hawaii or Owyhee. All sail taken
in at 11.30 A.M. Sea getting nice and smooth; atmosphere pleasantly warm. A complimentary address
from the saloon passengers was presented to Captain
Grainger after breakfast, and duly responded to in
champagne. At 1 P.M. we were off "Eastern Extreme,"
an abrupt rocky point or promontory on starboard side,
increasing in height towards Honolulu, with a continuation of lofty tors and peaks of volcanic appearance; then rises an abrupt headland at foot of the
hills and bordering on the sea, called "Diamond Head,"
after passing which the hills were gradually lower,
and opposite, on the port side, are very high hills,
being a continuation of ranges on the starboard side.
Signalled for pilot at 1.20 P.M. After passing "Extreme
Point," there are two or three small bays or inlets, and
at 2 P.M. a beach was discernible, and running behind
Diamond Head and at the bottom of the hills, apparently in a flat, a cocoa-nut grove was plainly seen,
with rows of graceful, bending, tall, slender palms, some
of them seemingly close to the beach, with huts and
buildings in the distance, and the flagstaff visible on
a very high hill above the town. The pilot boarded
us at 2.30 P.M. in midst of dinner, and brought news
of the Germans having entered Paris, but reported
that the boat to take us on to San Francisco, the 'Moses
Taylor,' had not arrived, but was hourly expected with

K

later news. Shortly after 3 P.M. we suddenly came in view of the harbour and town, with houses of wood principally painted stone colour, down almost to the edge of the water, the land near the water being in the shape of a crescent; the entrance, marked off by buoys, is very narrow and shallow, so much so that we could see the bottom on each side of the channel from the deck of the steamer. The steep hills towering above the town had a very bold and picturesque appearance. A great many persons were on the wharf, natives and white people, some in two and four wheeled buggies, and several, male and female, on horseback, with Mexican saddles, the women riding astraddle, one riding a very handsome white horse with silver-mounted saddle and long spurs. Many held brown silk umbrellas over their heads, which were certainly not required, for it was only moderately warm. The whites were well dressed, in the European style. Many of the native females (the natives are known by the name of "Kanakas") who are of a very dark copper colour, like the Maories, with jet black hair, had on long stuff black gowns, down to their heels, like clergymen's or barristers' gowns, and others with gowns of same shape of every description of coloured linen, some very gaudy, similar patterns to gentlemen's dressing gowns; some had small black or white straw hats on, with feathers or made flowers; others bare-headed and no shoes or stockings on, but unlike the New Zealand native ladies, they cut off their long black hair, too troublesome, they say, to keep in order, and do not display their charms like the Maories, no portion of the back or bust being visible, the gown being close up to the neck. We were alongside the wharf at 3.30 P.M., having run about 239 miles, making a total of 3902 miles from Auckland, the distance on the charts being 3858 miles. Most of us went on shore immediately, it being spring weather and fine. The wharf where the 'City of Melbourne' lay was half covered with huge piles of coal. This wharf is about 350 feet long, of timber, with piles sheathed with copper, and turning at an angle; wharfs run along the frontage of the harbour, altogether about a mile, formed of silt and coral rock, at the foot of the town, which is very irregularly built and is mostly on a flat. Found the streets generally narrow, with houses principally of wood, and many shops to attract the notice of the Kanakas, being filled with feathers, gaudy made flowers, hats, &c., from San Francisco and the States. Ready-made coffins of various sizes could be seen in shops, principally Chinese, plain, of wood; a ready-made supply, we were informed, was necessary, as Kanakas, young and old, die very suddenly, often dropping down in the streets from effects of drink and hereditary causes, although to all outward appearance they look healthy; two had died suddenly just before our arrival. Two or three streets are well macadamized and round as a barrel, with footways of sand; in a few instances bricks or tiles are used, the kerbs being formed of coral rock. Some irregular by-streets are sandy, dry, and pleasant to walk on, and most of the houses in the outlying streets have grass-plots in front, with a few shrubs and flowers looking green, but apparently wire or couch grass. Kanaka men and women were lolling easily on the grass, doing needlework, &c., as they get up early, and rest if they can in the afternoon, when it gets warm. Water is laid on; the inhabitants freely use the hose, which accounts for the plots looking so green. The natives do not tattoo, are very quiet, but generally not fond of work, although some work at various trades, as painters, lettering very well, carpenters, &c. Many females squeeze their large feet into boots, and walk rather stiffly and queerly, trying to imitate the walk of Europeans. Met several Kanakas carrying about bundles of hay for sale, made from wire grass, very fine in texture, put up into tall and slender bundles, the top part being large looking like a chignon, but not weighing 14 lbs. altogether. An American lady (said to be in a consumption) was driving a splendid buggy and pair, and a female Kanaka, married to an innkeeper, a white man, also drove a four-wheeled buggy, a very fine high-stepping horse, with tiger rug spread at the back of the vehicle, and had three children with her dressed European fashion. Most of the inhabitants, white and native, including shoemakers, tailors, and barbers, manage to keep horses, and ride everywhere they want to go about the town in a reckless manner, especially the Kanaka females, to the danger of pedestrians, many of them riding with Mexican spurs fastened to their bare feet in the stirrups, the females being particularly "wild" in their riding, and being astride like the men. The horses are generally about fourteen hands high, a few fifteen and a little over, many of them good looking, wiry animals from California and the States. Plenty of large luscious oranges about, but with very dark skins, selling for a dollar a hundred, and good-flavoured large strawberries twenty-five cents (quarter dollar) per quart. News received this evening by a smart craft from "Frisco," that terms of peace had been signed between Germany and France. Great commotion this evening amongst the few hundred German residents, who, throughout the evening and night made busy preparations to celebrate the event by festivities on the morrow, Saturday.

Saturday, 25th March.—Fine sunny morning, turned out at 6 A.M. About twenty native men and boys naked engaged in fishing with nets in a small inlet close to the shore for a small species of mullet. Some fried for breakfast; very good eating. Several male Kanakas came on board before breakfast touting for "washing." Some brought a neatly-printed list of prices, the principal one patronized being "Chelsea Laundry list of prices at reduced rates," including gentlemen's polished shirts, white or coloured, $1 50c. per dozen; collars or cuffs, 50c. per dozen; pants or vests, white, $1 50c. per dozen; white coats, $1 80c. per dozen; handkerchiefs, 36c. per dozen; socks or stockings, 50c. per dozen; ladies' plain dresses, 20c. to 30c. each; ditto, fluted or tucked, 50c. to $1 50c. each, &c., &c. Went to T. G. Thrums, 19, Merchant Street, who has a good assortment of stationery, books, music, newspapers and periodicals, &c., chiefly English and American, and fancy goods. Met, in his assistant, unexpectedly, a well-known Adelaide solicitor, who could get nothing else to do, and was earning a bare subsistence. Nearly opposite Mr. Thrums' shop stands the Post Office, built of concrete. It is 43 feet in length on the ground floor, 53 feet frontage to Merchant Street, and 33 feet high. Entrance up concrete steps into a corridor running whole length of front. Balustrading or portico of concrete supported by pillars of ditto. A native was reading aloud, to several of his brethren assembled under the portico, from the 'Ke Alaula,' native paper, the news of the entry into Paris, and peace between Germany and France. The Kanakas took a great interest in the war, the French having blockaded and occupied Honolulu for a short time in the year 1849. Education is conducted on a liberal scale, and every Kanaka can read and write, many of them very fluently. Every boy and girl must attend school daily, and if found straying about the streets, are taken up by the police, who are all Kanakas, dressed in white trousers, with sometimes a blue cloth jacket or a scarlet jumper. They each carry a rope, which they use as a lasso to catch stray dogs by the hind legs. The Germans and several others closed their stores to join in the peace festival. Service was held at 11 o'clock, by permission, in the American Protestant Church, Fort Street (the latter partly macadamized), where there are several nice private houses, with grass-plots in front containing flowers, shrubs, cocoa-nut, tamarind, bread-fruit and mango trees, the fruit of the latter coloured green, nearly ripe, looking like unripe pears, with long, narrow leaves larger than gum leaves. The Germans, having no pastor, had to get the services of Father Hermann, a spare, dark, dried-up French Jesuit priest from the Catholic church just opposite. The American church is a very neat edifice of wood, with wooden spire. The entrance is by seven wide concrete steps to a portico, and you then go into the building by doors to the right and left. At the top of the steps was the German Consul, Pffuger, dressed in a full suit of black, with a shirt of pearly whiteness, exquisitely frilled. As each entered he handed a very neat printed programme of the music and singing in German. Interior of building, including a gallery at one end, about 100 feet long, 40 wide, and about 30 feet high. Sides and ceiling plastered and whitewashed; cornice of wood, painted light green; open wooden pews, painted light oak; handsome organ-loft of wood, painted light oak; sweet-toned organ; a reading-desk, &c., with crimson velvet cushions; two handsome brass chandeliers with cut-glass lamps hung from the ceiling, other smaller lamps on brackets at sides; twelve Gothic-shaped windows of glass with blinds of light-coloured wood, Venetian style. Vases of flowers were placed on reading-desk and in organ-loft. The place was quite full of a medley of Germans, English, Americans, Kanakas dressed in all the colours of the rainbow, including John Chinaman, and nearly all the passengers from Australia and New Zealand. The singing and organ performances were excellent.

Father Hermann's sermon very long, tedious, and of course unintelligible to most of us. In the midst of it a salute of 101 guns was heard from the Punch Bowl, a height commanding the harbour, fired by permission of the King; he has twenty-one six-pounders there, but it is only safe to fire four of them, seventeen being in a dangerous state. Father Hermann had written his oration on half-sheets of foolscap, which he had before him in a loose state, and when he had finished one half-sheet he put it aside on his right. "Nun Danket Alle Gott," and "Ein' feste Burg ist Unser Gott," Luther's famous hymn, followed by prayer, was the grand finale, and well executed the chorals were. It was amusing to see the gentleman in the organ-loft anxiously watching Father Hermann remove a half-sheet to his right and thinking from the heap on the desk, that the time for "music" never would come. It was past 1 o'clock when the service was completed, and we had lost our lunch. The oration was evidently a warlike one, "Jena," "Quatre-bras," "Waterloo," "entry into Paris," &c., being often referred to. At night there was a huge bonfire at one side of the "Punch Bowl," which was a serious item, firewood being very scarce and dear, only a few small "sticks" for a quarter dollar. Sky-rockets were also discharged from this eminence. A torchlight procession of about 100 was also formed outside the consul's residence, Fort Street, in the evening, who marched round the town headed by the King's Kanaka brass band, who played English and German pieces of music admirably. There was also stationed in the small lawn in front of the Consul's house the Honolulu brass band (Kanakas), led by a young German, lately from New Zealand, the music being excellent. The Consul's house was thronged with visitors; respectable strangers being admitted to all parts of the house, except one balcony set apart for ladies and children. There was an excellent cold collation—poultry, hams, &c.—laid out, with lots of champagne, bottled ale and porter, &c., to which any one could help himself. The house was well lit up, particularly from the glare of ten torches constantly kept alight on the lawn. Some of the shipping and particularly a Hawaiian barque called 'Ka Moi,' S. Geerken, master, owned by Germans, but under the Hawaiian flag, and trades with London, Bremen, &c., were illuminated throughout the rigging. These festivities are said to have cost the German Consul over 400l.; but it was reported that he would be recouped by his Government. Some of us partook of tea at the Canton Hotel and Restaurant, a large plain wooden building sadly in want of paint, in Hotel Street, between Fort and Nuuanu Streets, kept by Achong and Akim, two heathen Chinee, where we had, at the charge of half a dollar, lean beef-steak, fried fish, cold meat, and coffee, with twenty-one bottles of pickles on one table and fifteen on another, and we were informed by the steward of the steamer that the Chinese pickle one so, because they cannot very well understand everybody, therefore they put on a profusion that you can take your choice. In consequence of this rather heavy "tea," the Consul's edibles did not suffer much at our hands; not so, however, his liquors.

Sunday, 26th March.—Beautiful bright morning and day, but rather warm. "Washing" brought on board, thoroughly clean and well got up. Left the steamer at 9 A.M. with Mr. Richard Lane, a passenger (formerly of Ludlow, Shropshire), and Adelaide friend, Mr. P., to go into the hills. Called and had a view, before service, of the Catholic church, in a large gravelled yard, opposite American church. It was built in 1840 of coral rock; getting greasy, and a dirty green colour; it is about 150 feet long, with a lofty steeple. Inside, on the floor, are imported Chinese mats, on which the natives "squat" during service. Other members of the congregation, termed "foreigners," sit in common chairs, painted black. There is a gallery of wood, painted white with blue stripes, all round the inside, supported on twelve large white painted pillars; ceiling of stretched calico; large organ-loft and powerful organ; handsome altar, with very tall plated silver candlesticks, &c. Yard spacious (no graves), well gravelled, and very clean; a handsome bronze fountain, close to entrance of Father Hermann's cottage in yard; a life-size bronze angel, with its wings over an olive-branch circle, about 2 feet in diameter, through which runs the water, and an inscription from John v. 13, 14. There is a large convent built of wood adjoining, with shingle roof and extensive verandah, with green painted lattice-work. A great many Kanakas were talking in groups about the yard, waiting for service to commence, most of them being Catholics. Father Hermann was standing at his door, comfortably smoking an immense German meerschaum pipe—a very long one—the bowl of which he held in his left hand, whilst his right was frequently engaged in shaking hands with the Kanakas and others, ourselves included, but principally the females. We then had a glance at Queen Emma's "town house," a plain edifice of wood, standing in a small lawn or grass-plot, with shrubs and flowers, in Beretania Street—a very quiet retreat, only a few private houses in it, and grass growing by the footways. There is a portico of wood at the entrance, and outside two very handsome tall china vases, containing flowers; a balcony to the house, with lattices painted green. We then went through Nuuanu Street, and along the Valley, a very pretty walk of about a mile, a nice wide macadamized road, with made raised footways; private residences on each side of the road, standing in lawns well irrigated by water-pipes, nearly all the way; a few Norfolk pines, tamarind, cocoa-nut, and other trees; flowering shrubs, roses, &c., scattered about in the various grass-plots—principally wire or couch grass, quite green, from being kept well watered. Crossed wooden bridge over a large running stream of clear-looking water, through boulders and gravel, with a stone wall at each end of it. A painted board was affixed, with painted letters on it in English, "1 mile from Honolulu;" also printed notices affixed, calling on defaulting tax-payers to pay up their arrears, or they would be proceeded against. No less than 1000 defaulters in Honolulu alone, owing to "bad times" and dissatisfaction. One large wooden house, the property of Mr. John Thomas Waterhouse, a leading merchant, is a very pretty spot; it has about 210 feet frontage; iron railed, fixed in brick; lawn nicely planted; ornamental vases of flowers, &c.; about half a mile from the town. Beyond the bridge is the British Consul's (Major Wodehouse's) neat residence of wood, close under the hills, and commanding a splendid prospect of the town, harbour, &c. The British standard was flying from the flagstaff. To the north of the valley very poor houses and country were seen, and there is a plain beyond that, but not visible from this road, many miles in extent, covered with the prickly pear or cactus. The stream of water we crossed rises in the mountains above, and is brought into two reservoirs, not far from here, from Maemae; and there are many very pure springs about. Observing a few yards to the right of the road a red, white, and blue flag at the top of a post near a large wooden house and buildings of irregular shape, with a balcony, we called there, and found it to be an inn kept by an intelligent, witty Irishman, called Ryan, from which a beautiful view of the valley, Honolulu, and harbour was obtained. Ryan's wife was a fine, stout, big Kanaka girl, who could talk English a little, and joined in conversation. We stayed here half an hour, as the weather was oppressive. We could only get lemonade, at 6d. a bottle, to drink, as no wine, spirituous or malt liquors are allowed to be sold on Sundays, licence being forfeited on first conviction: innkeepers being very heavily taxed, at 1000 dollars, or 200l. English per annum, to increase the price of liquors, if possible, and check the native fondness for strong drinks. Ryan had a profusion of illustrated and other papers to amuse his customers. He was very communicative and pleasant; had "burst" up (turned insolvent) several times during the last twenty years; and, to make the two ends meet, made bread, which he took in an open one-horse sort of phæton, and sold to the shipping, as also vegetables, bananas, and so on, as he could grow anything almost about his place. The engineer and first and second officers of the 'City' arrived, appearing very warm; but although well known to Ryan, no persuasion could induce him to supply any fermented or spirituous liquors. He said he couldn't afford to risk being "rounded," and indeed did not appear to care about selling anything. He was for a quiet day and "go in" at his papers. He also showed us an extract from section 2, chapter xxxv. of the Penal Code, as follows:—"The Lord's day is taboo: all worldly business, amusements, and recreations are forbidden on that day; and whoever shall be present at any dancing, public amusement, show, or entertainment, or take any part in any game, sport, or play on the Lord's day, shall be punished by fine, not exceeding ten dollars." Several dashing male and female Kanakas on horseback galloped past while we were here, and some at a furious rate. It is a favourite walk and place of call warm evenings. We then went down-hill to a narrow rocky path at the side of Ryan's, and walked up the gorge of the mountain stream, high hills with projecting rocks being on our right, and undulating ground with wild flowers and scented shrubs on our left, to a large bathing place of clear water in the solid rock, about the shape of a bowl. We had been walking on an ascending rocky path, the river flowing beneath us, midst rocks and boulders, forming now and then pretty cascades, and sometimes large pools of water surrounded by rock. A few natives, young and old, were bathing and sporting in the water, and now and then they would go up the path to a rock at the top, looking down on the bathing place, about 20 feet, and would dive from thence into the pool of water. We noticed about a quarter of a mile of wire fencing near the crown of one hill, and horses grazing. Close to here is the royal mausoleum, built of stone in the shape of a cross, protected by iron railing, very handsome, but kept sacred on a Sunday; and we could only get a view from the outside. Returned to the steamer for dinner; found it very close and oppressive down the valley, and very glad to get a bottle of cool ale. Met a great many people returning from places of worship; Kanakas in all colours—some on horseback. After dinner, several Kanakas hanging about the steamer; about twenty youngsters were sporting in the water, swimming and diving wonderfully after small bits of money, dimes, &c.; and races took place, from 100 to 300 yards—one big race for a dollar. Several had pieces of money in their mouths for a long time, as they had no other place to keep it, being afraid to come on shore and "plant" it in their scanty clothing. After the sports were over, we started to see the market, and on our way found lots of natives—male and female—riding "like mad" about the streets, dressed in their gayest colours. The market is a very rude one—only a few rough, dirty boards for stalls; vegetables, fruit, and flowers, &c., being sold principally on the ground. It is open for the sale of beef all day Sundays; vegetables, &c., morning only. There was only one shop well stocked with fat beef and mutton; the rest was all lean stuff. As you passed through you heard cries of "Will you have beefsteak or rumpsteak?" The whole looked dry and uneatable. Fat cattle (so called) were selling wholesale from 30s. to 40s. a head; sheep, about 6s. a head. Seeing cats at almost every native door, we were informed that the Kanakas had great faith in these animals in allaying pain—particularly wind in the stomach—by "cat treading," for which they are trained. Our Adelaide friend (the lawyer) volunteered to take us to a native whom he knew in the back part of the town, and endeavour to get us the sight of a "case in point." We found a middle-aged Kanaka and his wife lying leisurely on their mats on the ground. Kanakas don't want any furniture. After jabbering some time, the female caught up a thin white and black cat, and after coaxing it a little while, lay down on her back on the mat, and placed the cat on her stomach, who began to paw away rather gently for about a minute, and then suddenly jumped off and bolted away out of doors. The Kanaka made us understand that there was nothing amiss with her, and that the cat knew it. Turning from her, we went towards the King's Palace, in King and Richard Streets. The area is between five and six acres, surrounded by coral-rock walls, getting into decay, very dirty looking, and breaking down in many places. The house is of wood, in bad repair, and 20,000 dollars has been some time on the estimates to build a new one. The stables are much better than the palace, and there are some valuable horses there, well-matched chestnuts and bays, and beautiful American buggies and harness. The lawn is not well kept, and the trees, shrubs, &c., looked neglected: the large wooden entrance gates are out of repair, and difficult to open and shut. On knocking, a sentry, dressed in a blue jumper and white trousers, with Brown Bess and bayonet fixed, opened a door. A lighted cigar was tendered and accepted for our intrusion; and whilst we had a peep at the place for ten minutes, Mr. Sentry puffed away at his cigar, with his musket and bayonet carelessly thrown over his shoulder, more at ease than we ever saw a soldier before. There are several inferior wooden buildings on open ground at the side of the palace, used by "hangers-on" and runaways, principally children, who get dissatisfied at home, and run to His Majesty's hovels for protection. It was a beautiful evening, and the moon and stars shone brightly; so we went to have a peep at the Church of England at Hilo, in the suburbs, a neat wooden building, which will hold between 600 and 700, standing in about one acre of grass-plot, with shrubs, &c., apparently not long planted; seats of wood of American timber; a small but sweet-toned organ let into a recess in the wall on one side to give more space. Two clergymen officiated, but the congregation was small (only about sixty), and very few Kanakas attended. The Church of England service was strictly followed, except that, first, the King and Royal Family were prayed for; then a separate prayer for Queen Victoria; and, lastly, the President of the United States. One Kanaka woman belonged to the choir, which was very good. The bishop had lately resigned and gone to England. The ground was the gift of the late King (brother of present one); he laid the foundation-stone of new church, in the same ground, shortly before his death, and only the foundations have been put in. Several cases of wood containing imported cut stone for the contemplated new church were lying about the place. The church has been established too late; the American and Catholic churches having been "planted" so many years, have all the swing, the Kanakas generally preferring the Catholic, from its gorgeous display and lively services. We then went to the American church, and heard the close of the service. A new pastor, the Rev. Walter Frear, had been installed, charges delivered, &c. The first missionaries (American) arrived at Kailua on 4th April, 1820, and succeeded, after a long time and much labour, in getting the gods destroyed and idol worship abolished. Roman Catholic missionaries arrived at Honolulu from Bordeaux in 1827. They were persecuted and punished; and in 1831 the chiefs sent the priests away in the brig 'Waverley' to California, where they were landed. One came from Valparaiso in 1836, but was not allowed to preach. Some of those sent away returned in 1837, but were ordered on board ship. In June, 1839, the King issued orders that no more punishments should be inflicted on Roman Catholics, in consequence of threats of war by France. In May, 1840, a bishop and two priests arrived, others soon followed, and the Roman Catholic religion was firmly and permanently established on the islands. The Church of England only dates after Queen Emma's visit to England in 1855—is very weak, almost at a standstill—the Americans and Catholics having such a firm hold on the islands. The streets were very quiet, and not a drop of intoxicating liquor could be obtained on shore, but as much as one liked on board ship. The King's band played at sundown some good music—English and German pieces.

Monday, 27th March, 1871.—Weather about same as yesterday. Plenty of fish from 1 to 2 feet long, called banita, at the stern of the steamer this morning, and also a quantity of large gold-fish, which the banita were following and swallowing with some difficulty. Banita are also found on the coast of New Zealand. A large shark and some smaller ones were also seen. Natives again out fishing for mullet, and yet escape the sharks. At half-past 9 went to the Court House, in Fort Street, a nice commodious stone building, standing in a grass-plot of half an acre, planted with some ornamental shrubs and a few flowers. Interior of building well plastered, painted, and finished upstairs and down, Common Law,

Equity, and Criminal Courts being all in this building, also Attorney-General's Office, &c., &c. Outside is an ornamental fountain of ironwork, painted bronze colour, with lamp at the top, which burns kerosene. Prisoners for minor offences were engaged in cutting very close the Indian couch grass in the lawn outside, with sheaf knives, a slow process, but helped to pass away their time. The police room is rather small. The magistrate, Mr. Montgomery, an elderly Scotchman, with lavender kid gloves on. The Government interpreter, an intelligent, good-looking young man, speaking Kanaka, French, German, and English, was present. The first case was a charge of drunkenness against an Esquimaux sailor. Quickly disposed of. Magistrate: " Were you drunk?" Esquimaux, speaking loudly, in English, " Yes, drunk, sir." Fined five dollars, and paid immediately. A case of "burglary" was then called on, a native being charged with breaking into and stealing from a very old, skinny, dilapidated Chinaman's shop, in his absence, a box containing a very large ornamental pipe, a musical instrument, and other articles. Two interpreters were engaged, one for the prosecutor to translate Chinese into Kanaka, and the Government one to convert the Kanaka into English for the magistrate; and what with these conversions, and the turning the magistrate's observations into Kanaka and then Chinese, with the additional remarks of a native lawyer engaged by the prisoner, every sentence being translated after being pronounced, this short case really took up a considerable part of the morning. Prisoner was proved by the police to be an old offender, and found guilty: fined ten dollars, with two years' hard labour. Next case was a young Kanaka, charged with rushing out behind a fence at a Chinaman, hitting him a severe blow on the nose, which made it bleed; also with being drunk. Was defended by a native lawyer. Fined ten dollars: shortly after paid by his mother. Mr. Montgomery to interpreter: "Tell him I'm determined to put down assaults and outrages on the Chinese; and next time I will send him to prison." The Chinese are getting too numerous, and the natives have begun to be very jealous of them. Several lawyers were rushing in and out of the building; one, in particular, a Mr. Stanley, a Yankee "Attorney and Counseller at Law," Kaahumanu Street (said to be "wanted" at San Francisco by the police), with an immense bundle of papers tied with red tape, was rushing in and out, bent on Equity business we were told. He wore a white fluffy hat at the back of his head; immense blue tie, with white spots; very short pantaloons; white socks and thin shoes, tied with black ribbon; keeps no clerk, nor does any other limb of the law here. When they have occasion to leave their office, a card is tied to a nail in the door, "Gone to Court," or wherever it may be; "back in ten minutes," and so on. Sometimes Mr. Stanley, who is reported to be shrewd, is retained to go to the neighbouring islands on circuit to defend prisoners. He would then affix a card to his office door, "Gone on circuit, back in about six weeks." We then went to Richard Street, and inspected a large dilapidated wooden mansion called the Bungalo, walls of coral rock, plastered inside, but falling down. Rooms large and lofty. Approach by five granite steps to a wide portico, supported by seven high fluted wooden pillars. Large glass lattice windows; many broken. It stands in an acre of ground, and is almost a perfect ruin, far beyond repair. It was built by a great gambling man, who finding the place getting too hot for him, skedaddled to San Francisco, and it became the property of a rich man at the latter place, called "Sam Brennan." The theatre in King Street is a grotesque edifice, of galvanized iron, painted blue and red, looking like a large store. It is seldom used, there being no established company. Sometimes it is opened for a night or two, when the mail steamers call, having on board any professional singers, or actors and actresses, going to or from the Australian colonies and San Francisco. The former theatre, called "The Varieties," a large combustible place, was burnt to ashes on 7th July, 1855, with police station-house and stores of J. Cohn, Afong, and Watts and Company, supposed to have been the work of an incendiary, but never discovered. After lunch we walked down to the cocoa-nut plantation, under Diamond Head, about three miles from the wharf. The rows of palms, with their tall, naked, tender stems, the fruit being in the foliage, towards and at the top, had a very pretty appearance. We had to keep a little inland to get to it; the natives having here and there built their houses so close to the water's edge, prevented walking close to the water all the way. After dinner went to Fish Market, in Marine Street, a dirty locality — very primitive and scattered, only a few stalls, and the fish mostly small and inferior: also a few scraps of lean beef, with some tripe of a stale yellow colour, emitting rather a strong odour. Some natives were squatting about the street, selling flowers and garlands. Some well-to-do female Kanakas bought garlands, and placed them round their necks; others twisted them round their hats. Then strolled up the valley again, calling at Ryan's, having a rest and another peep from his balcony. Then visited a kalo or taro patch near. It is grown in small plots, out of which the soil is taken about a foot deep, then filled up with water, and the young plants put in, the natives being up to middle in mud and water in course of planting, &c. Some attention is required, and the place kept constantly irrigated to keep the plants alive. The root is about the size and colour of a parsnip, the top above the water being green, and looking in appearance like the top of a young sugar-cane. The natives bake the root, and pound it up into powder. It is then mixed up with water, generally put into gourds, or some vessel, and kept for three or four days till it gets sour, when the natives eat it with avidity, and almost subsist on it. It is called poi, and looks like "dirty" pea-soup. The King is very fond of it. Natives squat about with it in the streets for sale in gourds. It smells frightfully. Returning, went to a Chinese garden, about an acre of ground, near Mr. Waterhouse's; not a weed to be seen, nor an inch of ground wasted; long rows of onions, carrots, tomatoes, radishes; also cucumber beds, herbs, &c., from which the Chinese restaurant-keeper gets his materials to make his numerous bottles of pickles, &c. Irrigation easily obtainable from the river, close to the property; altogether a picture of neatness. In evening at Rev. Fletcher's lecture on "The Siege of Jerusalem" at American church, which was thronged, and it was evident that Mr. Fletcher had often dealt with that subject before. At half-past ten o'clock blue-lights were observed at sea. 'City of Melbourne' answered with rockets and blue-lights. An approaching steamer, supposed to be the 'Moses Taylor,' to take us to San Francisco. She turned out to be the Yankee boat 'Ajax'—the 'Moses' being laid up for repairs—and came alongside wharf, ahead of us, at 11 P.M. Some time before, and while she was being moored, the Native Glee Club sang very well and correctly several glees, and the wharf was covered with people.

Tuesday, 28th March.—Day sunny and warm. Mr. Lane, who had been perambulating the town before breakfast, brought the welcome intelligence that he had discovered that sound English draught ale could be obtained at Siders and Cluney's 'Bank Exchange,' Fort Street, below King Street, at 6d. per glass, having hitherto been paying 1s. for that article. Left 'City

of Melbourne' steamer at 10 A.M., and removed to the
'Ajax;' native porter charged half a dollar for taking
L.'s effects and my own in a hand-cart. Porters borrow
these carts from Yankees and other foreigners for a
dollar a week; one Yankee alone lets out forty. The
materials are mostly imported from San Francisco and
the States in parts, and put together in Honolulu.
'City of Melbourne' had been very busy up to last
night coaling, and taking in cargo—a small one, however; not much sugar, as Australia is principally
supplied from Mauritius, and the prices rule higher here
than there; and to-day principally Yankee buckets,
brooms, &c., *ex* 'Ajax' for New Zealand, &c. The
natives have been getting good wages (a dollar to one
and a half), working at night with good will, and very
noisy from sheer joy at earning money, with the prospect of spending it in drink. Coaling is dirty work,
the small stuff flying about and sticking to your clothes,
&c. At night coal fires were lit on the wharf, to facili-
tate the coaling. It had a pretty effect as the dark
forms of the natives, moved about with their wheelbarrows, singing, hooting, and making discordant noises.
Went on board the 'City' with the Government interpreter, cracked a bottle of ale, and said good-bye. She
left the wharf for New Zealand at 4 P.M., midst much
cheering and waving of handkerchiefs from numerous
spectators. She is a good boat, but not large or powerful
enough for the packet service; she is very well adapted
for "colonial" work, for which she was built. 'Ajax'
people very busy in discharging cargo, also in coaling,

natives besides the crew being engaged. Opposite side of the water is a landing stage for cattle from the other islands, whence they are driven through the shallow water to the shore, the most easy way of landing them. The Custom House, a large building protected with iron proof shutters to the windows, is near this wharf, also a large Government store and a very extensive Government shed on the wharf, with a shingle roof, supported by painted wooden pillars. The shed is open front and rear, and partly at each end ; shifting tramways from the store run under the shed and across the wharf, to ship and transship goods. This end of the wharf is planked, and the piles copper sheathed, the wharf being formed of coral rock and silt.

The "real estate" of Her Majesty H. K. Kapateuhaili, Queen Dowager, is advertised in the papers for sale by order of the Supreme Court (a small affair), and described to be 123 feet on Richard Street, and 168 feet deep; "large dwelling house on premises," containing five rooms and other necessary buildings ; J. W. Austin, C. Kanaina, administrators ; E. P. Adams, auctioneer. Went and inspected it; very plain place. The King would not attend her funeral, because he was not made executor, and could not finger any of the money, of which he is remarkably fond. Went and inspected the remains of the gas-works, near the corner of King and Maunakea Streets; chimney and portion of works only standing, which had been erected in 1859 by the Honolulu Gas Company, on a patent American principle ; was made use of by the hotels and a few other buildings for some months, the works being mortgaged by Mr. Tiffany, the resident manager of the company, who left for California under pretence of procuring more machinery, but never returned. The limited demand for gas was said to be the cause of abandoning the works. The apparatus is fast going to decay, the place full of filth, and the shed used as a stable, &c. Found it necessary to call in and taste Siders and Cluney's 6d. draught ale; it was Burton, very sound and good. The bar is neat, 32 by 20 feet, and a good billiard room with two tables. The bar of the 'Royal' is 50 feet by 30 feet; an harmonium inside some wooden railings, and nicely papered and painted. Two excellent billiard rooms, with two tables in each. Water tap, basins to wash in, and clean towels. These edifices are of wood. The largest inn is called 'Sailor's Home,' but is not used as such, and respectable persons go there to live, temporarily, and so on. It is a large old straggling wooden building, but the proprietor keeps a good table. Several of the passengers went to reside there for a change. Government are about to call for tenders to build a new hotel, as no private individual would risk doing so. Land had been purchased for over 9000 dollars, said to be a poor site, in a neighbourhood rather out of the way, but next to property of a member of the Government, a little jobbery being perpetrated. Tradesmen and many other respectable persons do not cook, but take their families to restaurants to get their meals; one reason being indolence on part of the females, and the other scarceness and dearness of firewood, three small pieces costing a quarter of a dollar; there being now no timber on this island, and only small stuff on some of the others, principally growing in declivities and rocky ravines, difficult of access. Formerly a large quantity of sandal wood grew in the mountains, but kings and chiefs exhausted it years ago, exporting it principally to China, getting rum and dry goods in exchange, and turning the produce into hard dollars, the value of which they were not slow to learn. Such was the greed of the chiefs that up to 1843 the exports to China alone amounted in value to a million of dollars. The natives were liable to be called on at any moment by the chiefs to cut the wood, and if a common Kanaka sold any wood or other thing to a ship, one half of whatever he received went to the King; also no valuable article was formerly considered safe in the hands of the lower classes, for if not directly plundered some form of taxation would be laid on, or some mode of suffering devised to obtain it; hence no commoner dared to live in a large house, cook a large hog, fish with a large net, or appear abroad well dressed, without forfeiting all. An adult would pay about five dollars a week for meals. Went in the evening and saw the "Adelaide ex-lawyer's" lodging; he has a good-sized room, nicely papered, Chinese matting over floor, mosquito curtains to bed, lamp, and kerosene found, for a dollar a week; good sitting-rooms, &c., in the house, kept by a Mrs. D., a widow, formerly from near Totnes in Devonshire; he took his meals at a Chinese restaurant. The "governor's" mother keeps a nice boarding house in Beltana Street, standing in a well-kept neat lawn, planted, &c. Several other respectable persons are obliged to do the same, on account of the "badness of the times." Owing to the effects of the English sixpenny, my companion, Mr. L., "turned in" with his trowsers and one boot on, his head where his heels ought to have been, in fact, nearly doubled up, a portion of his waistcoat having got entangled with one foot.

Wednesday, 29th March.—A gusty, dusty day, and the coaling day and night caused the atmosphere on board to be anything but pleasant. Many were awoke at daybreak by hearing Lieut. Verney calling loudly in a commanding tone for his boots. "Why the devil can't I get my boots? I want to go up to the bathing place." The watch came up and said, "Please don't make such a noise; you are disturbing the whole ship." "I want my boots to go and bathe," angrily replied the lieutenant, "when shall I have them?" No more satisfactory answer to be got than "You will get them when you have them." The man retired. A Yankee can be led, but not driven, and it was half-past six before the polish was put on the lieutenant's boots, for which he would have to pay half a dollar. The coloured assistant-steward, Wright, of 'City of Melbourne,' advised me not to put my boots outside my berth in the Yankee boat, as it would cost half a dollar a time, but always to look into your boots before putting them on, as scorpions are apt to get into them. I don't think the lieutenant repeated his experiment. After breakfast went and saw some old seedy-looking wooden buildings, standing in a yard, with some straggling trees, not at all attractive, being the department of foreign affairs, war, public instruction, &c.; the ministers looking more after their salaries than appearance or stability of the public buildings. The public accounts only appear about once in five years, and then no one can understand them. Also saw the Honolulu Iron Company's works. where all kinds of machinery, sugar-mills, steam-engines, carriage work, agricultural implements, &c., are manufactured on an extensive scale, the premises being large. Also the Pacific brass foundry in King Street; all kinds of brass and composition work cast, finished, and furnished to ships and plantations, by James A. Hopper, proprietor. Also some soap-works manufacturing many kinds of soap, yellow being in the ascendant. After dinner went over three shipping yards on a small scale, but craft had been turned out as large as 130 tons, and repairs effected to large ships in port. A new schooner about $36\frac{1}{2}$ tons, called the 'Maggie,' was shortly before our arrival launched from the shipyard of George J. Emmes; she looks strong, with nice bow, and was not built to order, but was for sale. When business is slack craft are built on spec. The King's schooner yacht 'Pauahi,' a smart-looking boat of about 100 tons, Captain Ballastierrie, a Guernsey man, was waiting His Majesty's "pleasure," and a change of weather, to take him to Molokai to see his sheep and cattle, which he breeds there, and sells as if he were a subject. The King is a bad sailor, and rough weather does not suit him. This yacht is also used to take cattle to market, and the King's ambition is to make a million of dollars. He has been losing on his sheep, the price of wool being so low, and His Majesty seems inclined to open a butcher's shop, as he says that the butchers get all the profit. It is the King's delight to retire to this island for two or three months together, where he loves to be in dishabille, recline on mats, eat with his fingers as his forefathers did, putting aside all royalty; his favourite dish is fat roast dog, highly seasoned, stinking poi from the taro root, and excessive indulgence in intoxicating liquors. Several large casks of sperm oil lying about the wharfs; very few whalers in harbour. October and November are the principal months for the whalers calling here to land their cargoes, which are shipped to New Bedford, in the States, but owing to the many modern inventions for lighting, whale oil is getting yearly less in demand. Within one month 150 whalers have been in this harbour; latterly not more than 40 on an average, which affects the trade of Honolulu very seriously, particularly the liquor stores. After landing their oil and effecting any necessary repairs and outfit, the vessels start afresh on another cruise. Went and saw several photographic establishments; many well-executed photos of Kanakas and others. We also noticed painted signs on boards of professors of French, English, German, and Native. Came across a dwarf close upon three feet high; scarcely any legs noticeable, nearly all being body; he was accosted and pulled about by the children in a good-natured way, as he walked on the footpath; he was exhibited in England when Queen Emma was on her visit there. Just after that a policeman was vainly attempting to capture with his lasso a poor-looking little brown bitch, evidently having a young family, without its registered badge on; she was too much for him, and escaped, after dodging and running through divers alleys and narrow streets. The dog-tax is a dollar a head per annum, with ten cents. added for a bit of white metal, with the number on it, fixed round the neck. There are several fire brigades, who have engine-houses in different parts of the town; they have different companies, numbered. We saw the apparatus at the engine-house of "Mechanic Engine Company, No. 2," in a square where the several companies usually parade annually in the month of February, in full uniform (helmets, &c.), with their fire apparatus, kept in creditable order, the engines, &c. (Yankee), being modern and good. Notice is given by the secretary, Charles T. Gulick, for parade. In evening went up the valley, with the intention of returning and attending service at native mission house; severe dust storm came on, succeeded by heavy shower of rain, perfectly blinding; some dust and mud got into my left eye, and I was obliged to return to the 'Ajax.' The mission house and schoolroom are very old wooden buildings; stand in a large yard; the walls are very low; and you can almost jump on the roof from the ground; the roof is of shingle.

Thursday, 30th March.—Heavy showers, like April weather in England; very acceptable, it not having rained for a year and a half, but always a plentiful supply of water from mountains for irrigation and domestic purposes. 'Ajax' still coaling; also shipping a large quantity of sugar in small, neat barrels, holding from 120 to 124 lbs.; the staves and light iron hoops are imported from San Francisco, and put together at Honolulu. Much cleaner to use barrels than mats, and no waste. Rats can't get at it so readily. The sugar was in the big store, and the barrels were placed in trucks and pushed on the tramway line to the side of the ship by Kanakas, who were very happy and noisy as usual in their work. Many natives were knocking about in their fragile canoes, some twelve feet long, very shallow, formed out of trees from the other islands, propelled by a paddle nearly the shape of a shovel. Went and saw a rice-mill worked by Chinese, who were naked from the middle upwards; it was worked by hand, two at a time; appeared to be no child's play; the perspiration flowing freely on their breasts and backs; a disagreeable place to be in, the husks and dust flying in every direction. Then attempted to get up to the cemetery beyond Ryan's, between the showers, but only succeeded in reaching the latter place, as it rained in torrents in the hills and mountains above, and heavy mists hung about them; here we were "fixed" for about two hours, as there are no omnibuses or cabs plying for hire, the country being so hilly and the roads very rough a mile or so from the town. Some of the passengers have been indulging in buggies and hack horses at livery stables. Hire of horses from $1\frac{1}{2}$ to

2 dollars per day; one or two large establishments, American traps, saddles, and harness. On hiring a buggy you have to deposit 50 dollars as security in case of an accident. Afternoon almost confined to the ship on account of the rain. Went round to the "Queen's" Hospital, 5, School Street, which is a Government institution, large, roomy, and clean, in an open, healthy situation, and was established in 1860. This is a free hospital, and a great boon to the lower order of Kanakas, sailors, &c. Also went over churchyard attached to the stone church (American); a great many Americans, chiefly young persons, buried there; numerous excellent tombstones and monuments. Several natives are also buried there, as also in the Catholic ground; in fact the American Churches and the Catholic appear to hold the sway, the Church of England being too late in the day, and the German and other sects nowhere. An open cart full of dead dogs passed, with their carcases besmeared with blood and brains. They had been lassoed and dragged with their feet drawn together through the streets, and then knocked on the head, being unlicensed, and thrown into the cart. Rain at night.

Friday, 31st March.—Raining occasionally in the town and up the valley, but heavy in hills. Saw native mode of repairing streets, or rather creating mud, between Thrums' and the Post Office this morning. Large quantities of so-called sand, but in reality three-parts earth, were brought in carts, deposited in the middle of the street, and spread by native prisoners for small crimes, in care of an overseer (a white man); then, notwithstanding it was raining, prisoners were turning the hose on and watering the soft and almost loose earth. A cart or two drawn by bullocks passed through this sea of mud with hard pulling and great difficulty, the overseer blowing up the Kanakas for putting on too much water in one place. These Kanakas have constantly to be watched—for instance, if the overseer told a Kanaka to water a particular spot for ten minutes, and he should be called away and return again in half an hour, he would find the prisoner still at the same place, watering away with all his might, washing holes in fact. If you hire a Kanaka to do a thing, he will do it with a vengeance; he won't stop, not even for food, until you tell him to; and instances have occurred where a native has been put to irrigate a garden in the morning, that he has gone on till his master's return from business in the evening, literally flodding the place; indeed they want constant watching, otherwise their labour is of little service. Now and then we saw two or three Chinese children peeping out from shops, &c. They were very shy, and on being noticed would retreat to an inner room. Some of them had already had the little hair on their heads shaved off, leaving at the back part the little tuft, thereafter to grow and form the "Chinaman's tail.". In the afternoon, a tall, dark-featured, bony man, with his son, called Lane, who had ridden in from their farm about ten miles distant on mules, inquired at the ship for Mr. Lane, to ascertain if they were relations; he had seen the name of Lane in the list of passengers in the newspaper, as he had two or three times previously, and he made a point of coming in whenever he did so on the chance of meeting with one of his family, but had never succeeded in doing so, and on this occasion he was again disappointed, for although Englishmen, the two Lanes came from distant counties in England, and were in no way connected. He had rented under the King, who wanted him to take a fresh lease, but Lane wished to sell off and leave the island, as he could not save any money. The King declines to let him go. We adjourned and had a social glass together at Siders and Cluney's. No one can leave the island without consent of the King, and natives leaving with consent are bound down to return One native Hilo lad, named Harry, an intelligent youth of eighteen, wishing to see Sydney, stowed himself away on board S.S. 'City of Melbourne,' on her previous passage; he was employed in the galley, spoke a little English, and was placed in the hands of the authorities by Capt. Grainger on the return voyage.

In the afternoon a bull, with a rope through his nostrils, a mule, and two ponies, arrived under the shed, each with little saddles on, from which projected two horns of wood, laden with bunches of pine-apples and bananas in a green state, for sale. They were packed in rough baskets of bark off small trees, and were in care of an old Kanaka and a young female, the latter in the usual " stuff gown," and she did more than her share in unloading. Afterwards a donkey, another mule, and eighteen ponies arrived from the country, loaded with oranges, bananas, and pine apples, of which the 'Ajax' took on board a great many for her use.

Saturday, 1st April.—Sharp showers all the morning; streets up to ankles in mud. At 9 A.M. the King took shelter under the shed from the rain. He was driving himself in a four-wheeled silver-mounted buggy, with hood to it, and a pair of nice bays in a very light harness, all American. He is a very burly, coarse, fat man, complexion very dark, looked to weigh about 16 stone. Shook hands with several of the passengers. He had on a plain black felt hat, blue cloth coat with velvet collar, brown tweed trousers and vest, spotted fancy shirt. He was accompanied by his intimate friend and companion, Captain Abe Russell, an American ship captain from New England, who wore a white felt hat, drab coat, &c., a stout man and common-looking; but no other attendant. In about ten minutes His Majesty waved his whip to the public, and drove off midst the cheers of the Kanakas and others. An American ship was discharging a cargo of ice. One could hardly imagine there would be sufficient demand for such a quantity; Goodfellow was taking in at his ice saloon, King Street, dray loads of blocks, which he retails at a dollar a pound, and an admiring crowd of youngsters were watching and snatching small bits from the drays, sucking them, and putting some down each other's backs, trying to make "April fools," and then pretending to have pain in their stomachs, &c. All Fools' Day is observed in the islands; it was introduced there by the Americans. At 11.30 the King drove on to the wharf, and handing the reins to his friend Russell, went on board his yacht, which left immediately for Molokai, midst a salute of twenty-one guns from Punch Bowl, and music from the band on the wharf; Captain Russell afterwards amusing himself in driving round the town. The 'Ajax' was appointed to leave the wharf at 4 P.M. The following is a brief account of the islands, derived from information obtained during the short stay. The Hawaiian or Sandwich group of the South Sea Islands on the great Pacific Ocean, lie in north latitude, between parallels 19° and 22°, and west longitude, 155° and 160°. Prior to 1794, the islands were separate kingdoms, but in that year and shortly after King Kamehameha I., entitled "the Great," became the master of the whole group by conquest. He attached to himself several foreigners, among whom were John Young and Isaac Davis, English seamen, who were treated with great kindness, they having more than once turned the tide of battle in his favour by their fire-arms. There have been numerous descendants of Young and Davis. The present King is Kamehameha V., born December 11th, 1830; ascended the throne Nov. 30th, 1863; he is unmarried; a son of Kinau, and grandson of Kamehameha I. Emma, the Queen dowager, widow of Kamehameha IV., paid a visit to Queen Victoria in 1855. Her father was a white man, a grandson of John Young. The present Constitution is limited monarchy. Failing a son to reigning monarch, his successor is appointed by the Privy Council with the assent of Parliament, convoked every two years, making laws and voting supplies. Present Minister of Foreign Relations, C. C. Harris; Minister of Interior, Dr. Hutchinson; Finance, J. Nott Smith; Acting Attorney-General, Frank Harris. The capital, Honolulu—containing, in 1860, 14,310 inhabitants; and in 1866, 13,521, a decrease in six years of 789—is situate on Oahu. All the islands are of volcanic formation. Owyhee, or Hawaii, is about twice as large as all the rest of the group, and is the place where Captain Cook, the celebrated discoverer, was massacred on 14th February, 1779, having discovered the islands on 18th January, 1778. There are three lofty mountains, one with nine cones, called Mauna Kea; another, Mauna Loa, with a smooth dome or top, and an enormous crater, estimated at more than two miles across; also Kuarari, with many volcanoes now extinct: these three lie in a great valley, almost uninhabited and not perfectly known. Kilanea, said to be the most wonderful of all in the islands, with no cone, is on an elevated plain, the summit being a huge black pit, three or four miles long by about three broad. It is about a thousand feet deep, with almost perpendicular sides, and a vast quantity of cooled lava within. From the official census of 1866, the population of the eight different islands comprising the group was:

	Square miles.	Feet high.	Population.
Hawaii, containing	4,000	13,953	19,808
Maui, „	600	10,200	14,035
Molokai, „	170	2,800	2,299

(Occupied by the King as a sheep and cattle run; a few leprous people there.)

	Square miles.	Feet high.	Population.
Lanai, containing	110	1,600	394
Oahu, ,,	520	3,800	19,879
Kauai, ,,	520	4,800	6,299
Niihau, ,,	80	800	325

(Held by Mr. Sinclair, a Scotchman, with his family and servants and their followers, and used by him as a sheep run, subject to Government supervision, but said to do as he likes.)

	Square miles.	Feet high.	Population
Kahoolawe (a barren rock),	60	400	Nil.

Total population, 1866, 62,959.

Foreign population was put down in 1866 (exclusive of Chinamen) at 4194. The total native population as compared with that of 1860 (six years) shows a *decrease* of 8901 natives and an increase of foreigners of 1621. Half-castes in 1866 numbered 1640. Vancouver estimated the population in 1793 at 300,000, so that a fearful reduction has taken place in the native race since their first intercourse with foreigners, and young and old are dying off like rotten sheep through drink and loathsome disease, principally introduced by the whalers, the great body of the people being contaminated either by direct contagion or hereditary. Few children are now born among the native population, and a large proportion born, die within a few months, the mothers, especially the younger ones, being often unwilling to look after them. They feel an infant to be a burden, interfering with their pleasures. The crime of fœticide is very prevalent, often resulting in the death of the mother, as well as of destruction to the future man. The riding astraddle by females on horseback is another most formidable cause, almost inevitably causing the premature expulsion of the fœtus in the early months. Young married couples seldom wish for children; they will tell you, if they had them they must stay at home; if not, they could go wherever they pleased and enjoy themselves. It is estimated that twenty years will decimate the native population, leaving a few half-castes and the Chinese to occupy the islands; the people being so thoroughly demoralized, and trade getting so bad, that Americans and Europeans are gradually leaving. The natives from their outside appearance look very clean, but in fact they are a filthy, lazy, lying race, most of them only thinking of the day and not of the morrow. They only look out for a day's food. Some will even eat fleas from dogs and vermin from their heads, and the females will lack food for a day or two to get a piece of finery to wear on the Sunday, such as a small hat with feather or made flower. No child is said to know its own father; it clings to the mother, who in case of charge of drunkenness, assault, or theft attends the police court and ceases no exertion until she has raised money to pay the fine. Very few Kanakas hold any land; most of them have sold it long ago, and squandered the money in drink. Prince Bill, a nephew of the King, has done his share in that line. He is tall, rather good-looking, and well educated. When flush of money and in his cups he will "shout" liquor to anyone he meets with, putting half-dollars and dollars in the bottoms of the pewters. He is also very fond of throwing his cap on the ground, exclaiming "Look here; there's the hat of a b——dy prince. You can't see that every day. I'll be on the throne yet, and will kick every b——dy foreigner out of the place." When sober he assumes the air of a prince, and passes his companions in debauch with disdain. The present King not being married, or likely to be, Prince Bill has made up his mind that he will, if living at the present King's death, be appointed King by the Parliament, as he is very much liked by the general public. If not, he will fight for it, he says. The soil of the island is mostly decomposed volcanic rocks, and although to appearance rich, requires constant irrigation. The valleys receive, through rains in the mountains, earth and *débris* washed from their sides, which create an extremely productive soil. Nature, however, here yields but little spontaneously, and much ingenuity and untiring industry is necessary in order to raise anything. The high mountains attract clouds and render the climate moist. On windward sides of islands vegetables are perennially verdant, but the leeward often suffer from long-continued droughts, and many places present a parched and desolate appearance. On Hawaii particularly, vast and rugged masses of broken lava have at various periods flowed from neighbouring volcanic craters, spread over the country, destroying every living thing, burying soil beneath black heaps of rock.

The indigenous and natural plants and fruits are:—

First.—Taro, banana, sweet potato, yam, bread-fruit, cocoanut, arrowroot, sugar-cane, ohelo (a mountain berry), ohia or rose apple.

Second.—Many varieties introduced. Irish potatoes

have been raised of immense size, largest from three to four pounds. Peaches will bear in eighteen months from the stone; they are not round, but the shape of a small pear, and sweet in flavour. Oranges, strawberries, raspberries, limes, mangoes, guavis, pine-apples, grapes, figs, citrons, tamarinds. Wheat of good quality has been raised on elevated lands of Maui and Hawaii. Rice, cotton, and coffee are grown and exported.

Not Indigenous. — Tobacco, indigo, and cocoa are cultivated, but not yet exported.

There are several rice plantations, large and small, one large one at Kauai called Lumahai. No less than thirty-nine sugar plantations, only a few of which are paying, wages being a dollar a day in place of a quarter dollar a few years back, and the Government not allowing rum to be manufactured, to check native intemperance, as it had been found to kill the men by inches. Among the largest and principal plantations are the "Makee," "Princeville," "Thomas Spencer" (also owner's name), "Waikapu" (H. Cornwall, proprietor), "Onomea." The owner of "Makee" is an old whaler, Captain Makee; he holds over 15,000 acres of freehold land, but a great deal of this of a volcanic character, and cannot be cultivated. This plantation has been worked over thirteen years, and is a payable concern. The machinery has cost over 100,000 dollars. Princeville is not paying its way; over 500,000 dollars has been expended in machinery and other ways; machinery said to be badly fixed, and money not judiciously laid out. Many plantations are over 2000 acres in extent. Very few birds, comparatively speaking, are on the islands; a few parroquets, and small birds with two bright yellow feathers under their wings, in the hills, very scarce, of which their war cloaks were partly made. There are no snakes or venomous reptiles, except scorpions; very few flies and mosquitoes at this period of the year. Rats are plentiful, being brought by the ships.

The climate is said to be generally salubrious, with a remarkable evenness of temperature, but earthquakes have been frequent, particularly from Mauna Loa, in January, 1859, the lava reaching the sea at Wainanalii in North Kona, distant between 40 and 50 miles, destroying in its course a village of thatched houses, and continued to flow for seven months. It got so hardened that pack animals and horsemen passed over in safety. The eruption in April, 1868, from the same mountain, was very destructive to life and property. A series of earthquakes began previously, and continuing for over a month with intervals, were felt on each of the principal islands, but on Hawaii, where the shocks were heaviest, a great deal of damage was done. At Kona fifty to sixty distinct shocks were felt in a day, and at Kua over 300 were reported. At four in the afternoon of 2nd April, the most severe shock of all took place. Its effect was instantaneous—in ten seconds almost every church, store, frame, or thatched house, and every stone wall in the district of Kau was laid flat with the ground; no one could stand, they had to sit on the ground, bracing together hands and feet to keep from rolling over; at the same instant with this heavy earthquake, at Kapapala, southern part of Kau, from a fissure burst out with a terrific explosion a stream of hot mud and water, which was driven fully three miles, varying in width from half to one mile, destroying men, animals, and trees. Thirty-one lives were lost, and over 500 head of cattle, horses, goats, and sheep. Following this singular eruption came a stream of clear, cold mountain water, issuing from the hole whence the mud had been expelled. There has also been tidal waves and inundations from time to time, the sea breaking on the shore, enveloping buildings, washing them several yards inland, then receding and sweeping the *débris* off to sea. Villages have been destroyed and many people killed from these tidal waves at Punaluu, Ninole, Kawaa, and others; also large cocoanut groves at Honuapo and Punaluu. There was a slight shock of an earthquake at Honolulu a couple of months before we arrived, but not sufficient to break any crockery.

In 1866 the number of Beef cattle on all the islands was					59,913
„	„	Sheep	„	„	100,625
„	„	Goats	„	„	56,980
„	„	Horses and Mules estimated at ..			100,000

	Dollars.
In 1870 the domestic exports were value	1,403,025
„ „ imported „	1,930,227
Oil exported (not produced here but brought and landed by whalers)	630,517

HONOLULU TO SAN FRANCISCO.

2080 Miles.

Weather cleared up in the afternoon of Saturday, 1st April, and the 'Ajax' left the wharf at four punctually, under a clear sunny sky; a multitude of people, male and female, had assembled to see her off, on foot, in buggies, and on horseback. Some Kanaka females in yellow and red gowns galloped from place to place to furthest extremity of the wharf, to see the last of us, midst a sea of waving handkerchiefs. The 'Ajax' belongs to the North Pacific Transportation Company, is 1354 tons and a fraction, was built at Brooklyn as a gunboat for the United States' Government, but the war ended just about when she was finished. She is strongly built and has a hurricane deck, covered with zinc, which makes her look very high out of the water. Passenger accommodation:—

Upper saloon deck	91
1st cabin (lower cabin)	120
2nd cabin	36
Steerage	166
	413

Saloon and lower deck of alternate layers of walnut and pine, about 2 inches wide, neat looking, and kept very clean; wide staircases, with ornamental balustrades of iron, and stairs edged with brass; roomy, well-ventilated cabins, carpeted, with a lamp between; two cabins on deck saloon, one in each below; all lights put out at 10 P.M. All the cabins, saloons, and doors painted with white China paint, as smooth as ivory, well finished and kept very clean, every dirty mark or stain being washed out every morning; not so much ornamental work as in colonial steamers, but more room. The ladies miss the comfortable hair seats and sofas, plated dishes, &c. She is provided with fifty-eight fire buckets, 450 feet of hose, and 450 life-preservers—laid out every night for use in case of accident. The captain, R. S. Floyd, is a smart thin Yankee, about thirty years old, wearing a blue tight-fitting frock coat. The stewardess, the only coloured person on board, about twenty-five years old, three parts negro blood, did nothing in port, and at sea the assistant-stewards made up the beds and kept the berths clean. Three meals a day, *i.e.* breakfast at eight, lunch (hot and cold) at 12.30 P.M., dinner at six, the gong sounding half an hour before each meal, making an awful noise, like at a pleasure fair, annoying many of the passengers. Meals not so substantial or good as in colonial steamers; numerous small dishes, with not much on them, but a greater variety of dessert, California apples being particularly fine; muffins and corn cake very good at breakfast; also preserved Oregon salmon, beefsteaks, rather tough and lean, boiled mutton and capers better, a lack of poultry, some "larkish" looking things, said to be chicken, on the table now and then, cabinet plum puddings and blackberry pie, excellent; ale and porter half a dollar pint bottle, quarter dollar for glass of grog or drink of spirits. We had additional passengers from

Honolulu, among them a coarse fat German, captain of a barque of 700 tons, called the 'Henry Hardley,' and his three passengers, two very stout young women and a young man for San Francisco. These people left in the barque in ballast, Melbourne, 5th October, 1870; went to Newcastle, New South Wales, obtained and brought to Honolulu 1000 tons of coal; then left Honolulu for San Francisco in ballast, but from head winds and cross seas the captain said he never could succeed in getting to his destination, and after knocking about, the ship sprung a leak within 90 miles of Frisco, and he could not get assistance, and had to return to Honolulu, where he left her with the first officer, &c., while he went to Frisco per 'Ajax,' to see the agents of the owners. He appeared particularly fond of the elder of the two girls, nightly taking their glasses of grog together. His interview with the agents didn't appear satisfactory, for a San Francisco paper of 17th April contained a notice to this effect, "Captain Hartmann, of barque 'H. H.,' not to be trusted," &c., &c.

We rounded Diamond Head and the eastern extremity at 5.30 P.M., the pilot having left us before this, as also the governor, who steered an excellent gig, manned by five hands, dressed in white trousers and shirts, with naval collars and blue cloth caps, with gilt letters round, "Hilo," using and feathering their oars in good style. We were rather close to the land and had a good view of the lofty mountains, peaks, and hills, the sides of some of them full of fissures, of large dimensions and various shapes. There is water lodged in extensive hollows or bowls amongst the hills and mountains, one piece of water termed a lake, but questionable whether permanent. We passed some nice little snug inlets now and then, adapted for picnics, but rather difficult to get at from the land. We commenced with a head wind and cross sea after supper, and the steamer began to pitch from stem to stern, but no actual rolling, although many passengers felt sick and turned in. It was a bright, cool, moonlight night, and the promenade on the hurricane deck was delightful. We had cleared the land some time, and at 9 P.M. we could scarcely discern it, and shall not see land again until we sight the Farralones, about 30 miles from San Francisco. Turned in at 9.30 P.M.

Sunday, 2nd April.—Morning bright and cool, one slight shower; still head wind and cross sea, pitching heavily fore and aft, the hurricane deck contributing to it; same weather all day, evening and night with showers. Only half a complement appeared at breakfast. English tracts were distributed at 10.30 A.M., by an agent of a Society at Honolula. The Rev. Fletcher was in his berth sea-sick, and therefore could not read prayers; Father Byrne in the same plight. The stewardess was bustling about, her hair frizzed up, with gilt earrings in her ears as large as saucers, a clean neat linen dress on in the morning, with a white apron up to her chin. In the afternoon a black stuff gown, with white collar and cuffs; she generally reads in the evening, but keeps to herself near her cabin. The steward and assistants usually read in a cluster at a distance—all intelligent young men, one a young German; all very chatty with the stewardess. A cup of coffee is brought to her between eight and nine, and sometimes she indulges in a glass of grog, and on these occasions polite exchanges were made as if in a drawing-room.

Observations, Noon.—Run, 117 miles; latitude, 22° 13′ N.; longitude, 156° 10′ W.

A few young albatrosses flying about; they are of a brown colour until maturity, two or three years old.

Seats at dinner ticketed, and napkins provided for use at table. All the courses, including dessert, were placed together on the table, except a large piece of beef, which was carved by the steward on an ante-table. The doctor, a fine fellow, standing about 6 feet, sat at the bottom of the table, and was particularly fond of boiled leg of mutton and capers. The doctor did not care much about the sea, declaring that he would rather live on shore, and would certainly do so if he could save an English half-crown a day; but he said the States and California were overrun with doctors, and he stuck to the sea from necessity. An elderly Irish lady, who sat opposite to me, did not take her napkin out of its gutta-percha ring (the colour and as hard as ebony), but used it like a shaving brush. She was very impatient, helping herself to anything near her, before the soup could reach her; sometimes she began with a fig, or some tart, or a slice of meat, or an apple, and never flagged until dessert was over, the "shaving brush" being much in use, keeping the young German constantly in attendance on her, and, as he said, he could do very little else.

Monday, 3rd April.—Morning cloudy and showery; about same sea and wind. 'Ajax' showing some agility, with the addition of a roll and a kick behind now and then. Engines stopped a short time at 11 A.M. to adjust and screw up machinery. Jib and mizen hoisted to keep her going a little.

Observations, Noon.—Latitude, 23° 18′ N.; longitude, 154° 3′ W. Distance run, 135 miles, proving herself a slow boat. Course, N. 61° 8′ E.

Heavy swell on from noon and remainder of day, evening, and night. Several vacancies at lunch. Many things moving without hands; some preserved cranberries went up one gentleman's sleeve. The most effectual way to save your soup on like occasions, is to hold your plate in your left hand, stick tight to your seat, and quickly convey that liquor to your mouth, per spoon in right hand.

Tuesday, 4th April.—Cloudy morning; afterwards pleasant and sunny a little while. Strong head wind and rough cross sea prevailed; pitching and rolling heavily. Special hop, skip, and jump at breakfast; many things thrown about and broken. Some passengers off their perch. The captain pitched under the table; taken on a ground-hop when he was earnestly conversing with Judge Lyons from California, who had taken a trip to Honolulu for his health, and who looked as if he had been raised in Virginia, as he was as yellow as a guinea.

Observations, Noon.—Latitude, 24° 43′ N.; longitude, 152° 6′ W.; distance run, 137 miles. Course, N. 52° E. Squally afternoon, evening, and night.

Jib, mizen, and mainsail set nearly all day; off her course, to avoid, if possible, head wind and cross sea.

Wednesday, 5th April.—About same kind of weather as yesterday. Jib and mainsail spread; steering two or three points off course to avoid head sea.

Observations, Noon.—Latitude, 27° 13' N.; longitude, 150° 41' W.; distance run, 168 miles. Course N. 27° E. Mizen only set during a portion of day, being in hands of "sails" repairing.

Thursday, 6th April.—Weather moderating; cool day. Jib, mizen, and mainsail set.

Observations, Noon.—Latitude, 29° 31' N.; longitude, 148° 21' W.; distance run, 185 miles. Course, N. 42° E. Over forty put in appearance at dinner. Watery sunset; night dark and cold.

Good Friday, 7th April.—Morning very cloudy; slight rain. Sea comparatively quiet; head wind not so strong. Trysail and jib set off and on. Engines stopped quarter of an hour at noon to examine and screw up machinery.

Observations, Noon.—Latitude, 31° 24' N.; longitude, 144° 56' W.; distance run, 210 miles. Course, N. 57° E. Fast day not noticed. Excellent spread at dinner. Calm afternoon, evening, and night. Steamer running steady.

Saturday, 8th April.—Reminded by Father Byrne (who had been confined to his berth, sick) that yesterday had been Good Friday; a circumstance that had escaped the memories of most, especially as no "fast" had been proclaimed. Eighteen years ago I passed Good Friday on board barque 'Nestor,' at sea, London to Sydney. Morning cloudy; sea calm, with light head wind, which continued all day, evening and night. No canvas spread.

Observations, Noon.—Latitude, 32° 43' N.; longitude, 141° 5' W.; course, N. 68° E.; distance run, 211 miles.

Easter Sunday, 9th April.—Fine sunny morning and day; smooth sea, and scarcely any wind. All sails set (except topsail) nearly all day.

Rev. Fletcher read Church of England Service up to Litany. The Bible was placed on flag, "Stars and Stripes." Prayers offered for President United States and Queen Victoria. Short sermon preached from Ecclesiastes—"May the end be better than the beginning;" wound up by prayer. Father Byrne held Catholic service at 2 P.M. The saloon was crammed, there being a great many Irish in the steerage. Heard the whole of the mumbling, uninstructive affair, from cabin.

Observations, Noon.—Latitude, 33° 37' N.; longitude, 136° 51' W.; distance run, 218 miles. Course, N. 76° E.

Monday, 10th April.—Wind freshened towards morning; nice sea on. Steamer rolling gently. Weather rather cloudy, but cool; came on to be squally in afternoon. All sails set (except topsail). Officers' steward and mess steward had a dispute, and fought a round or two on about equal terms, both being marked about the face when separated. Captain had them tied to the mainmast for four hours, with their hands behind their backs.

Observations, Noon.—Latitude, 34° 24' N.; longitude, 132° 32' W.; distance run, 223 miles. Course, N. 78° E. Large Yankee steamer 'Nevada,' from San Francisco to Honolulu, one of the packets of a new line in place of "Hall's," passed at 8 P.M., and threw up rockets, to which 'Ajax' responded; but no signals exchanged.

Tuesday, 11th April.—About same weather as yesterday, and similar canvas spread up to midday; then breeze freshened, producing a lively sea, with pitch-and-toss remainder of day, evening, and night. 9 A.M. sighted an American barque, all sails set except royals.

Observations, Noon.—Latitude, 35° 52 29" N.; longitude, 128° 37 2" W.; distance run, 210 miles. Course, 65° 19' E. South Farralone Lighthouse, 292-8^m W. 67° 56' E. Distance from San Francisco, 323 miles.

Wednesday, 12th April.—Rain early, very cloudy morning, and rough sea; fore-and-aft sails set.

Observations, Noon.—Latitude, 37° 19' N.; longitude, 124° 28' W.; distance run, 219 miles. Course, 67° E. South Farralone Lighthouse, 74^m.

San Francisco distant 104 miles; Honolulu, 1976, being 2080 miles between the two places, although some persons say it is 2120. Myriads of gulls on the Farralones; a few men earn a good living in collecting and selling the eggs.

At 6.45 P.M. off Farralone Lighthouse, with its revolving light, which looked very bright, the night being a dark one. Went through the Golden Gate at 10 P.M., and were alongside the wharf close on 11 P.M. Slept on board.

California is on the western coast of America, and is generally called "The Land of the far West." Climate said to be usually mild. The "Golden Gate" is the entrance to the splendid extensive harbour of San Francisco, about five miles from the city, which is protected by elevated forts in strong positions, mounted with heavy ordnance. This harbour is in fact a bay, about sixty miles long, extending into the interior, mostly surrounded by fertile land, with now and then excellent houses, &c. The city itself may be said to be built on sand, it having been a few years since a succession of sand hills and pits, which had to be levelled, filled up, or removed as occasion required, at a great expense, to get anything like a solid foundation; even now large pits are being filled up with sand, bought at some cost from owners of heaps, probably at a distance, who a few years ago were glad to pay to get rid of it, it blowing about very much on gusty days. The city, but little more than twenty-one years old, now contains a population estimated at from 157,000 to 170,000, the census having been taken twice, and the figures not agreeing; this includes Chinese, said to be about 15,000.

Thursday, 13th April.—Fine day. Turned out at 7 A.M. Custom-house officer slightly overhauled trunk, &c., on wharf. Went in pair-horse hack close carriage, silver mounted, and harness ditto, to the "Russ House," Montgomery Street—Pearson and Seymour, proprietors—about three-quarters of a mile, at a cost of 1½ dollar. This hotel extends from Pine to Bush Streets, and has a frontage to Montgomery Street, the fashionable promenade of the city, of 275 feet; it has over 250 lofty and airy bedrooms, very extensive, wide corridors, canvased and carpeted, sitting-rooms, and suites of apartments, all handsomely furnished. Water and gas laid on, saving a deal of labour to servants, particularly in the bedrooms, which contained grey and white marble washstands and toilet-tables, chests of drawers to put your things away, and everything very clean. Sixteen stores attached to the hotel on the ground-floor, in centre of which is wide entrance to hotel from Montgomery Street, up steps to commodious hall, with floor of white and black marble, diamond-shaped pieces interspersed. Public room carpeted over, fully supplied with newspapers; walls covered with advertisements and cards in frames; some cane-bottomed arm-chairs, others with easy damask cushions. A mixture of people, mostly smoking cigars; some chewing—spittoons provided. Handsome billiard-room with four tables. Very large breakfast and dining room, with ornamental ceiling, supported by wooden fluted pillars and handsome ornamental plaster caps; smaller room at side for use of those who come down late. Breakfast, 7 A.M. to 11 A.M.; lunch, 12.30 P.M. to 2 P.M.; dinner, 5 P.M. to 7 P.M.; supper, 9 P.M. to 10 P.M.; charges, 2 dollars a day. A dozen waiters, principally Irish; very attentive. No niggers on the premises. Good bills of fare; everything in season which could be had; butter particularly good. Fresh-printed bills of fare handed round every day. Entered name in book on counter in hall. Got "fixed" bedroom No. 237; key handed over, and, until return to clerk at the office, visitor liable for any loss. Had breakfast at 7.30; among other things, grilled Oregon salmon, very good. People constantly coming in and going out, consuming an extraordinary quantity of different viands—fish, flesh, fowl, &c. Montgomery and California Streets are very broad, with wide footways, principally of asphalt, and lofty noble buildings on each side, double tramways running through them in the middle; the cars carry from twenty-five to thirty passengers inside only, with pair of horses, which have small bells attached to their headgear; no turntables necessary, as both ends are alike, and the horses can be hitched or unhitched in a second; fare generally 5 cents, but tickets can be bought at a less rate. Some streets are laid with narrow pieces of Oregon pine; some with large round paving stones, and footways of wood. The Post Office is very large, the main building built of brick, cemented over; entrance up granite steps to portico supported by granite pillars. The private boxes, with a key to each, number 2142. The new Merchants' Exchange, in California Street, is an immense building of worked freestone, with square fluted pillars, very elegant. Some handsome banks in California and Montgomery Streets. A great many buildings are of brick, some of them cemented over. The markets are in Washington Street—four in succession—and very commodious; the interior, of wood, neat and clean. Plenty of Oregon salmon, mostly 8 or 10 lbs. in weight, sturgeon, perch, trout, lobsters, crabs, and a variety of other fish; plenty of fine geese, turkeys, fowls, rabbits, &c. The new Grand Hotel is a magnificent building, having its stores, &c., on basement. You pass from one wing to another through a gallery over a street, and, as regards capacity and accommodation, stands pre-eminent; has its telegraph office in a very handsome reception or reading room; very broad, handsome, and easy staircases, with spacious drawing-rooms, halls, and wide corridors, carpeted, &c., imparting to the entire place a palatial appearance; the furniture of the most costly description—arm-chairs with embroidery of different colours, plush cushions, &c. The billiard-room is a magnificent one, containing eleven tables, with luxurious couches and seats of rich crimson-coloured velvet.

The Occidental, only about half the size of the Grand, is another fine hotel, five stories high, facing three streets, frontage in Montgomery Street, 275 feet, 137½ in Bush Street, and 170 on Sutter Street. Contains 412 separate rooms and apartments, and can accommodate nearly 600 guests. Billiard-room, an immense one, very handsomely fitted up; has thirteen tables, Brussels carpet laid down, arm-chairs, crimson cotton velvet, and easy couches. At most hotels you can obtain lunch gratis in the bar, paying for your drink only, say quarter of a dollar. Some produce hot, others cold joints of meat, soup, boiled salmon, cheese, celery, radishes, pickles, &c. Many have hot drinks, others brandy smashes, &c., plenty of ice, limes, &c. At several bars, to keep the hogsheads of liquors cool, earth is placed on the tops of casks; grass grows on it, which is watered and cut to about 9 inches high. After lunch went and saw a young buffalo exhibited with two faces; some thought a sharp Yankee had been operating on it. Then went to Chinese Town, a steep and not very wide street, leading off Montgomery Street, yet a tramway was being worked up and down, a couple of extra horses being attached at the foot of the hill; coming down the hill a break was put on, and the car descended gently. This street occupied by Chinese on each side for about a mile, all shopkeepers, many of them selling meat and fish cut up into very small pieces, and every description of vegetables, fruit, &c. Then went and inspected stock of Chy Lung and Co., 640, Sacramento Street, containing a costly collection of Chinese fancy goods, beautiful carved ivory ornaments and silver ditto, ivory and lacquered wood fans, grass cloth, Canton crape shawls, Chinese ornamented shoes, &c. Lung could talk English, and we expressed our intention to call again some day. Excellent dinner at the Russ; salmon, boiled cod and oyster sauce, roast turkey, chicken broth, &c.; good dessert; apples very fine. Gentleman from Kansas walked into the edibles pretty stiff, but drank water. Said the Indians were decreasing very fast, principally from their fondness for "fire water." To his knowledge 15,000 Red Indians in Kansas alone had died within the last five years. Will all soon disappear before the white man. Claret was reasonable; had a bottle of Verdelias for 50 cents; pint bottles of ale and porter, English, 25 cents per bottle. After dinner took a stroll with Mr. Lane; some very large water-carts were employed, from five to ten hogsheads; two and four big horses. In evening shops and stores were brilliantly lit up with gas. Many did not close till near 10. Streets tolerably quiet. Went to Metropolitan Theatre, Montgomery Street, at 8. A conveniently-arranged place. French play, 'La Grande Duchesse de Gerolstein;' very good orchestra, French actors and actresses; very vivacious and full of excitement. 1 dollar to dress circle and orchestra; boxes, 5 to 10 dollars; gallery, 50 cents. House tolerably quiet.

Friday, 14th April.—Another fine sunny spring day. Went on tramway (double tram), for 5 cents, from corner of Market and Third Streets, for about two miles, then walked a quarter of a mile to suburban Mission Town, an old Mexican missionary place, said to be over one hundred years old; vehicles, &c., now and then crossed tramway with ease; not a horse shied, or took any notice of it, although bells are affixed to the horses' necks. Many nice villas, with lawns, &c., containing plenty of European and other trees and shrubs, in the suburbs and on sides of a belt of lofty conical hills. Pears, peaches, quinces, &c., in blossom. Several extensive laundries in suburbs, in which Chinese are engaged, being supplied by hotels, as well as private families; they turn their work out in beautiful order, superior to but at about the same prices as at Honolulu; the shirts in particular being beautifully "glazed," and got up in a superior manner. Mission Town, so called, is on a sandy strata, no footways formed, many good houses there, but several empty, persons having left to go into the city, &c. There is an ancient Catholic cathedral church, interior highly ornamented, with gilded altar, &c., and large burial-yard attached, containing many beautiful monuments of white marble, &c. The place is overrun with coarse long grass, and appeared to be much neglected. There is an engine-house in the town, containing a beautiful steam fire-engine, the steel parts being highly polished; hose wound neatly round a one-horse vehicle, very light; three fine upstanding bay horses, well groomed, ready harnessed; firemen in red jumpers, &c., sitting outside smoking and yarning, ready for any emergency. The engine was on a tram in the house, and single and double trams run through a street or two in this retired, quiet place. Went to the Pioneer Inn, a plain wooden structure, where we could only get inferior lager beer at 5 cents a glass; the bar and sitting-room were neat, oak paper varnished over, and the floors were strewed with sawdust, like country inns in England. Some quaint old paintings, in imitation of Dutch oil-paintings, were against the walls, in plain old-fashioned black, and some in gutta-percha frames; in fact every American copies very nearly from the English in clothing, living, and almost everything. The landlord was an Irishman, with bad eyes, who complained of the sand and dust flying about now and then, and also of badness of trade; he was evidently a Fenian. There was stuck against the wall in the bar a "Fenian Map of Ireland," and portraits thereon of "Fenian martyrs, Thos. F. Burke, Daniel O'Connell, and Robert Emmet," with intimations of revenge, &c., for their persecutions. On returning we had a peep at the new Mint in course of erection, corner of Mission and Fourth Streets. Walls up, and rapidly approaching completion; high base of grey or blue dressed granite rest of outside plain granite, all very substantial. Interior walls and partitions of brick. Went to north and south beaches, facing portion of harbour, in afternoon, about a mile and a half, in tramway car. Beaches very stony and difficult to walk on; some very good houses on sides of hills above, overlooking and commanding good views of harbour and the various bays and small islands adjacent. One ancient, villainous-looking storekeeper near the wharf at north beach has a collection of bears, monkeys, dogs, parrots, pictures and prints (the latter savouring strongly of the Holywell Street type), to attract custom to a miscellaneous display of goods; he also dispenses liquors. Pleasant ride back, the car going down hill easily and safely. The hack carriages and horses (pair) the best I ever met with, all so clean, looked like gentlemen's private carriages, the horses so well groomed, &c.

Saturday, 15th April.—Another fine day. Met with a very old friend, Mr. Andrew Jones, of the Imperial Insurance Office, whom I had not seen since August, 1854, at Adelaide. Went to Oakland, Alameda County, with him, about three miles across the bay, to deliver a letter from an Adelaide friend to his mother, Mrs. Armstrong, residing there. Walked into the large steam ferry-boat, on a perfect level with the wharf; roomy boat, hurricane deck, very convenient in stormy or extreme warm weather. Pleasant trip across; passed a small island called Goat Island. Landing very comfortable, the steamer's bow fitting like a glove into recess, quite level with wharf; then went by railway, long carriages, containing very easy armchairs, for about five miles, to Broadway, Oakland, crossing a viaduct nearly two miles long across an arm of the bay, and running into the very streets, which were very wide, with some wood and some sandy footways; plenty of good houses and shops; a Post Office, Telegraph Station, Town Hall, &c.; a very picturesque township; Broadway the chief thoroughfare. Many of the outlying streets like being in the country; trees principally scrub oak, smaller than English oak, being planted on each side, but affording good shelter, the foliage being thick. Some well-built villa residences on the banks of the Merra, a river or estuary from the bay, standing in midst of plots of green native grass, well cut and planted with rose-trees, laurestina, and other European shrubs and trees, weeping willows, &c., with here and there knots of heartsease, primroses, and other English flowers. Mr. Bacon's (a retired banker) house and lawn particularly good and well kept; we were shown over drawing-room by Mrs. B.; very luxuriously furnished, some splendid specimens of marble statuary there, elegant couches, &c.; stabling very good. The green native grass flats and sides of hills in distance looked very picturesque. Went to a very nice liquor store kept by a German, in a garden well stocked with flowers and shrubs, and looking into the river; seats under verandah and in garden; a pretty place; Allsop's bottled ale (quarts), half a dollar. Walked all over the place, the strata being generally sandy and dry, but did not succeed in meeting with Mrs. A.'s residence. It afterwards appeared that she lived with a married daughter, and that accounted for her name not being in the Directory; left note for her at Telegraph Office. Some liquor stores with very large bars here. The Broadway appeared to be the great place of business. Returned at 4; a very pleasant trip by rail and water.

Sunday, 16th April.—Raining heavily from 8 till 2. Went to north beach by tramway at 10, to spend the day with friend J. Passing through the Chinese quarter, several females, Chinese, handsomely dressed in silks and satins, but well painted, were peeping out of the doors and windows, with feelings of disappointment at the wet weather; all said to be harlots; Sunday being a great pleasure day, large steamers chartered for picnics, &c. Called at a liquor store kept by a German; very neat, clean place, liquors very good, a cold spread already laid out for customers, cold beef, sucking-pig, &c., with cheese, pickles, salad, &c.; had an hour's conversation about the war, and also on San Francisco topics; has a great hatred of the Yankees, and expressed his determination to "clear out" as soon as he could get a customer for his business; rain made the air quite chilly, and stoves were lighted; five minutes' walk in the rain found me at my friend's house, 206, Chestnut Street, nearly at the top of a steep hill; streets were very muddy, and large pools of water about; friend's house of seven rooms, well furnished, water and gas laid on, and a small yard at back, all rented at 190*l.* per annum; iron railings in front of the houses with little gardens containing in each a small May-tree, primroses, daisies, pansies, roses, &c.; two or three Australian gum-trees planted in front; the owner of the house, and of several others adjoining, is a ship captain, and on return voyages he brings young rooted trees and shrubs from different places. The backs of the houses are close to and look on the harbour, a very pretty prospect. Miss Theresa Longworth, otherwise Yelverton, or Lady Avonmore, was living in a house just opposite; she had been lecturing for some time, and considered herself as much ill-used and as great a martyr as ever; offered to be introduced to her, but declined. Found fire lit in dining-room, and that my friend had succeeded in obtaining a servant (Scotch) for 52*l.* a year; wages of female servants vary from 50*l.* to 60*l.* (some object to clean boots at the former price) per annum, and they are constantly changing places, getting married, &c. He had had three before the present one in about five months, but this one, from being extra ugly, was likely to remain longer; they generally leave without any notice; the last cut away in the midst of breakfast the previous Thursday, under pretence that her grandfather was ill up the country, leaving her mistress to wash up the breakfast things. Took a stroll in afternoon, before dinner; liquor saloons open all day; billiard-playing as usual; cold spreads for the customers laid out in every one; some cold roast pigs amongst the fare; these billiard fellows play nearly all day and night, now and then taking a snack, and drinking, chewing, and smoking, mostly standing, and never sitting down to a meal. Returned to the Russ at 9 P.M. by tramway. Streets comparatively quiet; only met with one man intoxicated, and he was too far gone to do much harm. Several places of amusement were open in the evening. The "California," the only theatre open, where Herr Bandmann, a German of some pretensions, was the chief performer in a five act comedy, "Ein Glas Wasser" (a glass of water). He has just arrived here from a tour through Australia.

Monday, 17th April.—Dull morning, threatening rain; afterwards turned out a lovely day. There are two very handsome buildings, corner Montgomery Street, built of dressed square blocks of granite brought from China twenty years ago; one is used by a celebrated firm of American forwarding agents, and the other (formerly the Pacific Bank) occupied as offices. Went and had peep at Exchange; great excitement, people rushing about in all directions. Then went to the Brokers' Exchange; a very large room, seated, where a President takes the chair on an elevated dais, and decides all questions on buying and selling shares, the owners and buyers of scrip (principally mining) being represented by brokers, who make a great clatter to get their business attended to first; it was more like the Tower of Babel than anything else, tongues going like greased lightning, midst constant interruptions, &c. Then went to a Yankee auction of boxes of boots and shoes. The auctioneer spoke so fast couldn't understand what he

O

said; now and then he read from a printed catalogue, and intending buyers following him from ditto, were enabled to understand sufficient to bid by, but we were completely at "sea." Lunched at Occidental Hotel, free; soup, fish, spiced beef, &c.; two drinks, English ale, for quarter dollar each. Went up in elevator, five stories, and inspected hotel; beautifully furnished; the large public drawing-room luxuriously so; surely the furniture must be hired, there is so much of it. The Cosmopolitan is another very large establishment, boasting a beautiful billiard-room with eight tables. In afternoon went over several large warehouses and shops, particularly a drapery and fancy goods shop and warehouse of J. W. Davidson and Co., 101 and 103, Kearney Street, held on a seven years' lease, at a rental of 5000 dollars, with right of renewal. It is three stories high, has its lift or elevator, 280 gaslights, forty girls working at Grover and Baker's sewing machines, principally making up clothing and ladies' fancy things; only three females behind counters, but several men. In evening went to "California" Theatre, Bush Street, a well-built place, the interior, about the shape of a punch-bowl, gradually rising from the orchestra to the dress circle, so that everyone could see and hear; paid a dollar. Crowded audience, principally Germans; a German called Joseph K. Emmet, taking the leading character of the young German Emigrant, in a three-act drama called "Fritz." Gods dreadfully noisy and ill-behaved, stopping the play twice for five minutes. A very strong company, twenty-six characters, well sustained, and excellent scenery.

Tuesday, 18th April.—Fine sunny day. Went to "Lone Mountain" by car, about two miles outside city. A queer conical-shaped large mound, covered with growth; below is the general cemetery, occupying a mile of undulating sandy country, commanding delightful views of portion of the bay and city, and of hills and mountains in the distance, at back, &c.; several wide winding avenues, named Oak Grove, Pioneer, &c.; paths branching off from main avenues, called Verbena, Angel, Hawthorn, &c., painted on boards, the better to enable persons to find out the graves; trained and clipped pines, Douglass spruce, and other ornamental trees; shrubs of laurestina, roses of many kinds, ivy in profusion, some Australian wattles in bloom, bearing yellow bunches of flowers, mignonette, ice plants, blue bells, carnations, daisies, marigolds, &c., &c., some in handsome china vases; hundreds of polished marble and granite monuments; beautiful full length figure of white marble, under a canopy resting on fluted pillars, bronze colour, marked simply "Sophy." White marble Egyptian lions sculptured in front, wide white marble steps at entrance; worked granite walls surrounding the whole, about six feet high; several tall white marble vases, with flowers growing at top of each at back. A very high handsome obelisk of white marble, with base and surrounding masonry of grey-spotted worked granite, to memory of Senator Broderick, of Washington, born 1820, died

1859; killed in a duel on account of a political dispute with some one. Some sea shells strewed about a few graves, evidently brought from a distance. Splendid mausoleum of cut stone, simply marked "my husband." Opposite is the Catholic cemetery, the tombstones looking like a forest of trees. Went to Woodward's garden in the afternoon; a fine spot, got up regardless of expense, with its enormous pavilion for dancing, &c., ornamental houses, grottoes, &c. Camel and its young, with bears and other animals, exhibited. Refreshments and liquors in profusion; is a favourite resort on Sundays. The grounds very well planted with shrubs and flowers, and well kept. In evening was introduced to a place called the "Colonial Club," to see a Mr. M., from Adelaide. It was on the first floor of the building. On knocking three times the door was unlocked, and on entering found ourselves in a large room, used as a gambling-house, and in it a liquor bar; after losing five or six dollars, and having two or three liquors, we managed to get away, on the score that we had a pressing engagement.

Wednesday, 19th April.—Fine sunny day. Went to Pavilion Skating Rink. Fast American female performer, one Carrie Augusta Moore, drawing large audiences; dressed in the height of fashion; a short dress, so as to give her feet and legs fair play; the skates were at her toe and heel. Very nice-shaped girl, and active, small feet, most graceful in her movements, and attractive; said to go beyond what has hitherto been considered perfection. Large funeral passed up Montgomery Street this afternoon; very difficult to get and keep in line, from great traffic. Hearse of most gorgeous description; gilt ornaments, plate-glass sides, and at door, so that the coffin could be seen; very gay trappings, &c. In the distance the hearse looked like a wedding equipage. Went with an agent, recommended by my friend J., and got tickets for railway to New York, by way of Chicago and Buffalo, about 3368 miles, 26*l*. 10*s*., first-class, and two nights in sleeping cars, 6 dollars. Agents get a percentage for introducing a customer, so it costs one nothing, and is safer for a stranger. Went to the court and saw Laura D. Fair, a bold, determined, middle-aged-looking woman, with remains of a handsome profile, who was and had been on her trial for many days, for shooting and killing Judge Crittenden (with whom she cohabited), in the presence of his wife and family in broad daylight, on board steam ferryboat, between Oakland and San Francisco, with a small pistol; she had a fan in her hand, was fashionably dressed in small hat, &c., and watched the proceedings narrowly, the court being crowded. Judge and counsel wore no wigs or gowns, and counsel mostly sat when examining a witness; indeed everyone appeared to take things easy; trial creating great sensation, and free bets exchanged that she would never be found guilty of murder by a San Francisco jury. During the week and to-day met with many females walking about, appearing careworn and consumptive, said to be brought about by drink, fast living, and dissipation.

Mrs. Fair looked like one of this class; she began her work young, and ruined many a man in her career. In the evening went to the Alhambra, in Bush Street, and saw the Emerson Minstrels, very pleasing and good; there was also a Miss Wren, a first-class vocalist. This place also opens Sunday evenings at 8. Bush Street is full of places of amusement.

Thursday, 20th April.—Same weather as yesterday. There are several "fortune tellers in San Francisco," who advertise and ply their trade openly, one in Bush Street has a board painted in white letters on a black ground, "Gipsy Girl Fortune Telling Establishment." Close to is Dr. W. F. Smith, oculist and aurist, where at eleven friend L. and self wound our way to have my left eye looked at and "fixed" prior to my departure by the big railway. A fat nigger, the first black servant we had met with in San Francisco, a perfect Dandy Jim from Carolina, dressed in a full suit of black, white frilled shirt exquisitely got up, opened the door and said that his "Massa" did not receive gentlemen till noon, so we had to retire, and to while away the time went to a new liquor store lately opened by a friend of L.'s, where we tasted and sipped till we were fit to go under any reasonable operation. Adjourned to the doctor's at twelve, where we had to wait in the ante-room about half an hour before we could get an audience. He was a keen-eyed, spare Yankee, about 5 feet 9 or 10, dressed in a tight-fitting black suit, with a shirt elaborately got up. Having put me on a chair, with strong injunctions to sit hard and fast as if I had to take root, the doctor proceeded to view the unfortunate left peeper through a strong glass, when he expressed his decided opinion that it must undergo an operation to clear it out, the chief pain of which would be keeping the "lids" open. During this "calculation" Mr. L. expressed his idea several times "decidedly so," which led the doctor to ask whether old L. was a doctor, to which he replied, "Oh dear, no," but that he had had considerable experience in the Bush in the blight. Doctor S. having requested my friend, the amateur, to shut up and be quiet, proceeded with great quickness and skill to keep open the eyelids with a pair of tweezers and then removed, with a small piece of sponge dipped in some liquid, all the dirt and matter from the eye, dropping some lotion into it, and tightly bandaging it up. He asked how I felt. I said "rather groggy," meaning stupid, but he took it in the real sense of the word, immediately taking out of a cupboard a bottle three parts full of pale Cognac, from which he gave Mr. L. and self a glass each, drinking it undiluted. He then wrote out a prescription for lotion and physic, saying, "my fee is twenty-five dollars, or 5*l*. 4s. 2*d*. English." A happy thought struck me that although I had the money about me, I would get my friend J. to settle, so telling the doctor that my cash was locked up in my friend's safe, I left an order with him for the amount, and then went to a German chemist and had the prescription made up, which cost several dollars. Afterwards met friend Jones, who was very annoyed at what he said was an exorbitant charge;

that he had "polished" the doctor off, who had taken fifteen dollars and given up the order. Went to north beach; dined with Mr. J. and spent the evening.

SAN FRANCISCO TO NEW YORK.
3492 Miles.

Friday, 21st April.—Beautiful spring day. Left San Francisco for Ogden, 882 miles by Union Pacific Railway from Oakland. Got up too late for the coach to take us to the ferry-boat. Carriage and pair belonging to the hotel quickly round—five inside (two ladies), one outside, at a dollar each, for about a mile run; barely in time for the ferry-boat at 8 A.M. Took a ticket for leather trunk to be sent direct to New York, No. 4280, taking only a valise into the cars, with change of linen for a few days. A great rush of passengers and baggage at the last moment; nothing to pay, the railway tickets clearing everything. Went to Oakland; train ready, and shown by guard into sleeping saloon car, No. 2. Cars very lengthy and roomy, something like 50 feet long, heated by steam, seats for four with easy backs to lean against, two sitting facing the other two, nice and soft, covered with fine fancy machine-manufactured carpet, of a pretty, lively pattern, looking similar to material used for ottomans. These seats are in a row on each side of a wide passage running through the whole train, so that when tired of sitting you can promenade up and down the extent of your car; there is a door at end of each car, neat closets out of sight, lavatories, toilet sets, &c.; easy chairs and small tables about. The roof lofty, sloping away gradually like an arch, nicely painted and ornamented with figures both male and female, and landscapes; each sleeping saloon car has its name painted in large gilt letters outside it, so that when you return from having a meal at a restaurant, you can readily find your car, as on such occasions you have no time to lose. Our car was named "Golden Gate." Train left punctually at 8.30 A.M., passing through Oakland and suburbs, midst nice orchards, kitchen and other gardens, and then well-grassed valleys, by excellent farms, up some moderate gradients and into a few insignificant cuttings and tunnels, with a succession of good agricultural land, and many acres of wild mustard scattered about, to Stockton, 90 miles from San Francisco, and 85 from Oakland, which was reached at noon, where we were only allowed ten minutes to dine. There was a plentiful supply of beef, pastry, &c. Chinese waiters; charge, six bits or three-quarters of a dollar; all dined with hats on, as there was no time to lose. Many decent brick buildings about the town, with some good orchards and gardens, and principally Chinese working in them. Stations between Oakland and Stockton are San Jose, San Jose Junction, Livermore, and Bantas. After leaving Stockton the country continued very good, up hill and down dale, in a moderate way, and well watered by numerous small streams; some land now and then fenced off, with posts and four rails of steam-machine-sawn timber, very neat. The small wooden railway stations, also used as telegraph offices, well-horsed coaches and vehicles, on leather springs, waiting for passengers at these small places, where only a few scattered houses of wood, mostly neatly painted, were to be seen. Passed Galt station and reached Sacramento, the capital of California, 48 miles from Stockton at two, a very scattered countryfied-looking place, infinitely inferior to Frisco. Many streets were bordered with trees, and some had tramways through them. Several houses midst gardens, trees, shrubs, &c. Many vineyards and large buildings in distance. There is a wide muddy-looking river, by which there is communication by small steamers with San Francisco, distant 125 miles by water, and a passenger sitting opposite me intended to return there by that route. A very large wooden station, with warehouses, &c. Stayed half an hour; very level country for miles after leaving Sacramento, with plenty of growing crops of spring wheat, maize, &c., and horses and cattle about, and some prairie land; the afternoon getting warm. Arrived at Rocklin at 3.30 P.M. A great quantity of projecting rocks scattered about here, the small country place appeared to be beset with them. Went thence up some steep gradients, at slow speed, to Auburn, 36 miles from Sacramento, and from there to Colfax into lofty hills winding about them midst beautiful scenery. Snow was now visible on the hill sides and mountain tops of the Sierra Nevada in the distance, many tall and slender pines and Douglass spruce being scattered about, some of them looking very minute, the view being magnificent. Well-horsed coaches were standing at the small stations; one had six bay horses attached, and the roads looked frightfully steep and difficult to get over. Still gradually ascending, crossed a ravine on a wooden viaduct at a very slow pace, sometimes almost at a standstill, and once "fixed" for ten minutes "to get breath." Rounded "Cape Horne" at a quarter to six, on the brink of a frightful deep hollow below, with stream of melted snow-water running through big boulders, a most romantic but dangerous place; nothing could be saved if train went off line; then on to Gold Run, through a portion of the diggings, a very extensive area, apparently well watered, large "races" being cut in the ground, as well as water carried through wooden "races," or shutes fixed on wooden supports about 5 feet from the ground. Many Chinese working about, and wooden huts seen every now and then. Reached "Alta," 70 miles from Sacramento at 6.30 P.M., where we were allowed twenty minutes for "supper;" very good, hot spread in large comfortably furnished room of wooden hotel. The waitresses were white women talking good English; charge three-quarters of a dollar. Stations between Sacramento and Alta are Arcade, Junction, Rocklin, Newcastle, Auburn, Colfax, Gold Run, and Dutch Flat. Almost dark when we left here, and passing Blue Canon, Emigrant Gap, and Cisco, through low hills and by mountain sides, we at length ascended to the summit of Sierra Nevada mountains, a distance of 105 miles from Sacramento, and at an elevation of 7042 feet above the sea level, where there is a small station called "Summit." Darkness having set in very little could be seen, and many "turned in" between nine and ten. Only two occupied the four seats from Sacramento, a Mr. Bousfield on a visit to England, who had been fifteen years, about half his life, in California, and myself; we had been wondering nearly all day how the beds or berths were to be "created," and as night drew near watched the "bedroom steward's" operations; he was a young, full-blooded nigger, over 6 feet high, the thinnest of his race we ever saw, talking English very correctly, and very civil and attentive, dressed in a neat grey tweed suit, with a short jacket. The two bottom seats were turned over and formed the foundation of a berth over 6 feet long, with room enough for two if needed, a very solid one, and underneath was a hollow place where I planted my valise, opossum rug, boots, &c., plenty of room for these and other things. With a stick or wand, with a key at its end, he touched a spring in the top or roof over, and down came a "top" berth, supported in front at each end by neat suspenders of brass; this recess contained two mattresses, sheets, and coloured blankets like fine horse-cloths, &c., &c., for the upper and lower berths. Handsome curtains were drawn against the berths on each side of the thoroughfare or passage, behind which ladies and gentlemen were supposed to disrobe; but the former must have a disagreeable task, and a room could and ought to be set aside for their use in undressing and dressing, as the gentlemen could retire to rest either last or first as might be agreed on, to avoid a collision or probable mistake in the passage. Mr. Bousfield occupied the top, and self the under berth, turning in at 10 P.M. The rocking soon sent us to sleep, which we did soundly till about six next morning. Boots were placed outside and cleaned just as if we were at an hotel.

Saturday, 22nd April.—A fine sunny morning, yet the snow was still seen on the mountains, seemingly close by. We were informed that during the latter part of the evening and night that after leaving "Summit" we had passed, at the crest of the mountain (Sierra Nevada), through a tunnel and along its side to the bank of the Truckee River. Truckee station is 119 miles from Sacramento, which river is the outlet of Lake Tahoe, whose surface is 6427 feet above the level of the sea. The railroad follows the banks of the Truckee to its big bend, a distance of 190 miles from Sacramento; from this point its course is north-east until it meets the Humboldt River. From Truckee to Humboldt, up to close on 7 this morning, we have passed the following stations:—Boca, Verdi, Reno, Camp, Clark's, Wadsworth, Hot Springs, White Plains, Brown's, Lovelocks, and Oreana. Breakfast at Humboldt at 7. A few Red Indians, adorned with feathers at the back of their heads, wearing mocassins, accompanied by some young girls clad in gaudy but mean attire, were loitering about the station, not at all warlike or dangerous in appearance, but looking careworn. The town consists of scattered wooden buildings in a flat, but mountains on both sides. The river flows about westward, and the railway follows up its banks to its source, and so on in the same general direction around the northern end of Great Salt Lake. Soon after breakfast we got on to a "sage-bush" plain many miles in extent, which although not at all well watered will fatten cattle, provided they can get water every three or four days. The feed, from six inches to a foot high, has a brown dry appearance very much resembling dried sage. No timber to be seen. Passing Raspberry, Winnemucca, Golconda, and Stonehouse stations, through about the same kind of country, we arrived at Battle Mountain, 101 miles from Humboldt, at 11.45, where we dined at a charge of a dollar, which we were informed would be the price for meals until we got to Buffalo. Passed some steep gradients between mountains, and now and then by side of a nice trout stream, with occasional beds of rushes by its side, to Palisades, 2.15, up steep gradients between rocky hills, the stream still running near us, in some places 20 or 30 feet wide. Some trout are caught six or seven pounds; but one mode of catching them is placing an explosive substance in the water, which generally destroys more than are brought to land. Stations between Battle Mountain and Elcho are Argenta, Shoshone, Be-o-wa-we, Carlin, and Moleen. We had twenty minutes allowed for supper at Elcho, 84 miles from Battle Mountain, and 607 from San Francisco, which we reached at 4 P.M. The same line of sage-bush country continued until we could see no more on account of the darkness, with very few trees, and those scrubby and small, and similar country we were told prevails up to Ogden, before reaching which place we passed Osino, Halleck, Tulasco, Wells, Independence, Pequop, Toano, Loray, Montello, Tecoma, Lucin, Terrace, Matlin, Kelton, Monument, Rozel, Promontory, Blue

Creek, Corinne, and Bonneville. Some passengers amused themselves by playing cards during the day, for boxes of figs and maple candy, eight cakes in a box for 25 cents, or parcels of sweetmeats for half a dollar, a few of which contained a prize in the shape of a greenback from 10 cents to a dollar, but more blanks than prizes; all offered for sale by the newsagent on the train, who also sold biscuits, and books of a miscellaneous character. Many passed away the time in reading poetical and other works; there were many admirers of Dickens, 'Pickwick,' 'David Copperfield,' 'Oliver Twist,' and other books being indulged in.

Sunday, 23rd April.—Morning dull and cloudy; snow on ground three or four inches deep. It had been snowing off and on the previous night. Arrived at Ogden 6.17 A.M. Turned out before that hour. Snowing a little. The Bear River running close by looked dirty from snow and rain. Left main line and went and had a good breakfast at restaurant close by; all nigger waiters; plenty of hot meat, corn cakes, and coffee; usual charge of a dollar. Mr. Bousfield and I went and booked ourselves at a small wooden station near, to go by the branch railway to Salt Lake City, State of Utah, 40 miles, all one class, for two dollars and a half; same commodious sort of carriages, but not so handsomely fitted up, and stoves instead of steam warming apparatus, which emitted a disagreeable smell. An immense plain or flat, partly sage bush, but apparently well watered, all the way from Ogden to Salt Lake City. Left at 7, and arrived at 9.30. Passed a few insignificant places on way. As we neared the city we found numerous small farms, peach and apple orchards, and gardens, with plenty of running water about, and mountains and hills in the distance, at the extreme back of the city, covered with snow. The station is large, built of wood, with plenty of waiting rooms, and fires lit in them. Yard of station not metalled, and, as well as the approaches, about six inches deep in mud, the snow having lately thawed. Got into a coach on leather springs, with a splendid pair of horses, crammed full of passengers. A large omnibus started just before us, loaded inside and out, and we were driven to Revere House, an hotel and restaurant of brick painted over, and boasting a "barber's shop;" within its walls, fully occupied, in Second South Street, with decent houses of brick and shops about it. Having deposited valise, &c., in a plain furnished but clean bedroom on the first floor — rather inconveniently situated, as I had to go through another room to get to it—we took a stroll. Some streets only partly metalled; footways wide, but mostly gravelled; streams of clear-looking water running on each side of many of the streets in the tables, and soft maple trees of a few years' growth on the edge of the footways of several streets. No business allowed to be transacted on Sundays, except in cigar and fruit shops, which were open, and the lager beer saloons are closed on Sundays. No spirituous liquors can be sold at any time. The suburbs full of gardens and peach orchards. Peaches and almonds were in blossom; snow hanging about the branches; very backward season we were told, nearly a month later than usual, such inclement weather in spring not having been known since the settlement. Very dirty walking, the snow having thawed, and the little snow now falling did not "lay," but was sufficient to make us put our top coats on. Some nice houses built at the foot and sides of the lofty hills in rear of the city, the tops being covered with snow. The Salt Lake is from ten to fifteen miles wide here; a steamer plies on it, and there are also some small craft. At the edges of the lake there are often three or four feet of salt so solid that one can walk on it. Brigham Young's house stands in a wide street, with very few houses in it. Its front is narrow towards the street, but extends a good depth into a large garden. On one side is a roomy paved yard, with large troughs, into which pure-looking water runs. A high wall next the street prevents people from looking in, but the upper story is visible, and the windows are furnished with Venetian shutters. The interior of the house forms in fact two houses, Brigham and his wives' harem being separated from the children and servants by an internal wall which runs right through the middle of the house. An imitation "beehive" is at the top of the main building, a spread eagle of plaster is placed over the entrance to the yard, and the representation of a lion over the portico of the house. The roofs are covered with chimneys, nineteen in number, each chimney representing a wife. There is telegraphic communication with the station, so that Brigham is constantly supplied with the latest news.

P

In consequence of the coldness of the weather Brigham had taken a few of his wives to a milder piece of country, about twenty odd miles down south by a river. We found the streets comparatively quiet. A few boys were playing marbles, and one or two galloping about on bare-backed horses, and a buggy or two in requisition, but otherwise everything was at a standstill. The theatre, a large building of rough stone, was closed. On returning to dinner we found the bar full of rough-looking diggers and miners of many different countries, with long boots on, all of them either smoking or chewing, and spitting on the floor, now and then taking a draught of very cold water, as they could get no beer or other liquor—a lucky thing from all appearances they couldn't, as they cursed and swore and made noise enough as it was. No Chinese among them; they have not ventured so far into the State of Utah as yet, and from what we could learn, if they attempted to do so they would meet with a rough reception and no encouragement. Besides, the climate would prove too cold for them in winter. The mines were said to be prosperous in the neighbourhood. Large piles of silver lead ore were outside agents' offices in one or two streets. A good dining room and excellent dinner; soup, roast breast of veal, bacon, asparagus, potatoes, and plenty of pastry and sweets for fifty cents; very cheap; charge for bedroom, seventy-five cents. After much coaxing we got the bar-keeper to fish out from below a pint bottle of Allsop's ale and some Byas's porter, very excellent, but at the monstrous price of half a dollar (2s. 1d.) per bottle. After dinner went to the Tabernacle about 2.30, it having ceased snowing, and passing Brigham's yard observed a neatly-dressed young woman milking a cow. To introduce ourselves we asked her the names of the fruit-trees in blossom, which having replied to satisfactorily, we went on our way. A great many visitors and miners were strolling about. Two tabernacles in a very large dirty piece of ground called a yard. The largest and newest a very big round building of brick, with a walk all round it under a portion of the roof supported on brick pillars, and with its roof looked in shape and appearance like a hippodrome. This was closed to-day, the weather being so cold, and the old one used instead. The latter, with shingle roof, is about 120 feet long, ceiling and walls inside plain, plastered and whitewashed over; a sweet-toned, although not very powerful, organ, and the singing was very good. Had conversation with one of the elders in the yard as to the wheat-growing capabilities of the State; he said, and firmly stuck to it, that 100 bushels had been grown to the acre, but it did not strike us to ask at the time whether he meant a Cheshire acre, and we left this elder and went into the Tabernacle with the impression that he was one of the greatest liars we had ever met with. About sixty well-dressed strangers attended, and were placed on forms to themselves, in a portion of one side of the church. The congregation were principally women and children, very plain in appearance and dress, but clean, reminding one of the style of the lower order of

Primitive Methodists in England some years ago. The choir were younger and better attired. Three or four men were reading newspapers, but whether they contained religious topics or not we could not see. There was no pulpit, but a raised desk used for reading, praying, and preaching, with a platform all round it. On each side the desk was arranged twelve plated silver quart cups and six cake baskets of a similar metal; also some large plain earthenware jugs, with a tumbler or two, for use of the elders and parson. The elders were old men, and looked very "seedy" indeed. Water was laid on beneath at one side of the desk. Whilst one of the elders gave out that sacrament was to be administered, and prayed, which he did in a very plain, uncultivated, and rather nervous manner, about half a dozen of his brethren were busily employed in breaking up into pieces about the size of a walnut, cakes of a light yellow colour, looking like sponge cake, and filling the baskets; but long before they had finished the elder had exhausted his yarn and another one had taken his place. Some of the elders in the midst walked off with the cups and proceeded to fill them with some liquid near the desk. Bousfield hearing a faint noise in filling the cups whispered to me, "Now we shall have a chance of tasting their wine and ascertaining whether it is as good as California." The elders having charged the cups, and being handed with the cake baskets over to a sufficient number of their brethren, they proceeded to distribute their favours. The strangers were dealt with to begin with.

The first, who looked like a Yankee schoolmaster, point-blank refused to touch either; second ditto; and so till it came to our turn, when Bousfield and myself declined, and the elders went off to the general body of the congregation, where they quickly disposed of the contents of their baskets and cups, the latter containing water only, and not wine. One child took a very long drink, the elder at last being obliged to forcibly take the cup away. A sermon followed, by a tall, well-spoken, grey-headed man, a companion of Brigham Young in the pilgrimage of 1847, who explained in a very fluent manner the difficulties in founding the settlement, the hardships they endured in dragging the women and children and their worldly effects from the then nearest seaport, Omaha, a distance of 1072 miles from the city, across mountains and the prairie, exposed to hunger and the attacks of the red man, driving wheelbarrows and dragging handcarts; their arduous task in forming the city, establishing farms and manufactories, and raising themselves to independence. Every now and then he would address himself to the elders on one side or the other by turns, "Did we not?" and the elders would cry out aloud "Yea, yea." After intimating that he was near exhausted from extra work in the Lord lately, Brigham their chief being away, he proceeded to lash notwithstanding everybody who he imagined did not recognize or believe in "Joseph Smith," the only true apostle, through whom they claimed. He was particularly hard on the Pope of Rome and the Czar of Russia, not forgetting the bishops (the English included); and, in fact, every one on the face of the earth, except themselves, was wrong. Notice of a lecture to the young by some Yankee was announced for 5, it being near that hour then. The evening was calmer, and we walked all round the place and found no narrow streets. Several dairies about, and farming in a small way, and making implements, &c., appeared to be the chief industries. About 7 we again passed Brigham's residence, where were assembled outside several girls and young lads, who had come from the lecture together, and were talking rather loudly and freely. One or two duennas were looking out from the balcony, smiling, but took no notice of the youngsters. One girl asked another for the key, apparently intending to go into their dormitory; she said that she had not got it, and so said all the rest. The key not being forthcoming it was proposed by one of the lads to take a walk, so they all started towards the hills, it being still light. Many shopkeepers and dealers had signs painted, some in gilt letters, over their doors, with words to this effect, "Holiness to the Lord," or "Zion's Co-operative Mercantile," or "Bank Institution," as the case might be, illustrated by a painted eye in the centre denoting "All-seeing Eye." On returning to Revere House we found the diggers gradually leaving for their huts in the vicinity of the mines; some still very noisy, but not sufficient quarrelling to come to blows. A darkie was employed with a "swab" cleaning the place from tobacco-juice, dirt, &c. After supper we retired to rest "beerless" at 10. The house was so full that one family of seven Yankee strangers were sleeping on the floor of the sitting-room. The bar-keeper told us that a new commodious hotel would pay very well, there not being sufficient accommodation for visitors to the city. Did not like the look of my next-door neighbour, through whose room I passed, yet could not bolt or lock my door, as bar-keeper was to call me in the morning. Slept with my leather belt round my waist under my shirt. Soon dozed off, being very tired.

Monday, 24th April.—Dry, but very windy and cold. Was awoke out of a sound sleep at 4.30 by bar-keeper giving me a grip in my throat; thought my end was near, but a light showed the object of the visit, and that I must "turn out" at once. Did so, and went down. Found Mr. Bousfield before me. The Yankee family were sleeping soundly on the floor, the door of their room being wide open. Had cup of coffee, and we were driven with a few others in the same coach to the railway station, leaving a little after 5 A.M. and arriving at Ogden about 7. The night had been very gusty, and several telegraph poles were blown down. Had an hour and a half for breakfast at Ogden. Observed an excellent walnut piano in dining saloon. Went to station, a little snow still on the ground, and purchased tickets for sleeping-car three nights to Chicago, 1525 miles, for eight dollars, and this was telegraphed to Omaha to keep place in saloon sleeping-car. Joined main line again of Pacific Railway Company, and left Ogden at 8.30 A.M. in sleeping-car 'Palmyra,' mountains being still in sight, along plains partly cultivated, running near a nice stream of water, a river in fact, passing Uintah, the Devil's Gate, Weber, the latter a thriving Mormon settlement in a large flat under some hills. Land, apparently good, under cultivation, and comfortable wooden houses, and cattle, horses, &c., about. Now and then through hills and between huge rocks, with steep precipices, snow lodging in declivities, and mountain streams flowing at foot—a pretty sight—brought us to about quarter past 9 o'clock. Then we ran through several short tunnels or sheds of wood to prevent the snow drifting on to the line in hollows. The "Devil's Slide" is a remarkable lofty smooth inclined plane of rock, gradually sloping towards the railway, with a rapid river running at foot, and a few straggling pine-trees. The scenery became very picturesque, countless quaint-shaped rocks, looking like Druidical remains, cropping out of sides of the hills until we neared Echo, a small station; then through a romantic gorge to "Castle Rock," another small station; after that through a short snow shed and up some very steep gradients and in a gorge to "Wahsatch," where we stopped at noon half an hour for dinner, 66 miles from Ogden. Snow was on the ground, and lay about the platform outside the restaurant. It was very cold on leaving the cars. The township small and scattered; all wooden houses. One man, who had been frostbitten, was laid on his back and his hands and feet vigorously rubbed with snow for five minutes until blood came from his nostrils, when he was got on his legs. Sometimes through hills and over extensive flats, crossing several nice streams of water, the Green River being often in sight, and passing through four or five snow sheds, snow lying on the ground nearly all the way, but the rails being perfectly free, we arrived at Bryan, 108 miles from Wahsatch, at 5.45 P.M., having passed through Almy, Evanston, Aspen, Piedmont, Bridger Carter, Church Buttes, and Granger. We had seen a quantity of wild fowl during the day, also some small herds of antelopes. Here we met the down train, the guards of which reported snow eastward all the previous night; and had "supper" in an excellent saloon kept by a German, the waitresses being also German. Capital repast of antelope steaks, very tender, with rich gravy and asparagus. Invested half a dollar in a pint of whiskey for use in the car. Air very cold outside, but comfortable in the cars. After leaving, the Green River was again in sight, and we passed the station of that name, also Rock Springs, and Salt Wells, when it was dusk.

Tuesday, 25th April. — Fine bracing morning. Turned out at 6 A.M., and found ourselves on the western slope of the Rocky Mountains, with the ground all round covered with snow, and alive with antelopes, which appeared in the distance to be huddled in herds, half frozen, and stationary. We passed last evening, and during the night, Point of Rocks, Hallville, Black Buttes, Bitter Creek, Table Rock, Red Desert, Wash-a-Kie, Creston, Separation, Rawlins, Greenville, Fort Steele, St. Mary's, Dana, Percy, Simpson, Medicine Bow, Como, Rock Creek,

Miser, Look-out, Cooper's Lake, and Wyoming. Breakfast at Laramie, 285 miles from Bryan, at 7.30, where we had a plentiful supply of antelope steaks, rolls, &c.; a good-sized, increasing township, of wood, having its bank, a small national theatre, machine shops, &c.; but the road and neighbouring country, far and near, was covered with snow. After leaving Laramie, we went through several long snow sheds, and up some steep gradients, to Sherman, having passed Fort Sanders, Red Buttes, and Harney, and seen a few buffaloes roaming about. At about 10.30 A.M. reached the highest point between the Atlantic and Pacific Oceans, 8242 feet above sea level. We had now got over the Rocky Mountains and reached the eastern slope. Passing Buford, Granite Canon, Otto, and Hazard, small stations, we arrived at Cheyenne, 57 miles from Laramie, at 1.30; a neat township. Excellent refreshment-room. Antelope steaks again; very good. A small covered waggon, drawn by a large pair of mules, in good condition, was waiting for passengers outside the station. Here we got the 'Cheyenne Daily Leader' for ten cents, from which we ascertained that Laura D. Fair, after twenty-seven days' trial, had been found guilty of murder of Judge Crittenden, in first degree. Also that John Boyer, a half-breed Indian, of the Sioux tribe, twenty-six years old, was hanged at Wyoming on the 21st instant, for shooting with his revolver, after a "frolic and dance," at a late hour, at Six Mile Ranch, near Fort Laramie, two men, named M'Clusky and Lowry. On the Sheriff asking him what he had to say, he stated that he died brave. "Look at me," he said; "I no cry; I no woman; I man; I die brave. I love Great Spirit, and am going to see him." After prayer, by Rev. J. D. Davis, the rope was placed round Boyer's neck, the black cap drawn over his face. In a moment he was dangling in the air, and was dead in about three minutes. He was executed inside the gaol, where a limited number of spectators only were allowed. A large crowd, however, assembled outside, who at times became very noisy and boisterous. Several cases of shooting, without a known cause, reported in that paper: one, a Miss Cunningham, not expected to survive her wounds. After leaving here, we continued on prairie land, an immense expanse of country, with no timber visible about, snow being on the ground for many miles; then none, except midst some low hills, for several miles; but it came on to snow heavily before getting to Sidney, 102 miles from Cheyenne, lying very thick on the ground, and on platforms, &c. Following stations between Cheyenne and Sidney: Archer, Hillsdale, Egbert, Pine Bluffs, Bushnell, Antelope, and Potter. Sidney is a very neat, rising township, with several good stores and refreshment saloons. We had "supper" at Dillon House, a large wooden building of Oregon pine, dovetailed, and painted over, with modern glass windows, boasting green painted Venetian shutters, and moreover four very good-looking, nicely-dressed, white waitresses. We had an excellent spread. Besides the usual antelope steaks, we had beef ditto, broiled ham and fried eggs, buckwheat cakes, and so on. Soon after leaving here, it began to rain hard, and continued to do so for many hours during the evening and night. We passed during this period a branch of a large river, called the Platte River, and the following stations, Lodge Pole, Julesburg, Big Spring, Brule, Ovalalla, Roscoe, Alkali, O'Fallons, North Platte, M'Pherson, Brady Island, Warren, Willow Island, Cayote, Plum Creek, Overton, Elm Creek, Stevenson, Kearney, Gibbon, Wood River, and Pawnee.

Wednesday, 26th April. — Still raining till about 7 A.M., when the weather cleared up, succeeded by a fine sunny day. The prairie looked brown throughout, with a little grass springing up here and there. No timber to be seen, or anything approaching to bush. Breakfast at Grand Island at 7; 260 miles from Sidney and 154 from Omaha. Some very good farms and houses in this neighbourhood, mostly a light sandy soil, with some dark loam; about the same description all the way to Omaha. A deal of ploughing going on, a pair of horses or bullocks being sufficient, the ground being light, and not ploughing deeper than 4 to 6 inches. Saw more horse-teams in use than bullocks. Quantities of geese, ducks, fowls, &c., about the farmyards, and plenty of birds about. A few fruit-trees, principally apples and peaches, here and there, with occasionally some small timber. A few cattle and horses seen.

Many waggons, travelling to and fro, each with pair of horses attached. We had gone by side of, and often crossed, a very wide river, called Main Platte, for many hours; sometimes in sight, and at other points not visible. Crossed a nice river, over a wooden viaduct, at North Bend township, 62 miles from Omaha. North bend of Platte River in sight, and signs of recent rains here. Stations passed—Chapman's, Lone Tree, Clark's, Silver Creek, Jackson, Columbus, Schuyler, and North Bend, reaching Fremont, 107 miles from Grand Island, at noon, where we dined; and a capital dinner, too — roast turkey, boiled ham, and so on. Now the railway is fenced off at intervals with timber (sawn by steam) posts and four rails. At and near Elkhorn large quantities of maize, stored in large wooden buildings, spaces of about 6 inches being left between the timber at sides to admit the air. We passed through a splendid country, nearly level for the last 20 miles, to Omaha, which we reached at 2.30 P.M., having seen a very scanty supply of timber for more than 1000 miles; but a great deal of splendid agricultural country, principally rich black loam, or light sandy soil. Omaha is 47 miles from Fremont, and the stations between those places are Valley, Elkhorn, Papillion, Gilmore, and Summit Siding. Here parted company with a few of the passengers, the wife of a German newspaper editor and her daughter amongst the number. They had travelled from San Francisco, were about to call on a relative in the country, and then proceed on a visit to friends in Germany, and try and induce some of them to emigrate. The mother provided herself on the journey with a full supply of brandy, the quality of which I can testify to, having found it "hot, sweet, and strong" more than once on crossing the prairie. Omaha has 14,000 inhabitants.

The town, mostly in a flat, contains many good buildings. The streets rather dirty from late rains. Observed a tramway in one street. Some hills overlook the town, and there are many nice residences on them, and at their feet and sides, with gardens attached. A large plain railway station, &c., of wood, and extensive plant here. After sundry shiftings and shuntings we were taken to near the side of a branch of the river Missouri (length of that river to Gulf, 4490 miles, supposed to be the largest in the world), and went on board an immense, roomy, steam ferry-boat, with hurricane deck, which at 2.45 P.M. took us across a narrow portion of the river, about two miles, I suppose, to join the Chicago, Rock Island, and Pacific Railway, which line passes through portions of the States of Iowa and Illinois. To show the extent of accommodation on board this boat (a river palace, in fact), two large four-wheeled baggage wagons, each drawn by four big horses, and laden with thousands of trunks and portmanteaus, apparently all leather, were on her deck, and were brought on board quickly and easily, the wharf being on a level with the steamer's deck. During our progress across, several passengers appeared to watch the waggons with some little anxiety, fearing that their baggage might be at the bottom of the pile and be crushed; but there's "nothing like leather;" ordinary boxes of wood would doubtless have been smashed like match-boxes, People would not like to travel by the inferior small boats on some of the rivers in England, after being accustomed to the Yankee boats. The train was waiting at a small station the other side of the river, and we had scarcely got into the car, when a heavy storm of rain and thunder came on. Left Missouri River, 493 miles from Chicago, at 4.40 P.M., having been delayed some time both sides of the river in shipping and transferring the baggage. Reached Council's Bluffs, 3 miles, about 5, where there is a large station and outbuildings of wood. A long and straggling town under a fine range of hills called The Bluffs, with a valley now and then. A very pretty, level, first-class agricultural country intervening, with here and there undulating land, some fenced off with wire. Crossed two beautiful streams of water, and went through a few short cuttings of soft strata, not very deep, and got to Avoca, 38 miles from the river, at 7 P.M. A small township, very muddy in appearance, from heavy rains, where we supped; after leaving which we proceeded through a good country, numerous mole-hills being seen up to dusk; and a great many four-railed timber fences about.

Thursday, 27th April.—Dull morning, but afterwards turned out a fine spring day. We were informed that similar country to yesterday afternoon was passed during the night and morning, also the following stations:—Atlantic, Anita, Adair, Casey, Dexter, De Soto, Boone, Des Moines, Mitchelville, Colfax, Newton, Kellogg, Grinnell, Malcolm, Brooklyn, Victor, Marengo, Homestead, Oxford, Iowa City, Downy, West Liberty, Atalissa, Moscow, Wilton, Fulton, and Walcott. We arrived at Davenport, 272 miles from Avoca, at 7.30 A.M., running right through a street of the city and stopping directly outside an excellent hotel, the river Mississippi (3200 miles in length) and Rock Island being in sight. This town has 22,000 people, and is prettily situated, containing numerous fine buildings, manufactories, shops, and places of business, with villa residences, gardens, greenhouses, &c., in suburbs. Going up some good stone steps at the entrance, we entered the hotel bar, and, signing our names in the visitors' book, proceeded to breakfast in a handsome large room, well attended by white male and female waiters, and were supplied with plenty of fish, beef and mutton, &c.; corn cakes as a matter of course. The Railway Company have a very large rolling stock here. Trees planted on each side of many of the streets, and indeed all over the place. Left Davenport at 8, and shortly after crossed over a branch of the noble river Mississippi by a wooden bridge, strengthened and kept together by iron suspending rods, &c.; about three-quarters of a mile to Rock Island, distant one mile; a very pretty spot indeed, surrounded by the river, containing very good buildings, some of them standing on elevated ground at the back. Leaving the island, we crossed another bridge of wood and iron as before, about a quarter of a mile over another portion of the river to the main land. Some good-sized steamers were plying on the river, and many rafts of timber were floating on it. Passing through the numerous orchards and gardens, and running, it may be said, almost by side of the river, we reached Moline, a thriving town, 3 miles from the Island; a few minutes' stay, and we passed on by orchards, farms, across streams of water, through a delightful country, to Colona, Geneseo, Atkinson, Annawan, Sheffield, Pond Creek, Tiskilwa, Peoria, Chillicothe, Sparland, and Henry, stopping occasionally at some of them, and arriving at Bureau, 69 miles from Davenport, at 11.30, where we were received with a very heavy shower. The township is small, in a beautiful valley well wooded on each side. Dining hall of restaurant well fitted up; first-rate dinner; chicken pie, &c.; slender Yankee-girl waitresses, dispensing their talk at a very rapid rate. Soon after leaving Bureau, we ran for a considerable way alongside the Chicago River, the narrowest part being about fifty yards, there being sufficient room on both sides for persons to walk on the sand. This river was in sight for many miles, as well as a canal very close to it, which in some places had overflowed its banks, and we had often to run through water three or four inches deep. Some barges were being towed by three or four horses; others were "steaming it." The rain had ceased, and a fine afternoon ensued, during which we passed some coal mines and several towns of some moment, but mostly scattered houses; the character of the country up to within a few miles of Chicago being generally light timbered, slight hills; principally flat, first-class agricultural land. Occasional valleys, well watered rivulets, good farm homesteads, plenty of horses, bullocks, milch cows, and pigs, a few small flocks of sheep, ewes with their lambs; some swampy land with surface water on nearing Chicago. Only went through a few short cuttings and a couple of slight tunnels all day. Arrived at Chicago at 4 P.M. (half-past 1, San Francisco time). Stations between Bureau and Chicago are:— Peru, La Salle, Utica, Ottawa, Marseilles, Senaca, Morris, Minooka, Joliet, Mokena, Bremen, Blue Island, and Englewood. Several passengers left here to go by other routes. The majority during the journey seemed to be persons above ordinary intelligence, being conversant with the works of many English and American authors, poetical and otherwise, particularly with the works of Charles Dickens, who was very highly spoken of by the Yankees, and several were engaged in reading his literature, a few only occupying themselves, male and female, in playing cards, but not for money. Population of Chicago in 1860 was 109,260; 1870, 298,983; now said to be over 300,000. Situate in a flat, on what was a swamp, on Lake Michigan. Full of shipping and steamers. Buildings of all sorts; "first-class" to the poorest; many of brick, but the greatest portion of wood. Tramways through the streets. Many very lofty spires to be seen, and chimneys of manufactories. Station and buildings very lofty and extensive, built of brick and wood; commodious refreshment ladies' and gentlemen's rooms; large printed notices posted up, "Beware of pickpockets and confidence men." These confidence men are smart, well-dressed fellows, who, seeing a stranger hesitate on getting out of a car, proffer advice as to the best and least expensive hotel to stay at, cheapest mode of getting there, &c., which generally ends in having your pockets emptied, and when you want your baggage, it has disappeared through confederates, as well as your kind friend. Paid three dollars for sleeping ticket, and left at 5.30 P.M. for Buffalo, 539 miles, per Lake Shore and Michigan Southern Railway, in sleeping saloon car, 'Golden Gate,' Mr. Bousfield going round to Detroit by another route. It had rained occasionally during the afternoon. After skirting one side of the city, going through streets, we went through flat, marshy ground, it and the railway in many places covered with surface water, Lake Michigan being visible for many miles, and so broad that one could not see the other side, and on by Englewood and Pine to La Porte, a small town, the country being scrubby and sandy, and much covered with soft maple, scrub oak, and some pines and firs, mostly small timber, from which the land in many spots was being cleared, and as it came on dusk the stumps on fire lit up the neighbourhood and had a pretty appearance. Scattered farmhouses could be seen, as also a saw-mill near one small township, with a large quantity of timber, cut and uncut, lying about. Supped at La Porte, 58 miles from Chicago, at 7.30. After leaving here, the country appeared to improve, much more being cultivated, but still "clearing" going on here and there, the timber appearing to be getting larger.

Friday, 28th April.—Fine sunny morning. We had passed during the night and early morning numerous townships, large and small, called Carlisle, South Bend, Elkhart, White Pigeon, Sturgis, Coldwater, Hillsdale, Hudson, Adrian, Sylvania, Goshen, Ligonier, Kendallville, Corunna, Edgerton, Bryan, Stryker, Wauseon, Swanton, Toledo, a large town containing about 29,000 inhabitants, Elmore, Fremont, Clyde, Bellevue, Monroeville, Norwalk, Wakeman, Oberlin, Elyria, and Berea, reaching Cleveland, a rapidly-rising manufacturing place of 100,000 inhabitants, the population of which was only 43,417 in 1860, at 7.30 A.M. We were close to Lake Erie. An immense lot of railway plant here. The town is well built, mostly on a flat, but partly on gentle slopes, with small orchards, gardens, &c., attached. Railway station about same dimensions and style as at Chicago, from which we are distant 356 miles, and 183 from Buffalo. Large breakfast and dining room, &c., in the station; plentiful supply of edibles in the shape of fish, &c.; nigger waiters. Felt very hungry this morning; disposed of fish, chop, steak, potatoes, poached egg and toast, roll, corn cake, &c. In the middle of repast caught the eye of Father Byrne at the other end of table; he was going to visit Niagara as well as myself, so we now travelled together. He related a chapter of accidents which had befallen some of our fellow-passengers, the principal being to the Rev. Fletcher, who, in endeavouring to show his agility in getting out of the car at Sacramento, broke a leg in two places, and had to be left behind to the tender mercies of Yankee doctors and exorbitant charges. Colonel Whitmore got the blight in both eyes, which blinded him for several days, and obliged him to stop at Ogden, Mr. Kitchener kindly staying and looking after him. The doctor ran up a bill of 26l. Continuing along a very good agricultural and pastoral country, and passing Euclid, Willoughby, Painesville, Madison, Geneva, Ashtabula, Kingsville, and Girard, we arrived at Erie, another large town 95 miles from Cleveland, at 11, the weather being very fine. Here we stopped a few minutes, and proceeded on to Ripley, Westfield, and Brocton Junction, a very neat station, where there was a nice greenhouse full of various flowers in bloom, including geraniums, polyanthuses, &c. We stopped at Dunkirk for five minutes, a bustling place, containing several manufactories for machinery, &c.; locomotive works here, and several branch lines springing from thence. It is 48 miles from Erie and 21 from Buffalo. The railroad runs by the outskirts of the town, and across and along streets. Passing Silver Creek and Angola, we arrived at Buffalo at 12.40 A.M. The character of the country between Chicago and Buffalo appeared to be about as follows:—Swampy, low, scrubby land for the first few miles, then good agricultural and pastoral country nearly all the way; but in some instances more expensive to clear, from the greater quantity of small timber and bush than on the land traversed between Omaha and Chicago, the soil not being so rich, and from its moist, wet nature, requiring draining. Drainage pipes were lying about on the ground at some spots, and men engaged in laying them. It certainly was a most delightful ride; now through a forest of soft maple, pines, &c.; then by farms neatly fenced off, some "dog leg;" peach and apple orchards and a small vineyard occasionally; a few sheep and lambs on almost every farm; nice streams of water, some narrow, but deep in places. There was a very small steamer on one. The great Lake Erie occasionally seen. This railroad appeared to be inexpensively formed, there being very few cuttings and bridges. Buffalo contains over 118,000 inhabitants. In 1860 it had 81,129; 1870, 117,715. The town is built on a large flat, and fronts the lake; some few craft on it. Contains some very wide streets, large buildings, public institutions, churches, &c., with tall spires. The railway station, &c., of wood, very large. Dined at "Centre" Dining Hall, part of the station; a very good spread for 75 cents. Waitresses, white; each had her table to attend to, and did not interfere with one another. Excellent bottled stout (Byas's) 25 cents, pints. Went in an omnibus three-quarters of a mile to station of New York Central Railway; charge, 50 cents. Left for Niagara Falls at 2.30 P.M., in a freight train; very slow affair. Did not arrive till 5 P.M.—only 22 miles—from frequent delays on road. We crossed two or three small arms of the lake over bridges; the lake was in sight most of the way. Country pretty good; about same as other side of Buffalo. Passed four very small stations: Lower Rock, Black Rock, Laselle, and Tonawanda. Niagara, a nice clean town, with good, wide, well-kept streets and footways, and excellent brick and stone-built houses and shops. Streets mostly macadamized; dull at present, the season for visitors not having set in. Two hotels—the 'International,' Niagara, and the 'Clifton,' on the Canada side, the latter containing about 500 rooms; only open during the season, commencing about 6th May, and then for about four months only. There is a town called Lewiston, about 5 miles below Niagara on the American side. Stayed at Spencer House, a commodious, comfortable hotel, close to railway station. Young nigger waiters. Meals, a dollar; bed, 75 cents. Gas and water laid on, and stove in bedroom. Same regulation with respect to key of room as at San Francisco. After a "wash and brush up," Father Byrne and I proceeded in an open hack-carriage and pair—a good turn-out—to view the Falls, close on a mile ride. Crossed the suspension bridge, about 1280 feet, at a walking pace, some 150 feet above the bed of the lake, the American and Niagara Falls being both in sight. Paid toll, 1½ dollar; and for the carriage, one hour and a half, 4 dollars. Ascended a tower about 60 feet high, free of charge, and had a fine view of the Falls and country around, which looked very green and picturesque; then we descended and put on, in a room where a dozen similar suits were hanging up, waterproof dresses and sou'westers, and went with a guide down a steep rocky incline and pathway, very rough and narrow, close to the lake, cut out of the solid rock, in sight of the cataract, and approached as close under the Canada or Great Horse-shoe Falls as the spray would allow us. They are 165 feet high, and occupy nearly the whole width of the lake. A rainbow was across them in a slanting direction, producing a pretty effect connected with the approaching sunset, and as the sun got lower shades of dark green appeared on the water. It was a nice bright afternoon for a view, the guide said. The charge for each waterproof dress, &c., was 1 dollar, on hearing which, what with the toll and the carriage fares, Father Byrne got very wrath, exclaiming, " Faith, when I get back to my parish, I won't stir out of it again in a hurry." We recorded our names in the visitors' book for nothing, which, I told him, was something towards expenses, but he couldn't see it, and no inducement could get him to visit the "hot springs," a mile or two beyond. One portion of the rock at top of the Falls had given way, and no water was flowing over it, which marred the effect a little; but the guide said there was every probability of its being again covered with water next winter. The Clifton Hotel, with its balconies, is a fine imposing building, commanding extensive views of the lake, Falls, &c. The township of Clifton is about 2 miles farther down the river. The Falls on the American side, about 160 feet high, are not so broad or imposing as the Canada Falls; but the "Bridal Veil" just below, is a sweet sight. Narrow and tapering from top to bottom, some 150 feet, its base was formed of ice, gradually melting; the fall of water dashing round and on it looking in appearance like frosted sugar on a cake. The spring was a late one, otherwise all traces of ice would have been removed ere now; very cold ride, particularly in crossing the suspension bridge. Met three of our Australian passengers at supper; very good spread; amongst other dishes, the old country "ham and eggs." The billiard-room was in full fling all the evening; the bar was next to it, and the billiard-marker also attended to the liquor department, with the assistance of a young nigger, but the players and spectators were very moderate with the drinks. At 10 P.M. received, through a young nigger, the compliments of Father Byrne, wishing to see me in his bedroom. On proceeding there found two smoking-hot glasses of whisky punch, which we soon polished off, the Father's countenance approaching a beaming character, having apparently forgotten the dollars expended in the afternoon. Turned in at 10.30 P.M.

Saturday, 29th April.—Fine morning. Up at 5.30. Father Byrne had a hasty breakfast, having been delayed in "shaving close." Saw him off by railway, as he intended to go to New York by water, down the Hudson River, about 324 miles in length. Went to Goat Island, American side, and walked around it, about two miles and a half, which has a good view of the Falls, &c. Left Niagara for Buffalo about 7.30, and arrived at 9, fare a dollar, which was paid on the journey; rain set in about half way, and continued to pour down steadily till noon. Went in omnibus for

50 cents to New York and Erie Railway Station, Michigan Street; left valise and opossum rug, and paid for sleeping car, 2 dollars; broad gauge, double track, and steel rails. Then went to Continental Hotel just opposite, to warm myself in the bar, it being very chilly and damp; had glass of whisky, hot; a large bar, walls covered with sporting prints, principally celebrated trotting horses in harness, "Dexter," "Shepherd Knapp," and others. Shortly after mounted overcoat and strolled about the city in the rain. Streets generally very wide, many paved with small stones, footways flagged, a few of wood. Walked through "Main Street," the principal one, very wide, and over three miles long. Tramways about Main Street and some others. Several small carts, drawn by large black dogs, the size and appearance of Newfoundland dogs, but surly-looking and muzzled. Women had the care of these carts, which were generally laden with washing. Grape-vines trained on trellis-work to most houses towards the suburbs; omnibuses and carriages numerous and well horsed. Saw the second drunken man since leaving San Francisco, he was being led by a child. Six very smart white waitresses at dinner; well-supplied table; soup, fish, fowl, &c., cost 75 cents. The afternoon and remainder of day turned out very fine. Left Buffalo by "Lightning Express" train at 2.45 P.M. Sleeping coach the most elegantly fitted-up I had met with; seats of carved walnut, with cushions of crimson velvet, Brussels carpets, curtains of tapestry, large mirrors,

paintings on sides or walls, ceilings in fresco, windows of French plate-glass; car lighted with gas, and warmed by patent hot-water furnace; a wash-room at each end well fitted up. Four sleeping coaches connected with this line, named 'Jay Gould,' 'Colonel James Fisk, jun.,' 'Morning Star,' 'Evening Star.' Went (car 'Morning Star') through same sort of level, good country, passing Lancaster, Alden, Darien, Attica, Linden, and Dale, and a long but slight cutting, on to Warsaw, a very pretty town, lying below the railway in a deep, long, beautiful valley, with small rivulets of water intersecting it; leaving here in a few minutes, we shortly afterwards went through a deep cutting, and then passed some nice waterfalls running into deep gullies, with very small streams of pure water every now and then. Passed over the Tennessee Valley Canal, and went through a large extent of good farming country, with charming views, passing Gainesville, Castile, Portage, Hunts, Nunda, Swains, Canaseraga, and Burns, and many excellent farmhouses, residences, &c., reaching Hornellsville, 91 miles from Buffalo, at 6 o'clock. Town in a narrow well-watered valley; signs of recent rains about; long plain station, excellent dining hall; a good hot supper for 75 cents; white waitresses; good dessert on table, including very fine apples. A succession of well-grassed flats, valleys, rocky hills by running streams, forest, &c., and some beautiful scenery, straggling farm-houses and cottages, and small towns, were passed up to dusk, and when the houses were lit up they looked very pretty in the distance. Now and then you would see a mother or elder sister giving the youngsters a Saturday-night's wash and scrub, as in the old country, and fathers ("hired men") doing the like to themselves outside their dwellings, on their return from work. Turned in at 9, the night proving a chilly one, in the most roomy and convenient berth I had slept in, everything being luxuriously fitted up, and the curtains exceedingly handsome, like in a drawing-room.

Sunday, 30th April.—Fine sunny morning. Turned out at 5.30 A.M. Conductor says passed through about same description of country during the evening and night, and following towns:—Canisteo, Adrian, Cameron, Rathboneville, Addison, Painted Post, Corning, Elmira, Wellsburg, Chemung, Waverley, Barton, Smithboro, Owego, Campville, Union, Binghamton, Kirkwood, Great Bend, Susquehanna, Deposit, Hancock, Callicoon, Cochehecton, Narrowsburg, Pine Grove, Lackawaxen, Shohola, Port Jervis, Otisville, Howells, and Middletown, the latter place 265 miles from Hornellsville. Went through several beautiful valleys this morning, with plenty of running streams and small rivers; moderate hills on each side, covered with small timber, principally pine and light bush, the country being green nearly all through; a few hills showed a bold, rocky face; some rapid streams and narrow rivers often ran close to and by side of the railway, in some places overflowing their banks, being swollen by recent rains; occasionally a weir was seen with foaming water running over its top. Many excellent farms, with orchards of apple, pear, and peach in blossom, and so on to Paterson, a fine town containing about 34,000 people, 51 miles from Middletown, having passed Hampton, Goshen, Greycourt, Oxford, Monroe, Turners, Newburg Junction, Southfields, Sloatsburg, Ramapo, Suffern, Ramseys, Allendale, Hohokus, and Ridgeway. We drove right through Paterson, and on a level country by Passaic and Rutherford Park, eight miles from New York, over a viaduct about a quarter of a mile long, on a river, and then in a tunnel cut through the solid rock, with deep cuttings about a mile and a half long, reaching Jersey City, one mile from New York, at 7.30 A.M., being thirty minutes late.* Jersey City is on the Hudson, directly opposite New York. It is a place of rapid growth, having only had 29,226 inhabitants in 1860, which increased to 81,744 in 1870. The railway station is a very extensive one, but built in the usual plain Yankee inexpensive style, of wood. Here my brass ticket for my portmanteau, given me at San Francisco, was exchanged for a paper one, to take me across in the ferry-boat, and my address was required, to know where to send it. I mentioned Lovejoy's Hotel, Park Road, to the conductor, who referred me to an agent, who said that that hotel was closed, and that the late proprietors, two Britishers, had taken the 'Cosmopolitan' hotel, corner Chambers Street and West Broadway, to which I determined to go. Having paid the agent a dollar to "coach" me to the 'Cosmopolitan,' walked a short distance and went on

* Population of New York in 1653, 1120; 1756, 10,530; 1868, 1,000,000.

board the 'Susquehanna,' a very large steam ferry-boat, where I was assailed by Irish porters and niggers, soliciting favour of introduction to hotels and restaurants without number; the answer "I'm fixed," was generally sufficient to stop further solicitation. The water was very smooth in crossing, and there was every prospect of a fine day. It is called the Pavonia Ferry. On landing the agent popped me, with two others, into a spruce coach on leather springs, drawn by a slashing pair of horses, and I was left at the 'Cosmopolitan' hotel, about three quarters of a mile from the waterside, at 9 A.M., my two companions having to proceed farther on, and I did not feel as much fatigued from my 3492-mile journey as I should have done after a 250-mile ride in a pent-up railway carriage in England. This hotel is kept by N. and S. J. Huggins, two respectable-looking young Englishmen, in the "European" style, seventeen niggers, old and young, being employed in the establishment, one witty old Irishman, "John," being at the head of the porters; servants upstairs, females. It is built of brick, painted drab colour, six stories high, and has its lift or elevator, worked by steam power. Being a corner house, tramways run in four different directions outside it. Entrance hall laid with black and white marble in large diamond-shaped pieces; counters of white marble, part sides pink-coloured ditto, with easy lounges and chairs, continually occupied by persons in and out all the morning reading the papers, just as on week days. A telegraph office in the hall. Very large bar open on

West Broadway side; floor and counters same as entrance hall, with refreshments, hot and cold, for the general public. The breakfast and dining hall for strangers visiting the house, termed the "Refectory," is on other side, looking into, and with entrance from, Chambers Street. It is a long and lofty, but rather narrow apartment, with ornamental gilt cornices, counter, floor, &c., same as entrance hall; small tables to hold four, are ranged on each side of the room. Having signed my name in visitors' book, and got "fixed" for bedroom, No. 96, on the fourth floor, went up in lift and took possession; charge, dollar and a half a day; meals in addition, paid for as you had them, the waiter in attendance giving you a ticket of what you "bolt," and you pay the amount to the clerk at the counter, the "niggers" not fingering any money. Had breakfast at 10; felt very hungry, having only had a few apples, which I took into the car from dessert at Hornellsville, last evening at 6. Had sirloin-of-beef steak and mushrooms, hot potatoes, corn cake, rolls and coffee, at a cost of 80 cents. Visitors, male and female, continually coming down to breakfast up to noon; a separate room for ladies if they wished. The head waiter, a pompous middle-aged nigger, in a full suit of black, and white tie, was engaged in teaching a young one to make up table-napkins into fantastic shapes. An excellent barber's shop, lavatory, and boot and shoe cleaning establishments on the premises. At about 11.30 the baggage-waggon brought my portmanteau safe and sound through its journey of 3368 miles, not having seen it since I left San Francisco. After a slight lunch at 1, went in car up Eighth Avenue to the Central Park, about three miles from the hotel, the favourite rendezvous of the New Yorkers, through very broad streets, at a charge of 5 cents. Fine open space of ground in front, and wide main carriage and horse entrance, where no pedestrians are allowed to walk, there being nice footways on each side formed of very fine sand and asphalt, the drives and walks being remarkably smooth and firm. The Park contains 843 acres, and is one of the largest in the world. It is bounded by Fifth and Eighth Avenues, and Fifty-ninth and One-hundred-and-Tenth Streets. Carriage roads completed 10 miles, the principal road or drive being sufficiently wide to admit of its being used by several vehicles at the same time, and long enough for an afternoon's drive without going over the same ground twice. Bridle paths, 5 miles; walks, 23 miles. Besides a reservoir containing 35 acres, called the old Croton Reservoir, and the new reservoir, 106 acres, there is a pond of 4 acres near Fifty-ninth Street, a lake between Seventy-second and Seventy-eighth Street, containing 20 acres, pool near Eighth Avenue, 2 acres, and the Lock and Harlem Lake, 14 acres.

A building, called the old State Arsenal, is now occupied as park offices; and a museum, in which are some splendid specimens of statuary and bas-reliefs. A great portion of the grounds is beautifully planted with ornamental trees and rare flowering and other shrubs, with here and there beds of flowers (tulips being in bloom). Certain roads are devoted to equestrians, to the exclusion of vehicles, and some walks entirely to pedestrians. There is a beautiful marble arch and several ornamental bridges of cut stone, &c., and pleasure-boats for hire on the lakes. In winter thousands of skaters enjoy themselves on the ice. There is a large level space of green sward prepared for and allotted to military exercises; also large plots for botanical and horticultural purposes; rustic houses to sit down and rest in — some very picturesque, on rising ground—and splendid views of the Hudson and palisades opposite. Sheep were depasturing on an extensive portion of land, not planted, termed the large lawn. Turned out a rabbit or two, midst grass, off a retired avenue. At half-past two, people, of both sexes and all ages, began to flock in, all well-dressed, but some very "fast" indeed, the carriage and horse drives being also well patronized, mail phaetons and carriages, with four-in-hand buggies, trotting-horses, &c., &c. Some sported livery servants, but the greater number drove their own vehicles; all being fashionably dressed, with well-appointed traps. Did not see a mean vehicle in the place. All went off quiet, without any disturbance, although some thousands were about. At four took a stroll in the neighbourhood, along its broad streets, and large piles of brick and other buildings, from seven stories downwards. The stars and stripes floated over numerous hotels and liquor saloons. Only druggists, fruit and confectioners' stores were open. The afternoon being very fine, there was a multitude of people about, the cars being quite full, which took a deal of traffic off the footways. Some were dressed very fast. Did not meet with a meanly-dressed person. In the evening the bells of many of the 255 places of worship known in New York were tolling for service. The Protestant Episcopal Churches are in the ascendant (53 in number); the Presbyterians next (41); then the Catholics (31). The Baptists follow close at their heels (27). There is also " the Dutch Reformed Congregational" (only 4 places of worship); " Methodist Episcopal Unitarian" (2); " Universalist" (2); " Friends" (3); " Jewish Synogogues" (16); " Lutheran" (9); " African Methodist Episcopal" (3). Miscellaneous includes — " Christian Israelites," Coloured Congregational," "Mariner's Madison," "Primitive Christians," " Welsh Congregational," and others. On returning to the hotel, during a slight shower in the evening, found " Old John " sitting in his easy seat in the entrance hall, watching his five young niggers, who sat in a row, waiting for custom. The duty of one consisted in receiving, at the hands of old John and one young " baggage " nigger, luggage, for which he gave a ticket, and entered it in a book. One attended to the lift, another brushed gentlemen's clothes in the hall, and the fifth attended to private rooms upstairs. When old John dozed a little, the five young niggers made all sorts of signs with their fingers, and grimaces with their faces, putting on ghastly smiles, grinning horribly, and rolling their eyes about as niggers only can. Suddenly he would awake, crying out, " Silence there, you boys!" and walk up and down the hall with an air of great importance; then, scratching his head, he would suddenly leave the hall as if on urgent business, but in reality to have a "go" of whisky at the public bar, which the young niggers knew well enough, and indulged in free laughter and play during his short absence, dislodging a skullcap from the head of one of them, disclosing a bald pate, his wool having been removed in consequence of a fever. Returning in about two minutes, the cry of " Silence there, you boys!" was repeated three times with vehemence, which had the effect of restoring order. One of the proprietors was present at the counter nearly the whole time, never interfered, and seemed to enjoy the fun as well as others. Only a few negroes, comparatively speaking, are employed at hotels, &c., the "Northerners" still hating that race as much as ever, although most of them are intelligent and can write and talk excellent English. One Yank told me at supper, in a most grave manner, that " a nigger has no brains:" also that when Queen Victoria dies, he guessed there would be a " tarnation" row about the throne in England. Tried American brewed ale, the best draught they could produce, called " Toby." It was heavy, and of a dark colour; not very good. A little brown jug, holding about three quarters of a pint, for 15 cents. English bottled ale or porter, pints, 25 cents, or quarter dollar. Spirits 10 cents a glass. Found bedroom neatly furnished, and very clean, especially the linen. Gas and water laid on. No mosquitoes, &c., to trouble one.

Monday, 1st May.—Fine morning, and also day. Rode about the "City of Bricks" in cars on tramways all the morning. Most of the buildings of brick; some painted over. Many of iron, painted over white or drab. The Great Central Hotel is an immense lofty building of iron, painted white. Elevation of a great many buildings very lofty. Went in Eighth Avenue car to 245, West Eighteenth Street, to I. Bawden's, from my native town, who did nothing else but turn out " vests " by sewing machines, and a few hands to complete the parts the machines could not. Does not take orders, but is employed by different houses, who supply the measurements and material. It being spring, was averaging about 1000 waistcoats a week, and during summer months would turn out about 700 per week. Lives in a nice wide street, in a well-furnished house, his own property, acquired by industry, since he left England, about twenty-four years since. Dined there, and in afternoon went to his brother-in-law (Mr. Bowden), 155, West Twenty-ninth Street, who has been in New York for thirty years, first as a cabinet-maker, but latterly with his son, manufacturing machinery and models. Went over premises, upstairs and down (Mr. Bowden's private property), and saw many ingenious pieces of machinery, steam-engines, &c., on a very minute scale, aiding in production of models, &c. In evening met at 'Cosmopolitan' a friend from Adelaide, Mr. Child, who purposed settling in Boston; passed very pleasant evening with him.

Tuesday, 2nd May.—Weather about same as yesterday. In the morning went to see the Astor House, the oldest hotel in New York; the interior like a palace of marble, stairs and all. It is situate in Broadway, opposite the City Hall; it is celebrated for its chops and steaks cooked in English style, and from the immense bar you can see the process of cooking going on, the cook and assistants in their clean white aprons and paper caps. The very long, winding counter with its white marble top is covered with edibles, solids, and sweets, and scores are constantly arriving and going, eating and drinking, sitting on tall cane-bottomed stools, similar to office stools. Although only the spring of the year, a favourite sweet called strawberry short-cake was exhibited in considerable quantities, and loudly called for at 25 cents. It consists of sweet cakes, interlaid with fresh strawberries, and is really a delicious morsel. There are book-stalls on each side of the lobby before entering the bar. Then went to the City Hall, standing in a small triangular park of ten acres, formerly called the "Common" or the "Fields," where military drills were held. On the evening of July 9, 1776, a brigade of the American army was drawn up here, and heard the Declaration of Independence read. It is surrounded by a strong iron fence, and is beautifully laid out with flowering shrubs and plants. The hall is a fine specimen of architecture, 65 feet high, 216 feet long, and 105 feet broad; it conbines the Ionic, Corinthian, and Composite order of architecture, rising in regular gradations. Front and ends from basement are built of white marble from Stockbridge, Mass.; the rear of freestone. Rising from the centre of the roof is a cupola, overlooking a large part of the city, in which a sentinel is stationed to give alarm in case of fire; on the top of the cupola is a figure of Justice. A little beneath is a four-dial clock, illuminated at night. By the side, in the rear, is a tower in which there is a bell weighing 9910 lbs., rung only in case of fire. The numerous rooms are occupied by the Marine Court, office of chief of police, sheriff's jury, mayor's office, county clerks, city library, clerk of the common council, &c. On the second story is the Governor's room, 52 feet by 20 feet, principally used as a reception room, decorated with some fine portraits of statesmen, &c. The writing desk of Washington, upon which he penned his first message to Congress, is exhibited. In the wings are the council chambers for aldermen, furnished with the chairs used by the first Congress, the mayor occupying the one used by Washington when inaugurated first President. Nine years in building, and cost 538,734 dollars; open all day to visitors, free. Within the Park also stands a building called the Rotunda, 54 feet in diameter, formerly used for exhibiting panoramic paintings, afterwards as a post-office, and now used by Croton Water Department. Fronting the City Hall is a magnificent fountain, the circumference of its basin being 300 feet; the central jet is very large and high, with numerous arching jets of extreme beauty. The jets rise from the flowers of the lotus or, Egyptian water lily, and the basin is surrounded by a white marble rim; this is encircled by a row of flowering shrubs and plants, and evergreens, the whole being enclosed within an iron railing. In afternoon went to Central Park, 3 to 5 being fashionable carriage promenade; many handsome equipages and some superior horses there; the attendance hailing from the "upper classes;" very few pedestrians; nurse-girls and children well represented; no "lower orders" of society to be seen. At 5 went in small boat from foot of Whitehall Street to Governor's Island in the bay nearest the battery, about 1090 yards distant; this island contains 72 acres, a pretty spot, sloping on all sides from its centre to the water. A fortification in form of a star, mounting 120 heavy guns, is on central summit, called "Fort Columbus." On north-west verge of the island is Castle William, a circular structure, with three tiers of port-holes full of cannon. It is about 60 feet high, and 600 in circumference. A battery on south-west part commands Buttermilk Channel between the island and the Long Island shore. Fort constantly garrisoned. Small boats are only used, and it would not be safe in rough weather to cross. Boatman's charge, including detention, 25 cents., lowest charge is 12½ cents. At "Minstrels," an excellent Darkie representation in evening.

Wednesday, 3rd May.—Slight shower in morning; cloudy, cold day. At New York Society Library, University Place, between Twelfth and Thirteenth Streets in morning; about 40,000 volumes, but affording room for 100,000; was incorporated in 1700; the present, a new building in the Italian style, having a frontage of 52 feet; approach up stone steps into entrance hall; the middle window contains a triple window with Corinthian pilasters. Going from the reading room up an iron staircase you approach two galleries, one on each side, with ornamental iron balustrades, divided into alcoves for books. The whole building is conveniently and comfortably arranged, but for space and beauty is very inferior to the Melbourne Library. Got "jammed" up twice in narrow busy streets like Cheapside and Cannon Street to get to it. Met Mr. Child by appointment, and went for a stroll. Visited one of the "fastest" liquor stores in the city; the girls, most fashionably and extravagantly attired, waited on by a host of admirers and spoonies; iced champagne, hock, &c., flying about; for a bottle, you would get no change, though, out of a 20-dollar piece, but you might retire and hold sweet commune with an elegant damsel. Went down Broadway and into Wall Street (as full of banking houses as Lombard Street); saw manager of Bank of British North America, No. 44, to get a draft cashed. No advice, through some error, from Sydney. The Treasury fronts this street. It is at the corner of

Wall and Nassau Streets, extending through to Pine Street; it is a beautiful building, the principal material being white marble from Massachusetts; Doric style of architecture, in imitation of the Pantheon at Athens; the building is in the form of a parallelogram, 200 feet long, 90 feet wide, and 80 feet high. Fronting on Wall Street is a portico with eight Doric columns, 32 feet high, and close on 6 feet in diameter, reached by a flight of eighteen granite steps from the street, extending the whole length of the building. The Rotunda, a principal hall for transaction of business, is 60 feet in diameter, lighted by a skylight from the top; the dome is supported by sixteen Corinthian columns, adorned with caps of exquisite workmanship. Whole eight years in building, at a cost of nearly two million dollars. Went up and down the real Broadway, but not so wide as expected; in fact, a third less than some colonial streets, but the great elevation of the numerous handsome buildings probably detracts from the appearance of the width. The Post Office is upon Nassau, Cedar, and Liberty Streets—narrow, busy streets; an old, low, rotunda-shaped stone and brick building, with plenty of internal accommodation, but exterior very mean in appearance. It was the place of worship of the Middle Dutch Church from the close of the 17th century until 1844. The British used it as a barracks when they first took possession of the city in 1776; afterwards converted into an hospital; subsequently used as a riding school; in 1790 again devoted to Divine worship. It was purchased by the Government in 1861 for a Post Office, for 250,000 dollars, but wants pulling down sadly, and being rebuilt. Opposite entrance to Wall Street, and fronting Broadway, is Trinity Church, a beautiful edifice. The "Corporation" is one of the oldest and by far the wealthiest of the kind in the States. The church is built of a handsome brown stone from New Jersey; the style is Gothic, of the chastest character; it is 192 feet in length by 80 in width, with walls 60 feet high; the tower and spire, the most elaborate and costly in the States, rise to an altitude of 284 feet; an excellent chime of bells in tower ; visitors may ascend by a spiral stairway of 308 steps to the height of 250 feet, from whence magnificent views of the city and surrounding scenery may be obtained. The first edifice upon present site was "reared" in 1696, during reign of William and Mary ; Queen Anne endowed it and presented it with silver communion plate. Building enlarged in 1735 and 1737; in great conflagration in 1776 was destroyed, and not rebuilt till after the war. The then new edifice was completed in 1790. In 1839 it was pulled down and the present costly structure was commenced; completed in 1846.

The yard is clean and the walks well kept; about an acre enclosed by iron rails and walls, and surrounded on every side by streets, and contains some very old tombstones. There is a handsome memorial cut-stone obelisk, the shape of a tower, in remembrance of the imprisoned American Independence men, during the war. It is surrounded with beds of tulips, now in full bloom. Mr. Child left for Boston this afternoon. Went to Niblo's garden, 578, Broadway, an extensive, well-got up pleasure place, but attendance not good, the weather being uncertain and cold.

Thursday, 4th May.—Raining morning and nearly all day; cheerless, muddy, and cold. Went to Mr. Bowden jun.'s and got draft endorsed, and reference to his bankers, the Second National, Fifth Avenue, West Twenty-third Street, for certificate that he was a customer. Walked there, about a mile. Got into omnibus just outside, and went down Broadway to Wall Street, $2\frac{1}{2}$ miles for 5 cents. No tramways on Broadway, but a constant line of large 'busses on to South Ferry; no conductor, no outside passengers; hold 20 inside. The driver opens and shuts the door by a patent strap of leather, which runs along ceiling of 'bus. When a passenger goes in he puts the fare up a small hole in the roof into the driver's hand; this causes a bell to sound communicating with a locked indicator, showing the number of passengers carried, and is a check on the driver for the cash taken. Very slow progress, Broadway being crowded with vehicles and people—sometimes at a walking pace only. Saw manager, British Bank, who said, "I heard about you from Australia this morning." Got draft cashed into English and American gold, the latter principally to pay passage-money, as shipowners won't take greenbacks; being an overdue draft on London, got all my money, no discount. Went to J. G. Dale's, 15, Broadway, and took cabin passage, in "Inman" line, for

Liverpool. Paid 75 dollars in gold and some odd silver = 15*l.* 12*s.* 6*d.* English. Had look at a very imposing structure, the Custom House, lying between Wall, William, Hanover Streets, and Exchange Place, the same site as the Exchange, which was destroyed in great fire of 1835. Building very substantial, of Quincy granite, and fire-proof. It is 200 by 171 feet, 77 feet high to the cornice, and 124 to the top of the dome. A recessed portico fronts on Wall Street, in which are eighteen Grecian columns, 38 feet high, and $4\frac{1}{2}$ feet in diameter at base, each formed from a single block, and weighs from 43 to 45 tons. Their entire cost was 55,000 dollars. The Rotunda, which is the principal room, is in the centre of the building; its diameter is 80 feet, and its height the same. It is surmounted by a dome, in which there is a large skylight, rising from the centre, resting in part on eight Corinthian fluted columns of Italian marble, 41 feet high and 5 feet in diameter. Its cost, including the ground, was 1,500,000 dollars. Then walked up Broadway to Astor House, and had a juicy steak from the grid, and some splendid Scotch ale at half a dollar a quart bottle. Went on tramway a considerable distance to near Harlem, and in steamboat across to Ward's Island, situated at junction of East and Harlem rivers, just above a whirlpool called Hell Gate, and opposite One Hundred and One Hundred-and-Fourteenth Streets. This island is small, and is used for the purposes of an emigrant hospital, but not very interesting. Then went to Randall's Island, which is larger and lies just to the north of Ward's.

There is an extensive nursery and school for pauper children, and an asylum for those who, from mental incapacity, cannot take care of themselves. These islands were places of encampment for a portion of the British Army in the autumn of 1776. A portion is used as a "Potter's-field," a burial-place for strangers. Did not get back to the 'Cosmopolitan' till after dusk.

Friday, 5th May.—Still raining all day hard, until evening. At New York Gallery of Fine Arts, corner Eleventh Street and Second Avenue, for two hours; said to contain some of the finest paintings in the country; a large portion of them belonged to the private collection of a Mr. Luman Reed. Several works of art from the pencils of Americans, particularly a series of pictures illustrating the "Course of Empire," by Cole; altogether a fine collection. The rooms of this institution are portion of the building of the New York Historical Society, which I could not see, as visitors must be introduced by members. Spent remainder of morning and part of afternoon at the Halls of Justice and City Prison fronting Centre Street, but covering the block of ground bounded by Centre, Leonard, Elm, and Franklin Streets. The main building is the only one in the Egyptian order of architecture in the city, and is 253 by 200 feet. It is built in the form of a hollow square, of granite from the State of Maine. The court-rooms are in front, and the prison (called the Tombs) in the centre. The prison is 142 feet long by 44 feet wide, and contains 173 cells. There is also a wing from the main building, used in part as a female prison, under the superintendence of a matron; the other part occupied for domestic purposes. Prison accommodation altogether for some three hundred. The police-court, in the north-east corner of the main building, is roomy and in daily use. A strong posse of police always on here. They are mostly a smart, tall, wiry body of men, many with not much "waist" about them; their clothing fitting tight and well. Feeling tired, took a long ride on cars, reaching Fifty-eighth Street. Subsequently walked about, looking out for a saddler's shop, to get a couple of leather straps for portmanteau. Observing the name of Beresford over the door of a small shop in Second Avenue, went in and saw him. Himself and an apprentice were at work in a very small space, scarcely room to turn round. He had no straps in hand, but made a couple in a short time for 50 cents, during which he said that he was the real Marquis of Waterford; that the De La Poers had no right to be recognized by Queen Victoria, but want of money prevented his proving his just claim. He was a very happy Irishman, had not much of the brogue, but accounted for it by stating that he had left Ireland when a child. Walked to Mr. Bowden's, 155, West Twenty-ninth Street, and dined at 6. Finished the evening at "Wood's Museum," for a dollar, a sort of half-and-half theatrical place, in a three-act drama, with a large, but well-behaved audience.

Saturday, 6th May.—Morning cloudy and showery up to 8 A.M. Streets very dirty, especially by side of tramways; full of holes, water, and dirt, some of the stones being displaced, and many of them, square blocks as well as large pebbles, being much worn. Walked to Inman Company's wharf, 45, North River, covered over for a considerable way, so that passengers can get alongside steamers with their luggage, in vehicles or otherwise, in the dry. Adjoining wharf had been lately burnt down; nothing but charred remains of timber to be seen. 'City of Washington,' steamer, in quarantine, having had a case or two of small-pox on board on last trip from Liverpool. Numerous liquor stores opposite the wharfs, full of half-drunken sailors and lumpers, although only 11 o'clock. Went to Central Park again in car, the morning turning out fine, and a great many were there, but only a few vehicles. Visited the Bowling Green after lunch, a small oval enclosure at the foot of Broadway. It was formerly a bowling place for the officers of the garrison of Fort George. The iron railing surrounding it was placed there before the Revolution; the round heads of the posts were broken off during that war and used for cannon-balls. In the centre, now occupied by a beautiful marble fountain, with a spacious bason, was erected a statue of George III., in 1770. In July, 1776, the patriots pulled it down and converted it into bullets, the material being lead, covered with gilding.

There are some good shady trees on this green; latter part of afternoon and evening turned out wet.

Telegraphed to Dale to know when steamer would leave; reply, "Monday afternoon at 4."

Went by tramway for 5 cents to the very doors of

Booth's Theatre. Saw Barrett in 'Winter Night's Tale,' which had been played with much success for 60 nights; well got up, beautiful scenery, and good acting; a very quiet audience, a contrast to San Francisco. Paid a dollar; perfect order in entering; no crushing; a policeman was stationed at a bar, and only let one in at a time to pay. The theatre is beautifully fitted up inside, and so constructed that everyone can see and hear. Returned to 'Cosmopolitan' by tramway in the dry—raining hard. You can get to any place of amusement cheap by the cars, thus saving cab hire.

Sunday, 7th May.—Morning and day fine, evening showery and gusty. After breakfast went by car to Astor House. Newsboys were vending papers, and fruit and other stalls were at corners of streets, like week days, principally kept by women. Liquor stores closed, but drink was to be obtained on the "sly." Got into a German saloon. Walked down Broadway, about three-quarters of a mile, and crossed over East River for South Ferry, Brooklyn, one mile, and on by car, about two miles and a half, to Greenwood Cemetery. A great many men were driving their sulkies about with fast-trotting horses; they meet on Sundays outside the city to make their bets on the quiet; they wore their caps, and dressed and drove in the same style as if bent on a race. The chief hotels were open for travellers, and liquors obtainable at the bars. The grounds of the Greenwood Cemetery, incorporated in 1838, comprise 250 acres, are situate on the Gowanus heights, Brooklyn. They are beautifully undulating and diversified, presenting continual changes of surface and scenery. The elevated portions afford interesting views, embracing the bay and harbour of New York, with its islands and forts, cities of New York and Brooklyn, New Jersey, Staten Island, numerous towns and villages, with a view of the Atlantic from Sandyhook to Rockaway. The various avenues (exclusive of paths) extend about 15 miles; a great many beautiful monuments, obelisks, tombs, &c., &c. Upon the hills of Greenwood a part of the battle of Long Island was fought in August, 1776. Brooklyn itself is a very large place, containing 400,000 inhabitants, with its 263 streets and avenues, facing the East River, which river runs between it and the eastern portion of New York, and its immense piles of buildings, public and private, would take days to see properly. Did not get back to Broadway till close on 4 o'clock. At four attended choral service and sermon at Trinity Church. Interior very commodious, arched and moulded like an English cathedral; handsome pillars of a sort of brown sandstone, highly polished, with ornamental caps; two organs—one a very large powerful one. The choristers wore white gowns, the service intoned, and everything conducted like an English cathedral; the service was over at a quarter to six. Walked back to 'Cosmopolitan;' streets very quiet. Old John and his youngsters same as usual. Hall and bar full on account of the rain. Newspapers and smoking, chewing, and liquors in great request.

NEW YORK TO LIVERPOOL.

3060 Miles.

Monday, 8th May.—Fine sunny day. Boiled cod and oyster sauce for breakfast. Walked to Pier No. 45, North River, and went on board the 'City of Washington,' lying alongside, 1908 tons register, of Liverpool, a well-provisioned, clean ship. Meat kept fresh at sea in ice. Number of passengers allowed cabins, 206; second, &c., 721. Captain, T. C. Jones, stout and jolly, from Devonshire; a perfect contrast to the slender Yankee captain of the 'Ajax.' Saloon lofty, 50 feet long, nicely fitted up with soft crimson cotton velvet seats; 125 can sit down; separate tables allotted to about fifteen at a table, like a family party; most commodious cabin I had been in, but no sofa or seats, trunk was sufficient. Went back to 'Cosmopolitan' and lunched on crab, very fresh and good. Got ready, and left for steamer in hack carriage at 3, charge one dollar. Old John had packed up some sensational illustrated papers to read on voyage; would like to see me again, he said. Quite a bustle on wharf and on board. Eight young Japanese men (jugglers), well-dressed in European costume, arrived about 4, accompanied by a bevy of porters and an extraordinary quantity of baggage; each carried a bowie-knife concealed about his person. Three Australians came on board, at 4.15, wishing to get a passage, as they wanted to see the "Derby," but their luggage being three or four miles away they had not time to fetch it, so they went on shore again. They said that all the passages had been taken by other steamers throughout next week, and they must therefore lose the Derby sight. Only forty-six passengers in the cabin. Steamed away at 4.30 P.M., midst cheers and waving of handkerchiefs from numerous friends on pier. In very smooth water down the harbour, midst beautiful scenery on each side of us, with views of Brooklyn, Jersey City, batteries, and islands, and fleets of vessels of all sails, inward and outward bound, with steamers crossing and recrossing everywhere, there being room enough for all. Substantial tea at six o'clock, in the colonial style, barring toughness, beefsteaks, chops, &c., being the principal portion. Sandyhook Lighthouse in sight. Off Sandyhook at 7 P.M., distant from Queenstown 2820 miles, Liverpool 3060. Smooth water all the afternoon, evening, and during the night. My companion (lower berth), a close-shaved, black-muzzled, tall, strong-built young Jesuit, a perfect Fenian, from Baltimore (Rev. J. A. Gallan, evidently of Irish extraction), was grumbling half the evening and night about his berth, complaining about his head being bumped against bottom of upper berth, there not being space enough, he said, between; he was also much annoyed at absence of seats; the fact was he was beginning to feel squeamish.

Tuesday, 9th May.—Dull morning and day; cold atmosphere; smooth sea; very little perceptible motion, yet several absent from breakfast, through sickness, my

Jesuit friend among them. Breakfast at 9; fish and flesh; butter excellent. Hot and cold lunch at 12; soup, roast tender sirloin beef, baked potatoes, cold meats, sardines, first-class cheese, &c.; bottled ale and porter, 6d. pints. Not sufficient sun to take observations at noon.

Dead reckoning.—Course, N. 85 E.; Distance run, 185 miles from Sandyhook; lat., 40° 44'; long., 70° 04'. Dinner at 4 P.M.; excellent spread; soup, boiled codfish, beef and mutton; prairie hens, very good eating, similar taste to a pheasant; pastry and dessert excellent. Tea at 7. Evening pleasant. Watched the captain and three gentlemen (one a young retired lieutenant in the army returning to Ireland from Canada, another an English solicitor who had been living in the States, and the third a young merchant from New York) playing at whist. Some played cribbage; others discoursing and disputing about Fenianism, Ireland, and America, and the probable downfall of England. Grogs were supplied at 6d. a glass, including plenty of lemon. Lights supposed to be out at 10. Got the purser, a north of Devon man, to give me another berth—one to myself; left Rev. Gallan to his own reflections. Night dark and cold.

Wednesday, 10th May.—Weather and sea almost same as yesterday. At 6 A.M. sighted large barque bound west. At breakfast "chopped" seats, out of the draught, to a better one, with a lady returning from Australia, who did not like sitting near the "heathen Chinee;" some of them were absent through sickness, but those who were well were constantly reading books and learning English; they appeared to have plenty of money, as they imbibed a considerable quantity of champagne, hock, and claret; they were allotted a table to themselves to-day. At 1 exchanged signals with large steamer of the National line, 'The Queen,' bound to New York, going west in latitude 41° 06', and longitude 64° 37'. Not sufficient sun to take observations.

Noon, Dead reckoning.—Wind, South; calm. Course, 85 E. Distance run, 260 miles. Lat., 41° 07' N.; long., 64° 22' W. At 1.30 P.M. sighted one of "Inman" line for N. Y. Raining part of afternoon, and all the evening.

Thursday, 11th May.—Dull morning; nice sea on; steamer rolling fairly; a good many absentees at breakfast through sickness; very cold gloomy day.

Noon, Dead Reckoning.—Wind, East-North; strong breeze; rain. Course, 85 E. Distance run, 270 miles. Lat., 41° 30' N.; long., 58° 28' W. Rather heavy "pitching" and "leakage" at tea. Very few at table to-day. The captain's whist party continued without flinching. Evening gloomy, cold.

Friday, 12th May.—Fine clear morning and day; strong breeze; high cross sea; rolling heavily; shipping water occasionally, but not on her lofty commodious poop; the Fenians forward kept within their cabin.

Noon.—Wind, N.W. Course, 85 East. Distance run, 304 miles. Lat., 41° 56' N.; long., 51° 43' W. (Totnes horse and cattle fair day.) Bancroft Library

Saturday, 13th May.—Morning fine; brisk sea on;

rolling evenly; promenading delightful; plenty of room to kick.

Noon.—Wind, West; moderate. Course, 63 E. Distance run, 304 miles. Lat., 44° 14' N.; long., 45° 33' W. Exchanged colours with a North German steamer at 1.30 P.M., in lat., 44° 22', long., 45° 55'. Wind, N.W.; strong breeze during afternoon; calm evening and night.

Sunday, 14th May.—Morning bright and fine; raining afternoon and evening gently. Captain read prayers, 10.15; good attendance; captain has a splendid voice, loud enough for a large cathedral; reading, very correct; and his manner of conducting the service was much admired, particularly by a (Scotch) lady, returning from a visit to Chicago.

Noon.—Wind, West-South. Course, 61 E. Distance run, 302 miles. Lat., 46° 40' N.; long., 39° 16' W. Fresh and light breeze. Rev. Gallan "discoursed" in the afternoon with his Fenian brethren in the second cabin, on "England shall bite the dust yet," &c., &c.

Monday, 15th May.—Sunny morning; slight rain between 10 and 11; lively sea.

Noon.—Wind, South. Course, 64 E. Distance run, 300 miles. Lat., 48° 52' N.; long, 32° 33' W. Fresh breeze, with rain; cleared up towards evening.

Tuesday, 16th May.—Cloudy morning; moderate sea; very smooth latter part of day.

Noon.—Wind, South. Course, 73 E. Distance run, 300 miles. Lat., 52° 20' N.; long., 25° 12' W. Fresh breeze, cloudy.

Wednesday, 17th May.—Morning dull; sea smooth, almost a calm.

Noon.—Wind, S.S.E. Course, 82 E. Distance run, 267 miles. Lat., 50° 57' N.; long., 18° 16' W. Light breeze, cloudy. Exchanged colours with American ship 'Sir Henry Pottinger,' bound west.

Thursday, 18th May.—Fine morning and day; scarcely a ripple on the water.

Noon.—Wind still calm, westerly. Courses, 89. Distance, 275 miles. Lat., 51° 02' N.; long., 10° 59' W.

Remarks: light and calm; passed Fastnet, 5.16 P.M., Old Head of Kinsale, 9.5 P.M. Sighted Roach's Point, with revolving lighthouse, 9 P.M. Signalled for steam-tug to take off passengers for Queenstown; tug 'Fanny' alongside, 10.15 P.M. Queenstown 236 miles from Liverpool. A few cabin but many steerage passengers landed at Queenstown; got rid of all the Fenians. The convict establishment on Spike Island looked very well lighted up, in the distance, the night being dark. One could imagine himself in the Emerald Isle, from the brogue and excitement of the hands on board the tug when she came alongside. The captain's whist party was broken up, the military man and the merchant having gone to "Ould Ireland."

Friday, 19th May.—Fine morning; occasional gentle rain from 1 P.M. during afternoon; A.M. 0.20, Ballycollin; 5, Coningbeg; 6.32, Tuskar.

Noon.—Wind, northerly. Courses, 69. Distance 55, Fastnet,—2817 miles.

Light breeze and cloudy. Abreast South Stack Lighthouse, Holyhead, at 1.30 P.M., erected on a bold round projecting rock, below the main land, but connected with it. At 1 the weather had got cloudy. It was hazy when first off Holyhead, but cleared temporarily on passing the South Stack, which, with its white-looking buildings, became distinctly visible up to passing the north portion, when the low, narrow neck of land in continuation became indistinct from rain and mist. Abreast north end 10 to 2 P.M.; off Moelfra Bay at 2 P.M., some 15 miles. A mast apparently rising out of the sea, indicating place of wreck of the 'Royal Charter,' with bold rocky coast in the distance, but not distinctly seen from the cloudy weather; abreast of the Skerries about 2.30 P.M.; sunshine again, portions looked very pretty and green. Some undulating land, which appeared to be divided into small farms. Coast not a very bold one, lying comparatively low in some places, the rock apparently of a soft nature..

The lighthouse a prominent object, about middle portion of the Skerries, on an elevated spot standing out from the rest, with a nice bay inside it, *i.e.* between it and the main land. Weather cleared up the latter part of the afternoon. Off N. W. Light-ship at 7.15 P.M., being now fairly in the Mersey. Engines stopped to wait for tide to take her over the bar; about an hour's detention. At 9.30 P.M. the passengers, except two others and self, were taken off almost in the dark, by a small steamboat, and landed. The 'City' then slowly steamed up the river to the Prince's landing stage. The town of Liverpool, also the houses on the Cheshire side opposite, looking very pretty, being well-lighted with gas, and the sky being cloudy.

Saturday, 20th May.—Landed at 11 A.M., with a good appetite—having never missed a single meal on any steamer between Australia and England—crossing a large steamer of the Inman line, having the inside berth, called the 'City of Antwerp,' to do so. Went in a cab about half a mile to Eberle's Alexandra Hotel, Dale Street. The Queen's birthday was being kept; plenty of bunting displayed on the river, &c.; a fine day, but rather cloudy.

HINTS TO TRAVELLERS BY SEA AND OVERLAND FOR THE CALIFORNIA ROUTE PARTICULARLY, AND STEAMERS IN GENERAL.

Leave Sydney not earlier than 1*st March*, to avoid probable cold and snow between Ogden and Omaha.

Choose, if you can, a top berth about midships.

Wear a suit of dark clothes on board, as smut from smoke of funnel and dust from coaling will not show so readily as on a light dress.

Only take what you actually require on voyage, &c., as the Yankees will make you pay smart for extra luggage (over 100 lbs. in first-class), and moreover, the "style" may be different by the time you get to London.

Take a wide-awake or Scotch cap, which you can easily pop into your pocket when not wanted.

I sent a large box from Sydney by a sailing ship, 'The Sobraon,' containing private papers and things I did not require on journey.

Had a cast-off dark suit, worn previous winter, renovated at Sydney, which answered every purpose, and lasted to San Francisco.

In a strong leather trunk took a strong grey-coloured tweed suit to wear on shore in cool weather; also two white silk coats for hot weather, half dozen pair commonest white socks, three pair woollen socks, very thick woollen stockings for cold weather, half a dozen white shirts and some paper collars, three wove under-shirts, one thick woollen regatta shirt, six pocket-handkerchiefs, stout pair of slippers with patent leather tops to wear on board, easily kept clean, and stand damp decks and salt water better than common leather.

Some foreign post paper and foolscap, "exciseman's" ink-bottle, pen-holder, and a few steel pens in waistcoat pocket; can get ink from the steward.

Only take gold and silver enough for use on board and on shore, as Yankees will deduct at rate of 5 per cent., same as at Honolulu.

Took drafts on London, which are eagerly sought after, and can readily be turned into cash all over the world.

Do not show or disclose to a stranger any money or valuables you may have, and avoid drinking with strangers.

Put money-bags and keys under bolster at night.

Take common digger's belt of leather with pouches, to put away your money, &c., and wear round your waist on shore. (Cost me from Adelaide to Liverpool 171*l*.)

www.ingramcontent.com/pod-product-compliance
Lightning Source LLC
Chambersburg PA
CBHW031944230426
43672CB00010B/2042